The Faces of Lee Harvey Oswald

The Faces of Lee Harvey Oswald

The Evolution of an Alleged Assassin

Scott P. Johnson

LEXINGTON BOOKS
Lanham • Boulder • New York • Toronto • Plymouth, UK

Published by Lexington Books
A wholly owned subsidiary of Rowman & Littlefield
4501 Forbes Boulevard, Suite 200, Lanham, Maryland 20706
www.rowman.com

10 Thornbury Road, Plymouth PL6 7PP, United Kingdom

Copyright © 2013 by Lexington Books

All rights reserved. No part of this book may be reproduced in any form or by any electronic or mechanical means, including information storage and retrieval systems, without written permission from the publisher, except by a reviewer who may quote passages in a review.

British Library Cataloguing in Publication Information Available

Library of Congress Cataloging-in-Publication Data

Johnson, Scott Patrick.
 The faces of Lee Harvey Oswald: the evolution of an alleged assassin by Scott P. Johnson.
   pages cm.
 Includes bibliographical references.
 ISBN 978-0-7391-8681-7 (cloth : alkaline paper) -- ISBN 978-0-7391-8682-4 (electronic)
 1. Oswald, Lee Harvey. 2. Oswald, Lee Harvey--Public opinion. 3. Kennedy, John F. (John Fitzgerald), 1917-1963--Assassination. 4. Assassins--United States--Biography. 5. Public opinion--United States. I. Title.
 E842.9.J6427 2013
 364.152'4092--dc23
 [B]
 2013034977

∞™ The paper used in this publication meets the minimum requirements of American National Standard for Information Sciences Permanence of Paper for Printed Library Materials, ANSI/NISO Z39.48-1992.

Printed in the United States of America

Contents

Preface	ix
Acknowledgments	xiii
Introduction	xv
1 Oswald as Lone Assassin	1
2 Oswald as Conspirator	19
3 Oswald as Patsy and Hero	43
4 Two Oswalds?	73
5 The "Russian" Oswald	89
6 Critical Analysis of Oswald's Role in the Kennedy Assassination	101
Bibliography	125
Index	131
About the Author	139

Preface

As a sophomore studying political science at Youngstown State University in 1982, I enrolled in a course entitled, The Executive Process, taught by one of my favorite instructors, Professor Larry Esterly. The course examined the office of the presidency and I was intrigued by a chapter written by James David Barber pertaining to the personality of President John F. Kennedy. Barber recounts Kennedy's early life and political career and describes how he possessed the personal characteristics and traits needed to become a great president. After reviewing Kennedy's early struggles as president involving the Bay of Pigs fiasco, the steel industry crisis, and the construction of the Berlin Wall, Barber documents how Kennedy skillfully handled the Soviets and Cuban Missile Crisis and then notes how Kennedy discovered his moral compass by supporting civil rights legislation in 1963. Barber portrays Kennedy as the unique individual who was capable of adapting to the office of the presidency and learning from his past mistakes. Barber concludes the chapter by stating that Kennedy was on his way to becoming a great president when November 22, 1963, changed the course of history and all of a sudden Lyndon Johnson was president. It was as if the United States had been denied a leader who perhaps comes along once in a lifetime. Political scientists have since traced the public's apathy and alienation toward government and politics to the Kennedy assassination.

In 1983, the twentieth anniversary of the assassination of President John F. Kennedy provided an opportunity for the media to revisit the event with news footage. I recall viewing the Zapruder film on television for the first time and heard family members reminisce about where they were on November 22, 1963, and whether Kennedy was assassinated as a result of a conspiracy.

In 1992, on winter break from graduate school, I read Mark Lane's book, *Plausible Denial*, which argued that the Central Intelligence Agency (CIA) and the military-industrial complex assassinated the president because he opposed the escalation of the Vietnam conflict. I have always enjoyed attempting to solve a mystery and, as a youngster, I was drawn naturally to the Sherlock Holmes and Ellery Queen novels. The Kennedy assassination provided perhaps the greatest mystery in the history of the United States. Who killed the president? Why was Kennedy killed? Who was Lee Harvey Oswald? Who was Jack Ruby? Why did Jack Ruby murder Oswald? These are the fundamental questions that everyone thinks about concerning the Kennedy assassination and I was fascinated by them.

The Oliver Stone film, *JFK*, debuted in 1992 and, while it was a great cinematic experience, it was clear that Stone had created the film as a counter-myth to debunk the myth of the Warren Commission, the official government investigation of the assassination published in 1964. At this time, I made a conscious decision that I would read as much of the material related to the assassination as possible and then I would arrive at a conclusion for myself. Gerald Posner's book, *Case Closed*, read like a prosecutor's brief, but it was nevertheless an effective and powerful argument that Oswald acted as the lone and disturbed assassin. Other books followed such as Jim Garrison's *On the Trail of the Assassins*, Gaeton Fonzi's *The Last Investigation*, Michael Eddowes's *The Oswald File*, John Newman's *Oswald and the CIA*, James Fetzer's edited book, *Assassination Science*, Norman Mailer's *Oswald's Tale*, Seth Kantor's *The Ruby Cover-Up*, Jim Marrs's *Crossfire*, and, most recently, Vincent Bugliosi's *Reclaiming History*, an excellent summary and analysis of the assassination literature. The list above only scratches the surface. I had developed quite a collection of Kennedy assassination books and received quite a bit of teasing about my interest in the assassination from my colleagues in the political science department at Frostburg State University where I was hired as an instructor in 1999.

In August 2001, when the chair of my department, Dr. Steve Simpson, was promoted to the Provost's Office, he asked if I would cover his Personality and Politics course which began in the fall semester less than two weeks away. He easily convinced me to teach the course because I would be able to spend a considerable amount of time lecturing on political assassins in the course. James Clarke of the University of Arizona had written a book entitled, *American Assassins*, which Dr. Simpson encouraged me to use for the course. The book has since been reissued under the title, *Defining Danger*, and is a superb textbook for undergraduate students who are interested in examining the psychology of political assassins in American history.

I have taught Personality and Politics now for twelve years and used the course as an opportunity to entertain my obsession with Lee Harvey Oswald and the Kennedy assassination. In 2002, I presented a paper at the November in Dallas (NID) conference which was entitled, "Lee Harvey Oswald and the Logic of Conspiracy." The paper presentation made an effective argument that Oswald acted alone but I left open the possibility that there may have been a conspiracy based upon circumstantial evidence. However, I maintained that no concrete evidence existed that Kennedy was assassinated as a result of conspiracy. Needless to say, the paper was not well received by the organizers of the conference and an audience of individuals who were convinced beyond any doubt that a conspiracy was responsible for the murder of the president. In 2007, I published a version of the NID paper in the *South Texas Law Review* under the title, "The Prosecution of Lee Harvey Oswald."

In presenting Lee Harvey Oswald and the Kennedy assassination in my lectures in the Personality and Politics course, I ultimately would be asked by students about my own thoughts concerning Oswald and the assassination. I realized that I could make a convincing argument from a variety of perspectives. I was able to present strong evidence that Oswald was the lone assassin, the conspirator, the patsy, the hero, or even a Russian impostor. In short, I realized after decades of reading, researching, and writing about Oswald that his life story has more than one narrative. Oswald has evolved within American culture over the last fifty years in a number of ways and the American public, including myself, is unsure about the identity of the alleged assassin and his role in the assassination. Hence, I decided to write this book. It is probably one of the first books on Oswald and the assassination that attempts to present the information from an objective perspective. While I arrive at some tentative conclusions in the final chapter, I encourage readers to think for themselves in order to get beyond the myopic viewpoints of researchers who consistently portray Oswald in a single dimension. Whether he is depicted as the lone assassin, the conspirator, the hero, the patsy, or the Russian impostor, most books and articles refuse to include the entire story and ultimately provide the reader with a biased perspective. After fifty years, the true story concerning Oswald and the assassination may be lost to history. But, hopefully, this book will provide some insight for the public regarding the evolution of Oswald as a historical figure and make a contribution toward understanding his life and his part in the most dramatic event in American history.

Acknowledgments

First and foremost, I would like to thank Lexington Books who have provided me with a wonderful opportunity to publish my research on Lee Harvey Oswald and the assassination of President John F. Kennedy. The book project, *The Faces of Lee Harvey Oswald: The Evolution of an Alleged Assassin*, is the product of more than a decade of research and writing so it is satisfying to have the chance to present the results of my work in published form, especially given the fact that the book is being published in concurrence with the fiftieth anniversary of the Kennedy assassination.

Of course, I am indebted to the mentors who have been integral in my development as an instructor and researcher. Christopher E. Smith of Michigan State University, Thomas R. Hensley of Kent State University, and Stephen J. Simpson of Frostburg State University have greatly influenced my academic career through their advice, encouragement, and positive example.

I am also fortunate to have colleagues in the Political Science Department at Frostburg State University who provide a healthy environment for conducting academic research. The professional relationships and friendships that I have made at Frostburg State have enhanced my academic career and personal life in such a way as to make "work" more enjoyable.

Jennifer Murray, currently an Assistant Professor of History at the University of Virginia at Wise, is a former student who shares my enthusiasm for investigating the Kennedy assassination and I enjoyed presenting research with her at the November in Dallas (NID) conference in 2002. It also has been rewarding to observe her development over the years from a student into a professional academic.

I am grateful to Ronald Chrisman of the University of North Texas Press who read an early version of the manuscript and offered encouraging comments and suggestions. He was also instrumental in the publication of the book because he recommended that I contact Rowman & Littlefield as a potential publisher.

I have been fortunate enough to establish wonderful friendships that have enhanced my professional career as well as my personal life. In particular, I would like to express my gratitude toward Hans Hacker, Jack and Ruth Armstrong, and Dennis and Suzi Mills for their support and friendship over the years.

My family has always been supportive of my academic career. My parents, Dale and Kathy Neely and Robert and Nancy Johnson, have always been important forces in my life by providing much needed love and support over the years and I am forever grateful. My wife, Phaiboon Ladkubon Johnson, has provided unconditional love and support over the years and continues to tolerate the amount of time I devote to my research projects. Hence, I dedicate this book to my wife, Phai, whose life story will always remain a source of inspiration for me.

Introduction

The assassination of President John F. Kennedy on November 22, 1963, has spawned a host of conspiracy theories based largely upon intriguing questions, speculation, and inference. Thousands of books and articles have been written about the assassination with a large majority of the published material arguing for a conspiracy of one kind or another. However, only a few researchers have argued that Lee Harvey Oswald acted alone. Moreover, a relatively small volume of literature has been written from a scholarly and academic perspective.[1] The end result has been a massive amount of literature that is subjective and myopic in its treatment of the assassination.

THE LONE GUNMAN THEORY

Although discounted by conspiracy theorists, the case against Lee Harvey Oswald is stronger than most would admit, simply because such researchers have chosen to ignore facts related to the assassination. As documented in the Warren Commission Report, Oswald displayed a pattern of behavior throughout his life that indicated a strong probability he was involved in the Kennedy assassination.[2] The Warren Commission Report also provided a comprehensive analysis of the physical evidence which most likely would have been used against Oswald to find him guilty beyond a reasonable doubt before a jury in a criminal trial. While there is a strong likelihood that Oswald was involved in the assassination, it is not an absolute certainty. Hence, it is imperative to address the possibility of a conspiracy given the strange and mysterious circumstances surrounding the life of Oswald and the events of November 22–24, 1963 in Dallas, Texas.

CONSPIRACY THEORIES

Conspiracy theorists have been drawn to the Kennedy assassination since Jack Ruby, a Dallas nightclub owner, murdered Oswald within forty-eight hours of the assassination. The apparent silencing of Oswald contained all of the trappings of a conspiracy and cover-up. The murder of a young and charismatic president in broad daylight also added to the intrigue as well as the fact that Kennedy had made enemies with some of the most powerful elements across the globe, namely the Mafia, the Central Intelligence Agency (CIA) and the "military-industrial complex," Cuba and Castro, the Soviet Union, the ousted Diem government of South Vietnam, anti-Castro Cuban exiles, and Southern conservatives who opposed the civil rights movement. In 1964, the Warren Commission Report produced a conclusion that was largely based upon the physical evidence against Oswald and the testimony of key witnesses, such as Oswald's wife, Marina. But, the Commission also contributed to the conspiratorial mindset by conducting an investigation that was influenced by political factors such as the approaching 1964 elections as well as the fact that the government refused to explore Oswald's alleged connections to the CIA, the Federal Bureau of Investigation (FBI), and other government agencies. President Johnson and the Commission members were also extremely concerned that Oswald's international links to the Soviet Union and Cuba might cause an international conflict of epic proportions. Hence, the Warren Commission chose not to investigate the possibility of a conspiracy because of the potential for domestic and international unrest. At the behest of President Lyndon Johnson, the Commission members hastily concluded that Oswald acted alone in the assassination of President Kennedy and portrayed the alleged assassin as a loner and disconnected Marxist. In addition, it concluded that Ruby and Oswald did not know each other and Ruby also acted alone in the murder of Oswald. Clearly, the Warren Commission Report was designed to produce a credible investigation but it was also constructed, in part, for political purposes to put to rest a traumatic event in American history.

The fact that the Warren Commission produced a finding based, in part, upon political considerations did not necessarily mean that the government was involved in a conspiracy and cover-up of the Kennedy assassination. However, this fact, in and of itself, inspired conspiracy theories implicating the CIA, FBI, Secret Service, and even presidents Lyndon B. Johnson and Richard M. Nixon. In the post-assassination era, the Senate Church Committee investigations of the 1970s produced evidence that the U.S. intelligence community had been involved in assassination plots against foreign leaders and also was known to use counter-intelligence propaganda to overthrow democratically-elected leaders of foreign countries, not to mention its use of domestic surveillance against its own citizens.[3] Such findings made the public even more suspicious that Kennedy may have been assassinated by a rogue element of the U.S. intelligence community perhaps composed of CIA members, organized crime figures, and anti-Castro Cuban exiles operating in coordination with each other.[4] In fact, the "CIA/Mafia/anti-Castro Cuban" coalition under the supervision of Attorney General Robert Kennedy had worked closely together on assassination plots against Fidel Castro and was aggressive in carrying out intelligence operations in support of U.S. interests throughout Latin America.[5] Interestingly, Robert Kennedy hypothesized that he may have unwittingly played a role in the death of his brother by creating such a covert organization capable of assassination.[6] Researchers have theorized that such a covert organization may have turned on President Kennedy and carried out the assassination because Kennedy did not support wholeheartedly their aggressive policy of invading Cuba and challenging the Soviet Union.[7] To make matters worse, this covert organization would have been shielded from any government investigation because Robert Kennedy could not have revealed the existence of such an organization without implicating himself in its illegal activities. Hence, while it is plausible that a rogue element of the intelligence community assassinated Kennedy, the evidence in support of such a theory is, at best, circumstantial.

Beyond the intrigue and mystery produced by the plausible scenario described above, other motives exist for conspiracy theories involving the intelligence community.[8] Some conspiracy theorists have probably chosen to blame the U.S. intelligence community for the assassination simply because the sensationalism associated with this idea allows authors, researchers, and publishers to reap financial rewards through the sale of books as well as the opportunity to gain notoriety as "conspiracy superstars."

Finally, it is obvious that theorists who blame the U.S. government in some capacity for the Kennedy assassination have relished creating a "counter-myth" to what they believe is the "myth" created by the Warren Commission Report. In fact, Oliver Stone often has stated that his popular movie, *JFK*, was such a "counter-myth." These researchers operate from the premise that the U.S. government and its intelligence agencies routinely lie to the American people, withhold information, and engage in illegal and unethical activities at home and abroad. Therefore, it is appropriate to have the Kennedy assassination laid at their doorstep as punishment for their past deeds, regardless of their guilt or innocence. By blaming the CIA, FBI, or any other intelligence agency for the assassination, these researchers have furthered their cause by damaging the reputation of the intelligence community, a segment of the U.S. government despised by many intellectuals.[9]

Researchers also have focused on conspiracy theories advocating communist involvement in the Kennedy assassination. Lee Harvey Oswald's defection to the Soviet Union in 1959 and his return to the United States in 1962 raised concerns that perhaps Oswald, or someone "doubling" as Oswald, was instructed to commit the assassination by the Soviet State Security Service, also referred to as the KGB. In fact, a 1962 film, *The Manchurian Candidate*, based upon the premise of a U.S. soldier brainwashed by Communists to carry out a political assassination, was initially shown in theaters but later banned from further release because of its eerie similarity to the circumstances surrounding the Kennedy assassination.[10] Oswald's mysterious trip to Mexico City in September 1963 just eight weeks before the assassination also implicated the Soviets because Oswald met with a KGB agent at the Soviet Embassy who was in charge of its infamous "Department 13," renowned for carrying out political assassinations.[11]

Oswald's devotion and loyalty to the Communist revolution in Cuba and its leader, Fidel Castro, is also a popular explanation utilized by conspiracy theorists. Throughout his life, Oswald presented himself as a Communist and it is believed that he wanted to serve in Castro's revolutionary army. Oswald's wife, Marina, testified that Oswald's trip to Mexico City was based upon his desire to enter Cuba and serve as a military officer for Fidel Castro. During Oswald's trip to Mexico City, Oswald visited the Cuban Embassy in an attempt to gain entrance to Cuba, but he told Cuban officials that he only wanted to travel to their country as a means to re-enter the Soviet Union. The fact that Oswald met with Cuban officials in Mexico City only weeks prior to the assassination has caused some conspiracy theorists to argue that Oswald received orders from Fidel Castro to commit the assassination. As noted above, it is well documented that the Kennedy administration tried on several occasions to assassinate Fidel Castro and conspiracy theorists provide a compelling argument that Castro may have acted out of self-preservation by ordering the assassination of Kennedy.

The organized crime syndicate, or Mafia, is also a prime suspect among many conspiracy theorists.[12] President Kennedy and his brother, Attorney General Robert Kennedy, targeted Mafia leaders by prosecuting organized crime figures at an increasing rate in the early 1960s.[13] The Kennedys went as far as having Carlos Marcello, the Mafia kingpin of New Orleans, deported to Guatemala only to have him return to his organized crime empire in the United States. On the day of Kennedy's assassination, November 22, 1963, Marcello was involved in an immigration hearing related to his deportation. Researchers have also alleged that Marcello spoke of eliminating both John and Robert Kennedy because of how aggressively the Justice Department had been prosecuting organized crime leaders. Marcello supposedly went as far as saying that a "nut" would be picked up on the streets and blamed for the assassination. Interestingly, Oswald's uncle, Charles "Dutz" Murret, was employed as a bookie for the Marcello crime organization and it has been hypothesized that Oswald was set-up as a "patsy" to take the fall for organized crime.[14] Coincidentally, Oswald grew up in a neighborhood in

New Orleans that was controlled by Marcello and his organized crime operation.[15]

It is also well documented that President Kennedy and Sam Giancana, the Mafia boss of Chicago, shared a mistress, Judith Campbell Exner.[16] President Kennedy received several visits by Exner according to White House logs,[17] and her involvement with both Kennedy and Giancana may have created an additional motive for the assassination.

A final motive for the assassination by the Mafia may have been Kennedy's decision to cancel Operation Mongoose, a second attempt at invading Cuba after the failure of the Bay of Pigs in April of 1961. The Mafia leaders had planned on the Kennedy administration ousting Castro which would have allowed organized crime to return to Havana and re-establish their lucrative casinos. During the Cuban Missile Crisis of October 1962, Kennedy's "behind the scenes" deal, where he promised not to invade Cuba in exchange for the Soviet Union removing nuclear missiles from Cuba, most likely outraged Mafia leaders, particularly Marcello of New Orleans and Santos Traficante of Florida, who stood to make millions of dollars from the Havana casinos.

In 1964, the U.S. government did not even recognize the existence of the Mafia and the Warren Commission Report refused to consider the possibility that organized crime played a role in the assassination. However, in the most recent investigation of the assassination, the House Select Committee on Assassinations (HSCA) in 1979 concluded based upon the acoustical evidence at the time of the assassination that a high probability existed that shots were fired by two gunmen from separate locations within Dealey Plaza, specifically the Texas School Book Depository and the grassy knoll area.[18] The HSCA found that Kennedy was probably murdered as a result of a conspiracy and named the Mafia as the likely culprit because organized crime had the means, motive, and opportunity.

GOAL OF THE BOOK

The goal of this book is to analyze the Kennedy assassination in an objective manner by presenting five chapters with each offering a different paradigm, or lens, from which to view Oswald's role in the assassination and a sixth, and final, chapter evaluating the unresolved evidence as its relates to the various perspectives on Oswald. The impetus for the book is that any of the theories discussed above can appear as convincing as the next, particularly when researchers advocate a theory with apparent certainty. In reality, however, the Kennedy assassination offers little certainty based upon the complexity and ambiguity surrounding the event. Hence, after reading the following chapters, readers should decide for themselves as opposed to a preconceived idea, or theory, delivered as an absolute certainty.

Chapter 1 documents the idea that Oswald acted alone in the assassination. While conspiracy theorists fiercely maintain that Oswald did not act alone (or may not have acted at all), an empirical pattern of behavior demonstrated by Oswald throughout his life suggests that he committed the assassination. In addition, the physical evidence against the alleged assassin presented in chapter 1 is compelling. Chapter 2 examines the possibility that the assassination was a result of a conspiracy based upon empirical patterns of behavior demonstrated by a variety of suspects, specifically segments of the U.S. intelligence community, members of organized crime, and the Cuban exiles opposed to Fidel Castro. Because conspiracies do occur and certain individuals may have had prior knowledge of the assassination, Oswald's connections with and movements among suspected conspirators are examined. Chapter 3 lays out the circumstantial evidence that Oswald was not involved in the assassination, except for the idea that he was framed for the crime. This chapter also explores the historical evolution of Oswald who has been viewed by some conspiracy theorists as a heroic figure. It begs the question whether Oswald was employed as a government informant and/or contract agent for the CIA and assigned the task of thwarting the assassination and saving the president, only to be turned into a "patsy" by sinister forces. Chapter 4 examines the various Two Oswalds theories involving alleged impersonations and sightings of Oswald leading up to the assassination that are viewed by many researchers as evidence of conspiracy. The Two Oswalds theories provide complementary evidence to support the existence of a conspiracy involving Oswald or perhaps to suggest the possibility that Oswald was framed for the assassination. Chapter 5 discusses the Russian Oswald theory based upon the idea that Oswald defected to the Soviet Union but did not return to the United States. Instead, it has been argued that Oswald was replaced by a "double" who committed the assassination as part of an international communist conspiracy to murder President Kennedy. While most readers will scoff at the idea of a "Russian" Oswald, it is interesting to note that in the world of intelligence and counter-intelligence, such a ploy is not unprecedented. Finally, chapter 6 attempts to draw conclusions from the various perspectives of Oswald with a critical evaluation of the most compelling evidence that researchers have failed to resolve in the last fifty years.

NOTES

1. Diane Holloway, Ph.D., *The Mind of Oswald* (Victoria, B.C.: Trafford Publishing, 2000); James Fetzer, Ph.D. ed. *Assassination Science: Experts Speak Out on the Death of JFK*

(Chicago: Catfree Press, 2001); Scott P. Johnson, "The Prosecution of Lee Harvey Oswald," *South Texas Law Review,* 48 (2007), 101-127.

2. *Investigation of the Assassination of President John F. Kennedy: Hearing before the President's Commission on the Assassination of President Kennedy*, 88th Congress (1964) [hereinafter WCR].

3. Karen DeYoung and Walter Pincus, "CIA Releases Files on Past Misdeeds," *Washington Post*, June 27, 2007, A01; Frank J. Smist, Jr., *Congress Oversees the United States Intelligence Community, 1947-1989* (Knoxville: University of Tennessee Press, 1990).

4. David R. Simon, *Elite Deviance* (Needham Heights, Mass.: Allyn & Bacon, 1999).

5. Lamar Waldron and Thom Hartmann, *Ultimate Sacrifice: John and Robert Kennedy, The Plan for A Coup in Cuba, and the Murder of JFK* (New York: Carroll & Graf, 2005), 225-239.

6. Richard D. Mahoney, *Sons & Brothers: The Days of Jack and Robert Kennedy* (New York: Arcade, 1999), 293-296.

7. Jim Garrison, *On the Trail of the Assassins* (New York: Sheridan Square Press, 1988).

8. Richard M. Mosk, "Conspiracy Theories and the JFK Assassination: Cashing in on Political Paranoia," *Los Angeles Lawyer,* November 1992.

9. Most scholars of American politics trace the loss of public confidence and trust in U.S. government to the Kennedy assassination. David Simon, *Elite Deviance* (Needham Heights, Mass.: Allyn & Bacon, 1999), 305-328. A modern example of the loss of faith in the CIA involves a poll conducted of 1,000 adults by Rasmussen Reports (April 30-May 1, 2007) which found that 52 percent believe the CIA was "Not Very Truthful" or "Not at All Truthful" leading up to the Iraq War in 2003.

10. The 1962 film starred Frank Sinatra and Angela Lansbury and was based upon a novel. Richard Condon, *The Manchurian Candidate* (New York: McGraw-Hill, 1959).

11. Oleg Maximovich Nechiporenko, *Passport to Assassination: The Never-Before-Told-Story of Lee Harvey Oswald by the KGB Colonel Who Knew Him* (New York: Carol Publishing, 1993).

12. John Davis, *Mafia Kingfish: Carlos Marcello and the Assassination of John F. Kennedy* (New York: McGraw-Hill, 1989), 118-145.

13. Waldron and Hartmann, *Ultimate Sacrifice,* 417-418.

14. Waldron and Hartmann, *Ultimate Sacrifice,* 499-500.

15. Peter Dale Scott, *Deep Politics and the Death of JFK* (Berkeley, University of California Press, 1993), 77-82.

16. Judith Exner, *My Story* (New York: Grove Press, 1977).

17. Waldron and Hartmann, *Ultimate Sacrifice,* 422-423, 427-428, 675-676.

18. *Investigation of the Assassination of President John F. Kennedy: Hearing Before the House, Select Committee on Assassinations* (HSCA), 95th Congress (1979).

Chapter One

Oswald as Lone Assassin

The circumstances surrounding the assassination of President John F. Kennedy have provided fertile ground for conspiracy theorists.[1] Whenever a traumatic event occurs such as the assassination of President Kennedy, there is always a segment of the population that finds comfort in explaining such events with a conspiracy because it balances the political significance of the event with an explanation that is as important as the event itself.[2] A current example of a conspiracy theory being used to explain a dramatic event is the terrorist attacks of September 11, 2001. Many people refuse to accept that radical Islamic terrorists committed the 9-11 attacks out of sheer hatred for America. Instead, the events of September 11th also have found conspiracy theorists arguing that the federal government was behind the terrorist attacks to gain public support for military operations in Afghanistan and Iraq or perhaps the Israeli intelligence agency, Mossad, orchestrated the 9-11 attacks in order to blame the event on their sworn enemies, Islamic fundamentalists.[3] Many conspiracy theorists refuse to accept a simple explanation for a dramatic event because it diminishes the importance of the event. For example, a lone and disturbed assassin could not have murdered President Kennedy because such an explanation appears senseless and lacks any significance. However, an elaborate conspiracy justifies the assassination because perhaps then Kennedy died for a cause such as his desire to put an end to the Vietnam conflict, the Central Intelligence Agency (CIA), organized crime, or the Cold War itself.[4]

However, researchers who approach such events with rationality and hard evidence usually conclude that the explanations are quite simple. This chapter examines the assassination of President John F. Kennedy from an objective and logical perspective and concludes that prosecutors would have had a strong case against Oswald if he had lived to face the charges filed against him by the District Attorney of Dallas, Texas. The prosecution's case against Oswald would have rested largely upon the presentation of a behavioral pattern demonstrated throughout his life as well as a mass of physical evidence which would have been used to prove beyond a reasonable doubt that Oswald assassinated President John F. Kennedy on November 22, 1963.[5]

BEHAVIORAL PATTERN OF THE ASSASSIN

Lee Harvey Oswald demonstrated a pattern of behavior throughout his life that would have influenced a jury to conclude logically that he was responsible for the assassination of President John F. Kennedy and the murder of Dallas police officer, J. D. Tippit. Throughout his life, Oswald exhibited a pattern of behavior wherein he sought attention in order to compensate for his low self-esteem and feelings of inadequacy. As described below, Oswald was known to behave in a dramatic and self-destructive manner, particularly after he experienced major disappointments in his life.

Oswald led a strange and mysterious life. He was born in New Orleans on October 18, 1939, and his early childhood was characterized by loneliness and emotional detachment. Oswald's mother, Marguerite, was portrayed by many as an overbearing and self-absorbed woman who neglected her children.[6] Oswald's father, Robert Oswald, Sr., died of a heart attack two months before Oswald was born and this provided an unstable environment for the young Oswald. Marguerite Oswald remarried after the death of Oswald's father to a local businessman, Edwin Ekdahl, who acted as a father figure assuming the role of the stepfather for Oswald. However, the marriage ended in a divorce after a few years and Oswald again was left alone with his mother. During his childhood, Oswald spent a brief time in an orphanage with his older brothers, while his mother worked various jobs in sales or nursing to provide for the family. Marguerite Oswald admitted to holding more than a dozen jobs and being fired from several of them.[7] Oswald had one full-blooded brother, Robert, Jr., and a half-brother, John Pic. His brothers both joined the military at a young age which left Oswald to be raised exclusively by his mother. According to some researchers, Oswald developed a personality similar to his mother because she was the only parent, and role model, in his life. Priscilla Johnson McMillan argues that Oswald's behavior was based upon an unconscious Freudian type rejection of himself because he was so similar to his mother in terms of personality.[8]

While living at home with his mother, Oswald spent much of his childhood alone watching television, reading books, and attending many different schools in various places from New Orleans to New York City. His mother lived a very transient lifestyle and frequently moved Oswald in and out of school at a moment's notice. While Oswald and his mother were living with

John Pic and his wife in New York, Oswald was picked up by the police at the Bronx Zoo and given a truancy hearing in August 1952. At this time, a psychologist evaluated Oswald and found that he was above average in intelligence, but demonstrated a passive-aggressive personality with a great deal of frustration and hostility toward his mother and society because he was deprived of affection. During his stay in New York City, Oswald was known to strike his mother on occasion and he also threatened John Pic's wife, Marge, with a knife. When Marguerite Oswald intervened in the knife incident, Oswald struck his mother in the face. Because of his lonely and difficult childhood, Oswald had difficulty relating to other people and was diagnosed as quite disturbed because of his emotional isolation. He also appeared to have delusions of grandeur that were somewhat detached from reality, such as fantasizing about having great power and control over people.[9]

During his short stay in New York as a teenager, Oswald supposedly was handed Marxist literature by someone on the street during the Rosenberg kidnapping trial and began to develop an interest in the workers' revolution and Marxist ideology. Oswald developed a strong hatred for the capitalist system in America which he viewed as exploitive of workers and the poor, which obviously included his family. Ultimately, Oswald was portrayed in the Warren Commission Report as a disconnected Marxist with few friends.[10]

Oswald joined the Marines when he was 17 to emulate his older brother, Robert, but also to escape his mother's domination. Robert Oswald was quoted as saying that Oswald joined the Marines because he looked up to him. Robert Oswald joined the Marines in July 1952 when Lee Oswald was 12 years of age. Oswald's half-brother, John Pic, however, stated that Oswald joined the Marines to gain freedom from his mother. John Pic stated that he himself joined the Coast Guard in 1950 to escape his mother's domination.[11] As a Marine, he began teaching himself the Russian language and subscribed to Communist publications and Russian newspapers. Oswald was stationed for a while at a U.S. airbase in Atsugi, Japan, where he worked as a radar operator on the secret U-2 spy plane project. During his time in the Marines from 1956–1959, Oswald began to demonstrate an empirical pattern of behavior that would surface repeatedly throughout his life. Oswald's behavioral pattern was characterized by responding to failure with dramatic behavior to gain attention and recognition, thus proving his importance and worth as a person. Robert Oswald actually points to this pattern of behavior prior to Lee Harvey Oswald's service in the Marines. After Oswald quit his job as a messenger and office boy in 1956 working for a company, Gerald F. Tujague, Inc., Oswald followed his failure with an attempt to join the Communist Party.[12]

Oswald's failures and frustrations in the Marines produced a dramatic response that had serious repercussions for the U.S. government during the height of the Cold War. After Oswald was reprimanded by the Marines for possessing an illegal weapon, a revolver that accidentally discharged and wounded him in the arm, Oswald was court-martialed. In July 1958, he was sent to the brig for a month after he poured a drink over an officer's head in a bar during a heated discussion. Oswald's resentment and dissatisfaction over these experiences and other conflicts with military superiors caused him to apply for an honorable discharge from the Marines in 1959, supposedly to take care of his ailing mother. However, Oswald stayed with his mother in Fort Worth, Texas, for only a few days before leaving home and defecting to the Soviet Union at the age of 19 with the promise of turning over military secrets to the Russians. After the Soviets granted him a six-day visa to visit their country, Oswald applied for citizenship to the Soviet Union. When Oswald was denied an opportunity by the Soviets to become a citizen, he subsequently attempted suicide by slitting his left wrist.[13]

Oswald's failure in the Marines and his failed attempt to gain entrance into the Soviet Union were followed by dramatic attempts to gain attention and recognition. After he was humiliated in the Marines, his defection to the Soviet Union obviously shocked his family and gained him some notoriety in newspapers across the United States. His failed suicide attempt also created a stir internationally for both the U.S. and Soviet Union. Because the Soviet government sensed an international controversy, Oswald was admitted a work visa and given employment at a radio factory in Minsk.[14] Oswald lived in the Soviet Union for nearly three years from 1959–1962 and was supplied with a stipend and also a nice apartment by the Soviet government. He dated many Russian women and ultimately married Marina Pruskova in 1961. Oswald returned with his wife, Marina, and an infant daughter, June, to the United States in 1962.

Oswald had become disillusioned by the Communist system in the Soviet Union because he found that the party elites maintained all of the advantages within the Russian bureaucracy, while the workers lived an existence of monotonous labor. Oswald felt that the "drab, daily routine" was "unbearable" despite the fact that he was given an allowance to supplement the wages that he earned in the factory.[15] He also was disappointed to find that the brand of communism practiced in Russia had abandoned Marxist principles. Oswald found this unbearable and returned to the United States having been unsatisfied by both the capitalist and communist ways of life.

Oswald returned to his family in Texas after his failed adventure abroad and entered into tense relationships with his mother and closest brother, Robert. After a brief reunion with his family, he withdrew from them, thus continuing a pattern of self-isolation. His marriage to his wife, Marina, became strained by his various dead-end jobs as well as the transient life of moving the family from one apartment to the next. There also is evidence to suggest that Oswald was physically abusive to his wife during their time spent together in the United States.

In early 1963, Oswald's disillusionment with the U.S. and Soviet political systems caused him to focus intensely upon the Communist revolution in Cuba and its new leader, Fidel Castro. Cuba presented an opportunity to begin anew with a political system untainted by the imperialism and exploitation of the United States or the bureaucracy and corruption of the Soviet Union. In March of 1963, as Oswald's political interests were shifting to Castro, he ordered a 6.5 millimeter Mannlicher-Carcano rifle from a Chicago mail-order company using an alias, "A. Hidell." At roughly the same time, Oswald also ordered a Smith and Wesson .38 pistol from Seaport Traders using the same alias.[16] In April 1963, Oswald was fired from his job with Jaggers-Chiles-Stovall, a commercial photography business, which was one of the few jobs that he enjoyed because it was interesting work that did not involve manual labor. Shortly after his firing, Oswald followed the failure at Jaggers-Chiles-Stovall with an assassination attempt on the life of General Edwin Walker, an extreme right-wing militant who was staunchly anti-communist. Oswald shot at Walker while the general sat at a desk in his Dallas home working on his tax returns. Firing from about thirty yards outside of Walker's home, Oswald's shot barely missed because it was deflected by the wooden frame of a window.[17] The testimony of Oswald's wife, Marina, provided strong evidence that Oswald did, in fact, attempt to assassinate Walker.[18] It was not until the following day that Oswald heard on a radio broadcast that he had missed Walker with the rifle shot. Oswald again had repeated a pattern wherein he reacted to the failure of losing his job at Jaggers-Chiles-Stovall with a dramatic attempt to gain recognition and attention. Oswald had planned to become a great leader in Castro's army and the assassination of Walker would have proven his loyalty to the Cuban leader and also would have established himself as a communist revolutionary.

Immediately after the assassination attempt on Walker, Oswald left Dallas because his wife feared that the authorities might link him to the act. Oswald gained employment at a coffee processing plant in New Orleans and wrote to the Fair Play for Cuba Committee (FPCC) requesting literature and permission to start a chapter of the FPCC. After his pregnant wife and daughter joined him in New Orleans, Oswald was fired from his job at the coffee plant in July 1963, after only a few months of employment. Oswald's failure again produced more dramatic behavior such as his attempt to infiltrate an anti-Castro organization and, later, his arrest in August 1963, for his involvement in a scuffle while passing out pro-Castro leaflets. The local media noticed Oswald's antics and he appeared on two radio debates discussing Marxism and U.S. foreign policy toward Cuba.

In September 1963, Oswald allegedly took a trip to Dallas with two Cubans to visit Silvia Odio, a Cuban refugee whose father was being held in a Havana prison for criticizing Fidel Castro.[19] Odio stated that the two Cubans and Oswald arrived at her home asking for help with their anti-Castro movement. Odio was suspicious of the visitors and said that one of the Cubans called himself "Leopoldo" while Oswald was introduced as "Leon Oswald," a former Marine. Odio cautiously ended the conversation but then Leopoldo contacted her by telephone the following day asking about her impressions of "Leon Oswald." Leopoldo indicated that the ex-Marine was a bit crazy and stated that "Leon Oswald" had criticized Cuban-Americans for not being more outraged at President Kennedy for the Bay of Pigs fiasco. Leopoldo informed Odio that Oswald said the Cubans had no guts or else they would have killed Kennedy by now. Oswald then supposedly went further and stated that perhaps he would assassinate Kennedy.[20]

Conspiracy theorists have used Oswald's visit to Silvia Odio's home and the subsequent telephone call from one of the Cubans accompanying Oswald as proof of a conspiracy to assassinate President Kennedy. Robert Groden and Harrison Livingstone state that Sylvia Odio's story is "among the strongest witnesses to conspiracy" in the assassination of President Kennedy.[21] Silvia Meagher claims that Oswald's visit to Odio's home was "proof of the plot."[22] Some conspiracy theorists have even gone further and argued that Oswald had infiltrated an extremist organization planning the assassination and was in the process of being framed for the murder of President Kennedy. However, researchers who argue that Oswald acted alone have raised doubts concerning Odio's story because she was receiving psychological counseling at the time of the alleged visit and had a history of emotional problems. In addition, Odio's claim that the Cubans introduced her to "Leon Oswald" could not be corroborated by a second person and she was unable to provide a positive identification of Oswald when she was shown photographs of Oswald by members of the Warren Commission. It is also very possible that Oswald was in Mexico City during the time frame when Odio supposedly received the visit from Oswald and the Cubans.[23]

It is well documented that Oswald made a trip to Mexico City by bus in late September of 1963 to obtain an in-transit visa from the Cuban Embassy to travel to Cuba. Oswald had hoped the publicity that he received in New Orleans would gain him entrance into Cuba and Fidel Castro's army as an elite officer. In Mexico City, he contacted the Cuban and Russian embassies repeatedly in a desperate attempt to obtain a travel visa to Cuba.[24] After being denied several times over the course of a few days, he broke down emotionally in front of officials at both the Cuban and Soviet embassies.[25] After his failure to enter Cuba by way of Mexico, Oswald returned to Dallas on October 3, 1963, where he filed for unemployment compensation and spent the night at the YMCA. The next day he hitchhiked to Irving, Texas, where his pregnant wife and young daughter were staying with a friend, Ruth Paine.

Oswald obtained a job at the Texas School Book Depository in Dallas during October 1963, from a friend and neighbor of Ruth Paine's, Buell Frazier, who worked at the Depository. Oswald was interviewed by the manager, Roy Truly, for the job and began working at the Depository by filling book orders for $1.25 per hour.[26] During the final weeks of his life, Oswald worked at the Depository and rented a room in Dallas for himself during the week. On Fridays, he would travel the thirty miles from Dallas to Irving with Frazier to spend the weekends visiting with his wife and two daughters at the Paine house. Oswald's second daughter, Audrey Marina Rachel Oswald, was born on October 20, 1963, during the time when Oswald had just begun working at the Depository. Oswald was dependent upon Frazier for transportation to visit his family on weekends because he never learned to drive an automobile, although Ruth Paine was in the process of giving him driving lessons with the hope that he would secure a driver's license.

Oswald had continued a pattern of self-isolation by staying at the rooming house alone in Dallas while his wife, Marina, and his daughters stayed at the Paine home in Irving.[27] During this time of isolation, Oswald lived under an alias, O. H. Lee, because he feared harassment by the Federal Bureau of Investigation (FBI) who had been keeping tabs on him since his return from the Soviet Union. Oswald believed that the FBI had him fired from his previous jobs and when a special agent for the FBI, James Hosty, made contact with his wife, Marina, he marched into the FBI's Dallas office and left a note for Hosty. The contents of the note were never revealed because Hosty destroyed the note upon orders from a superior after Oswald was murdered by Jack Ruby. A receptionist, Nancy Fenner, stated that the note said Oswald would blow up the FBI office if Hosty did not stop bothering his wife, Marina. Agent Hosty claimed that the note read, "[i]f you have anything you want to learn about me, come talk to me directly. If you don't cease bothering my wife, I will take appropriate action and report this to the proper authorities."[28] The note was not reported to the Warren Commission and it did not become public knowledge until July 1975.

During the weekend prior to the president's visit to Dallas, Oswald did not visit Marina and the children because Ruth Paine's husband, Michael, was at the house celebrating a birthday for one of the Paine children. Oswald and Michael Paine did not like each other and Marina thought that it was best that he not visit that weekend. When Marina attempted to contact Oswald at the rooming house the following Monday, November 18th, the landlord told her that no one by the name of Lee Oswald lived there. Marina was infuriated when she found out that he was living under an alias because she thought that he was up to his old "spy tricks" again. On Thursday, November 21st, Oswald appeared unexpectedly at the Paine house after requesting a ride with Frazier in an attempt to reconcile with Marina. After Marina rejected his attempts at reconciliation, he indicated that he would not be visiting her and the children during the upcoming weekend because he had visited that Thursday evening.

Prior to the assassination, Oswald had experienced a series of failures and most likely was seeking a dramatic way to gain attention and recognition. Oswald's failure to gain entrance into Cuba to serve his hero, Fidel Castro, and his failed attempts to reconcile with his wife suggests that Oswald was in a mood to commit the assassination based upon the history of his behavioral pattern. Oswald had tried unsuccessfully to reunite his family in the weeks prior to the assassination and his wife belittled him by talking about her past lovers. Oswald's most recent argument with his wife over his use of an alias apparently was the last straw for Marina. Oswald left behind his wedding ring in a Russian tea cup and all of his cash, $170, for Marina when he left for work on the Friday morning of the assassination. This was a symbolic gesture to his wife and an act designed to make her feel guilty for rejecting him.[29]

Oswald left the Paine house on Friday morning, November 22nd at 7:15 am with a small package and drove with Buell Frazier to work at the Depository. Oswald placed the package in the backseat of Frazier's car and told him that it contained curtain rods for his rooming house in Dallas. The Warren Commission concluded that Oswald had dismantled the Mannlicher-Carcano rifle which he had stored in the Paine's garage and concealed it in brown wrapping paper that he had brought the previous evening from the Depository.

At 11:40 am, Oswald was seen on the sixth floor of the Depository by two different employees of the Book Depository shortly before the president's motorcade passed in front of the Depository.[30] At 12:30 pm, two workers on the fifth floor of the Book Depository heard the cartridge shells from the rifle hit the floor above them. Howard Brennan, who was watching the president's motorcade from the street-level, saw the shooter in the sixth floor window of the Depository and gave a description to the police that roughly matched Oswald.[31] Oswald fled the Book Depository within three minutes of the shots being fired and boarded a bus headed for the Marsalis district but, when the bus became stuck in traffic, Oswald exited the bus and hailed a taxi cab. The taxi driver, William Whaley, took Oswald to the 700 block of North Beckley, roughly a five minute walk to his rooming house at 1026 North Beckley where he retrieved a handgun and a light beige jacket which altered his appearance. At 1:00 pm, Oswald fled on foot from his rooming house until he was approached by a Dallas police officer, J. D. Tippit, who was driving along Tenth Street in the Oak Cliff district of Dallas. At 1:15 pm, Tippit stopped to question Oswald through the open front window on the passenger side of his patrol car and then got out of his patrol car and walked around the front of the car toward Oswald who was curbside. Oswald proceeded to shoot at Tippit five times from close range with the handgun that he had retrieved from his rooming house. Tippit was shot twice in the chest, once in the forehead, and once in the temple of his head. Oswald fired a fifth shot that missed.[32]

Several eyewitnesses saw Oswald shoot Tippit. Helen Markam was roughly a half of a block from the shooting and was able to select Oswald out of a line-up at the police station. Two other eyewitnesses, Virginia and Barbara Davis, observed Oswald shoot Tippit and then watched as he ran across their front lawn. Both women selected Oswald out of a police lineup. A taxi driver, William Scoggins, was parked in his vehicle about a half of a block from the shooting and he also was able to pick Oswald out of a lineup. Scoggins recalled Oswald saying something like "poor damn cop," or "poor dumb cop" which was a phrase that was familiar to Robert Oswald who had said that he had heard Oswald use this expression before on occasion. Domingo Benavides was only five yards away from the shooting in his pickup truck and said that he "really got a good view" of Oswald after he fired his handgun at Tippit.[33] Lastly, Ted Callaway, Sam Guinyard, Warren Reynolds, and William Arthur Smith were additional witnesses who identified Oswald at the scene of the Tippit shooting.

Oswald fled the Tippit murder scene heading east and he hid his light beige jacket underneath a parked car in a gas station, supposedly to alter his appearance a second time. Then, Oswald entered Hardy's Shoe Store to hide momentarily and, after exiting the shoe store, he walked fifty yards to the Texas Theater and entered without paying for a ticket. Within an hour of the assassination, the Dallas police quickly descended on the theater and arrested Oswald after a scuffle wherein Oswald punched an officer, tried unsuccessfully to shoot another,[34] and was punched by an officer himself. During an interrogation of Oswald, he did not confess to the murder of the president or Tippit and, for the most part, was evasive and uncooperative during questioning.[35] However, when asked by a reporter whether he killed the president, Oswald said, "No, I have not been charged with that."[36] Interestingly, Oswald omitted what he had done and answered a different question than the one asked by the reporter. In yet another instance where a reporter asked Oswald if he murdered the president, he again avoided answering the question directly by stating, "I didn't shoot anybody, sir. I haven't been told what I'm here for."[37]

Oswald's answers to the reporters perhaps demonstrated an example of habitual lying.[38] For example, an innocent person would have responded emphatically that he didn't kill the president. Oswald's habit of lying surfaced when he repeatedly told the police during his interrogation that he did not own a rifle, never used an alias,[39] had not taken a trip to Mexico City, did not say anything to Buell Frazier about the package containing the curtain rods, and was not connected to the FPCC. Oswald also denied that he brought a package to work. Instead, Oswald stated only that he brought a lunch bag with him. Oswald was caught in another lie when he said that he ate lunch at the lunchroom of the Depository but the persons that Oswald cited as being in the lunchroom at that time denied his presence.[40]

Further evidence of Oswald's habitual lying occurred when he stated that he had no knowledge of the name "Hidell," that he had not been dishonorably discharged from the Marines, had not lived at 214 Neely Street, had not posed for the backyard photographs, and had never used a post office box. According to Ruth Paine, Oswald also lied to the police when he stated that he visited the Paine house on Thursday, November 21, 1963, to avoid being in the way of a birthday party planned for the upcoming weekend of November 23–24, 1963, for one of the Paine children (Lynn Paine who was four years old). In fact, the birthday party had already been held the previous weekend.[41]

While in custody, Oswald's statement to the reporters that he was a "patsy" has been used by conspiracy theorists who have argued that Oswald was framed for the assassination. However, if you judge Oswald's statement within the context of his many false statements, it is quite possible that he was lying about being a pasty. Moreover, Oswald's words should be analyzed within the context of his entire statement. In one of the many instances where reporters asked Oswald if he shot the president, he answered, "No, they have taken me in because of the fact that I lived in the Soviet Union. I'm just a patsy."[42] Arguably, Oswald was not implying that there was a conspiracy to assassinate Kennedy with this answer. Instead, he was simply stating that law enforcement had been mistaken by focusing on him because he had lived in the Soviet Union.

After nearly two days in police custody, Oswald was murdered in the basement of the Dallas police station by Jack Ruby, a nightclub owner who supposedly was distraught over the assassination of President Kennedy.[43] Oswald was in the process of being transferred from the city jail to the county jail when the murder occurred in the presence of over forty law enforcement officials.

PHYSICAL EVIDENCE AGAINST OSWALD

The physical evidence against Oswald would have been viewed by any jury as compelling. Oswald's Mannlicher-Carcano rifle was found hidden between boxes on the sixth floor of the Depository at 1:12 pm and three cartridge shells from the rifle also were found on the floor. Oswald's fingerprints were found on the brown wrapping paper and his prints also were found on the boxes where a sniper's lair had been created near a window on the sixth floor. His palm print also was supposedly found on the butt of the rifle.[44]

According to an updated analysis of the Zapruder 8–mm film, Oswald's first shot missed its target because it struck an oak tree branch and then hit a concrete curb wounding James Tague who was watching the motorcade near the triple underpass. The first shot occurred between frames 160 and 166 of the film when Kennedy's motorcade was passing in front of the Book Depository. Oswald's second shot was fired 3.5 seconds after the first shot and it wounded both Kennedy and Governor John Connally of Texas between frames 223 and 224 almost simultaneously. This shot has been named the single bullet theory, or magic bullet theory (according to conspiracy theorists), which argues that the second shot caused seven wounds between the two men. Initially, the second shot passed through Kennedy's throat grazing a vertebra in his neck and causing a spinal injury. Because of the injury, Kennedy's arms were forced upward in an abrupt fashion. The instantaneous movement of Kennedy's arms as seen in the Zapruder film is known as the Thorburn position, a neurological reflex caused by injury to the spine. After traveling through Kennedy's throat, the second shot continued through Governor Connally's shoulder and wrist, and finally landed in his thigh. The third shot was fired 8.4 seconds after the first shot and this final shot mortally wounded Kennedy in the back of the head. Oswald clearly had enough time to shoot three times at the motorcade in 8.4 seconds because the Mannlicher-Carcano rifle had a bolt action that recycled a cartridge in only 2.3 seconds. The telescopic sight on the rifle made Kennedy appear only 25 yards from Oswald at the time of the third shot and Marine records indicated that Oswald was skilled with an M-1 rifle at distances of nearly 200 yards without the use of a telescopic sight. Failure Analysis, a computer-generated 3-D reconstruction of Dealey Plaza, determined that the single bullet theory was feasible and likely caused the seven wounds to Kennedy and Connally based upon the trajectory angles and physical models of the presidential car and Kennedy and Connally.[45] In addition, Marina Oswald testified that her husband had practiced with the Mannlicher-Carcano rifle and, therefore, he was familiar enough with the weapon to pull off the assassination.[46]

In regard to the Tippit murder, four shells were found at the scene of the crime and the shells were matched to Oswald's revolver found in his possession when he was arrested at the Texas Theater. A ballistic expert concluded that Oswald's revolver was the only weapon that could have been used in the murder.[47]

Authorities also obtained a warrant to search Ruth Paine's house and garage for evidence and they found the controversial photographs of Oswald taken by his wife, Marina. Oswald had posed in the backyard of his home on Neely Street with the Mannlicher-Carcano rifle used to assassinate Kennedy and the .38 revolver used in the murder of J. D. Tippit. Oswald maintained during interrogation by the Dallas police that the photographs were not real, but rather pictures of someone else with Oswald's head superimposed onto the body. This has led conspiracy theorists to suggest that Oswald may have been framed for the assassination of Kennedy.[48] However, the House Select Committee on Assassinations (HSCA) in 1979 produced a scientific study of the photographs that proved their authenticity.[49] The testimony of Marina Oswald, who admitted taking the photographs of Oswald, also proved that they were most likely genuine.[50]

While a great deal has been made about the autopsy conclusions drawn by Dr. James Humes at the Bethesda Naval Hospital and the postmortem photographs and X-rays of President Kennedy, the physical evidence in this area also supports the conclusion that Oswald was the lone assassin. The autopsy report as well as the photographs and X-rays indicate that Kennedy was struck by two bullets from above and behind the presidential motorcade.[51]

The acoustical analysis of the gunshots fired during the assassination at Dealey Plaza has been a source of debate for researchers because a number of scientific studies have produced contradictory results.[52] At the time of the assassination, the Dallas police were using two radio channels for communication purposes. Channel 1 pertained to routine communication and it was recorded on a Dictaphone belt recorder. Channel 2 was assigned to the presidential motorcade and it was recorded on an Audograph disc machine. Each channel had a dispatcher that announced the time at one minute intervals. Channel 2 established that the assassination occurred between 12:30 pm and 12:31 pm while Channel 1 was taken over between 12:28 pm and 12:34 pm by a radio microphone from a police motorcycle that was stuck in the "on" position during the time of the assassination. The motorcycle was judged to be one of eighteen in the presidential motorcade. At roughly 12:30 pm on Channel 1, static-like noises occurred in sequence and these sounds have been interpreted by some researchers as gunfire.

In 1979, the HSCA hired an independent laboratory to analyze the acoustic evidence found on Channel 1 of the Dallas Police Department radio recordings.[53] The laboratory's results showed that a sound pattern on Channel 1 might be attributed to one shot being fired from the grassy knoll area. Therefore, the HSCA concluded that the assassination of President Kennedy was probably the result of a conspiracy. A second laboratory was hired to review the evidence and it agreed with the findings of the first study.[54] Both laboratories estimated that the chances of the static-like sound patterns being random radio noises were roughly 5 percent. In other words, the sound patterns were probably not random, but most likely evidence of a second shooter firing from the grassy knoll.

The HSCA called upon the Justice Department to conduct an investigation of the acoustical evidence. The Justice Department assigned the National Research Council (NRC), part of the National Academy of Sciences, to review the acoustic evidence. In 1982, the NRC Committee on Ballistic Acoustics published a portion of their report in the journal, *Science*.[55] The NRC report challenged the results of the HSCA findings, and argued that an instance of crosstalk heard on Channel 1 from Channel 2 existed on the recordings at the time of the alleged shots. Crosstalk is when sounds from one channel are picked up by a microphone tuned to a second channel. The acoustic patterns used by the HSCA to prove a shot from the grassy knoll could not be of the assassination gunfire because the crosstalk from Channel 2 to Channel 1 happened roughly one minute after the assassination. The crosstalk from Channel 2 to Channel 1 allowed the NRC to synchronize the two channels at least for the moment of the alleged shot from the grassy knoll area. The NRC report also illustrated a timeline of events on both channels and corrected such factors as the speed of the tape and location of the microphone from the police motorcycle. The NRC argued for a competing theory that the sounds on Channel 1 were most likely random noise and estimated that the likelihood that the sounds on Channel 1 were random noises was about 22 percent.

In March 2001, D. B. Thomas published an article in a peer-reviewed journal from Britain.[56] This article renewed the debate over the acoustic evidence. Thomas challenged the assumptions of the NRC by arguing that it would be highly unlikely for sound patterns akin to four gunshots from the Book Depository and one shot from the grassy knoll area to be random noise. The fact that such random noises appeared nowhere else on the recordings and occurred within a time span of eleven seconds called into question the NRC findings. By using a different instance of crosstalk to align the two channels after the shooting began, Thomas found that the shots could be placed at the actual time of the assassination. After correcting for the statistical errors of the NRC, Thomas concluded that the probability for a grassy knoll shot was actually set at 97.3 percent.[57]

Finally, and most recently, Michael O'Dell issued a report demonstrating that D. B. Thomas's analysis used an incorrect timeline, and made false assumptions that when corrected did not allow for the identification of gunshots on the Dallas police recording.[58] According to O'Dell, Thomas's use of crosstalk to align the two channels is incorrect because the crosstalk used in his analysis occurred further ahead in time than the crosstalk used by the NRC. Thomas's reliance on crosstalk that occurred further ahead in time from the assassination than the NRC crosstalk creates a serious problem because Thomas's findings are based upon the faulty assumption that Channel 2 did not stop at any time after the shooting. However, because both channels were equipped with an activation system to stop periodically when dead air existed for four seconds, O'Dell provides evidence that the recording of Channel 2 did stop and, therefore, the crosstalk used by Thomas cannot be used to align the noises on Channel 1. O'Dell argues that the most accurate instance of crosstalk to use in aligning the channels is the one closest to the assassination which was used by the NRC. As Thomas moved further away from the time of the assassination in aligning the channels, the instances where the two channels stopped and started increased which produced recordings that were asynchronous for the Thomas analysis. O'Dell concludes that the sounds relied upon by Thomas occurred too late to be connected to the assassination and Thomas simply found a sound pattern on the HSCA analyses of the acoustical data to match a sound pattern from the grassy knoll area. In sum, there cannot be a 97.3 percent probability associated with a gunshot being fired from the front and to the right of the presidential motorcade.

OSWALD AND RUBY

Having established that Oswald was involved in the assassination of Kennedy based upon his behavioral pattern and the physical evidence, it is imperative to address the murder of Oswald, within forty-eight hours of the Kennedy assassination, by Jack Ruby, a Dallas nightclub owner. The murder of Oswald by Ruby, more than anything else, convinced a majority of the public that Kennedy was assassinated as a result of a conspiracy because it appeared that Oswald was being silenced to protect either his co-conspirators or the real assassins who had framed Oswald.[59] If Oswald acted alone, then why did Ruby shoot Oswald on November 24, 1963?

Jack Ruby stated soon after the murder of Oswald that he acted on behalf of the First Lady, Jacqueline Kennedy, because he wanted to save her the trauma of having to testify at Oswald's trial. Ruby stated that he did not want Mrs. Kennedy to have to return to Dallas for Oswald's trial and be subjected to "this ordeal for this son-of-bitch."[60] Along these same lines, Ruby expressed admiration and respect for President Kennedy after the murder of Oswald.[61] Another basic motive may have been Ruby's desire for fame and attention. The Assistant District Attorney stated that Ruby thought he would be hailed as a hero for murdering Oswald and would gain notoriety by absolving the city of Dallas of any stigma from the Kennedy assassination. Ruby may have viewed the murder of Oswald as a way to gain publicity and, in turn, a financial reward that would end his economic problems which always seemed to exist.[62] Other assassination researchers have argued effectively that Ruby was emotionally imbalanced as evidenced by the fact that he became increasingly unstable during his time in prison. Jack Ruby's full name was Jack Rubinstein and he was born an Orthodox Jew on March 25, 1911. Ruby's sister, Eva Grant, referred to him as mentally deranged as evidenced by his paranoia and obsession with the idea that the Jewish people would be exterminated by President Lyndon Johnson, who Ruby referred to as a Nazi.[63] His fixation upon the discrimination of his Jewish people was a significant part of his mindset before and after the murder of Oswald. For example, Ruby had become obsessed with an advertisement attributed to Bernard Weissman in the *Dallas Morning News* on Nov. 22, 1963, which accused President Kennedy of supporting the communist movement. Ruby surmised that the Jewish name "Weissman" was listed to disparage Jewish people who would be blamed for the assassination. Ruby also became obsessed with a billboard calling for the impeachment of Chief Justice Earl Warren because he mistakenly thought a post office box number on the billboard was the same as a number on the Weissman advertisement. Ruby went as far as to photograph the billboard and three photos of the billboard were found in his pocket after his murder of Oswald. Finally, immediately after Ruby murdered Oswald, he was quoted as saying that "I guess I just had to show the world that a Jew has guts."[64]

Ruby's testimony before the Warren Commission representatives in Dallas showed that Ruby emphatically denied being part of any conspiracy and he requested and was administered a polygraph which proved that he had never met Oswald, that he acted on his own in shooting Oswald, and that he decided to murder Oswald spontaneously without premeditation. Ruby was convicted on March 14, 1964, and sentenced to death for the premeditated murder of Oswald. Ruby's attorneys had failed miserably in their attempt to have Ruby declared innocent by reason of insanity. An appeals court overturned the verdict but, after being diagnosed with cancer, Ruby died of a blood clot on January 3, 1967, before a second trial could commence.

CONCLUSIONS AND ANALYSIS

In the final analysis, Oswald's assassination of Kennedy was personal in the sense that he was an individual who could not separate his personal life from the political world. Political scientists define this type of personality as the "political personality."[65] Oswald had displaced his personal motives for the assassination on to a public object, President Kennedy. Oswald had rationalized his motive for the assassination toward a larger public interest. In reality, Oswald was seeking power to compensate for low self-esteem. The exercise of power by way of assassinating a political leader generates the attention and recognition that the person has been deprived of their entire life. Oswald once was quoted as saying, "[t]here is no borderline between one's personal world and the world in general."[66]

Oswald had delusions of becoming a great leader in a utopian society. He often compared himself to Lenin, who led the successful Bolshevik revolution in Russia. While Oswald did not hate Kennedy, he saw Kennedy as the embodiment of U.S. foreign policy toward Cuba as well as an obstacle to Oswald's greatness. Kennedy offered hope to a capitalist system which was a source of Oswald's poverty and frustration. In short, Kennedy was too good and the utopian revolution that Oswald envisioned would not come about if Kennedy was allowed to continue serving as president of the United States.[67]

While Kennedy became the object of his personal frustrations, the assassination also provided Oswald with the attention and recognition that he was denied during most of his life. Whether it was his failure in the Marines, his disillusionment with the political systems in the United States and Soviet Union, his several dead-end jobs, or the rejection from his wife, Oswald consistently reacted in dramatic fashion with behavior that was designed to prove his importance as a person. The opportunity to kill Kennedy was the most important moment in Oswald's life and it offered him the type of attention and recognition that, in his own mind, he deserved.

If a future generation of researchers is able to reveal a conspiracy in the assassination of President Kennedy, this would not absolve Oswald of his role in the assassination based upon the demonstrated pattern of behavior throughout his life as well as the physical evidence discussed above. In short, prosecutors would still have been able to prove in a criminal court that Oswald committed the assassination beyond a reasonable doubt, albeit with the assistance of co-conspirators.

NOTES

1. James H. Fetzer, ed., *Assassination Science: Experts Speak Out on the Death of JFK* (Chicago: Catfree Press, 2001); Jim Garrison, *On the Trail of the Assassins* (New York: Sheridan Square Press, 1988); Mark Lane, *Rush to Judgment* (New York: Dell, 1966).

2. Gerald Posner, *Case Closed: Lee Harvey Oswald and the Assassination of JFK* (New York: Random House, 1993), x-xi.

3. Michael Dobbs, "Myths Over Attacks on U.S. Swirl through Islamic World: Many Rumors Lay Blame on an Israeli Conspiracy," *Washington Post*, October 13, 2001, A22.

4. Mark Lane, *Plausible Denial: Was the CIA Involved in the Assassination of JFK?* (New York: Thunder's Mouth Press, 1991); *Investigation of the Assassination of President John F. Kennedy: Hearing before the House, Select Committee on Assassinations* (HSCA). 95th Congress (1979) [hereinafter HSCA].

5. James Clarke, *Defining Danger: American Assassins and the New Domestic Terrorists* (New Brunswick, N.J., Transaction Publishers, 2007).

6. Jean Stafford, *A Mother in History* (New York: Farrar, Straus & Giroux, 1966), 24-25.

7. *Investigation of the Assassination of President John F. Kennedy: Hearing Before the President's Commission on the Assassination of President Kennedy*. 88th Congress., Vol. I, 253-255 (1964) (testimony of Marguerite Oswald), [hereinafter WCR].

8. Priscilla Johnson McMillan, *Marina and Lee* (New York: Harper & Row, 1977), 223-228.

9. WCR, Vol. VIII, 217 (testimony of Renatus Hartogs); WCR Vol. XX, 89-90 (Hartogs Exhibit 1); WCR, Vol. XIX, 308-323 (Carro Exhibit 1) (summary of John Carro's psychiatric report created on 5/1/53).

10. Clarke, *Defining Danger,* 108-112.

11. WCR, Vol. 1, 375-76 (testimony of Robert Oswald); WCR, Vol. XI, 4 (testimony of John Pic).

12. Robert L. Oswald, *Lee: A Portrait of Lee Harvey Oswald by His Brother* (New York: Coward McCann, 1967), 75.

13. WCR, vol. XVI, 94-95 (Oswald's Historic Diary, Warren Commission Exhibit 24).

14. Ibid. (Oswald's Historic Diary, Warren Commission Exhibit 24, entry for Nov. 17-Dec. 30, 1959).
15. Clarke, *Defining Danger,* 109.
16. WCR, vol. XVII, xx & 635 (Commission Exhibit 773—photograph of a mail order for a rifle in the name of "A. Hidell").
17. WCR, Vol. XI, 405-410 (testimony of Edwin Walker).
18. WCR, Vol. I, 16-17 (testimony of Marina Oswald).
19. Sylvia Meagher, *Accessories After the Fact: The Warren Commission, the Authorities, and the Report.* (New York: Vintage, 1992), 376.
20. WCR Vol. XI, 368-373 (testimony of Sylvia Odio).
21. Robert Groden and Harrison Livingstone, *High Treason: The Assassination of President John F. Kennedy and the New Evidence of Conspiracy* (New York: Conservatory Press, 1989), 399.
22. Sylvia Meagher, *Accessories After the Fact: The Warren Commission, the Authorities, and the Report* (New York: Vintage, 1992), 376.
23. Posner, *Case Closed,* 176-178.
24. Oleg Maximovich Nechiporenko, *Passport to Assassination: The Never-Before-Told-Story of Lee Harvey Oswald by the KGB Colonel Who Knew Him* (New York: Carol Publishing, 1993).
25. HSCA, vol. III, 33-60, 130-147.
26. WCR, vol. III, 213-216 (statement of Roy Truly).
27. Thomas Mallon, *Mrs. Paine's Garage and the Murder of John F. Kennedy* (New York: Pantheon, 2002), 41-45.
28. Posner, *Case Closed*, 215.
29. Clarke, *Defining Danger,* 122-124.
30. WCR, Vol. XXII, 681-682 (statement of Bonnie Ray Williams, Commission Exhibit 1381); WCR, Vol. VI, 354 (testimony of Charles Givens).
31. Howard Brennan and J. Edward Cherryholmes, *Eyewitness to History: The Kennedy Assassination as Seen by Howard L. Brennan* (Waco, Tex.: Texian Press, 1987), 8-15.
32. Jim Bishop, *The Day Kennedy Was Shot* (New York: Funk and Wagnalls, 1968), 256-258.
33. Posner, *Case Closed*, 276.
34. Oswald's revolver actually misfired. Edward Jay Epstein, *Inquest: The Warren Commission and the Establishment of Truth* (New York: Viking, 1966), Appendix A, 176.
35. WCR, Vol. IV, 209-225 (testimony of J. W. Fritz).
36. WCR, Vol. XXV, Commission Exhibit #2166.
37. Diane Holloway, *The Mind of Oswald* (Victoria, B.C.: Trafford Publishing, 2000), 214.
38. Ibid., 230-231.
39. Posner, *Case Closed*, 92. Oswald was known to use the alias, "Alex Hidell." The first name, "Alex," was given to him as a nickname during his time in Russia because many Russians were confused in calling him by his real name, "Lee," because it sounded as if it was a Chinese name. The last name, "Hidell," had its origins either in the last name of a fellow Marine of Oswald's or some have speculated that the last name, Hidell," may have been used by Oswald because it rhymed with the first name of his hero, "Fidel" Castro.
40. Holloway, *The Mind of Oswald,* 218.
41. Scott P. Johnson, "The Prosecution of Lee Harvey Oswald," *South Texas Law Review,* 48 (Spring 2007), 679.
42. Holloway, *The Mind of Oswald*, 215.
43. Gladwin Hill, "One Bullet Fired: Night-Club Man Who Admired Kennedy Is Oswald's Slayer," *New York Times*, Nov. 25, 1963, 1a.
44. Posner, *Case Closed,* 264-272.
45. Ibid., 317-318.
46. WCR, Vol. I, 54-65 (statement of Marina Oswald).
47. WCR, Vol. III, 511-513 (statement of James D. Nicol, ballistics expert).
48. Jim Marrs, *Crossfire: The Plot That Killed Kennedy* (New York: Carroll & Graf, 1989), 450-454.

49. HSCA, Vol. VI, 182-206.

50. WCR, Vol. I, 15.

51. Dennis L. Breo, "JFK's Death: The Plain Truth from the MDs Who Did the Autopsy," *JAMA* 267 (May 27, 1992), 2794.

52. The most frequently cited scientific studies of the acoustics evidence are as follows: HSCA, vol. III, 49-50 (finding a shot from the grassy knoll was likely); 2) Committee on Ballistic Acoustics, National Research Council, "Reexamination of Acoustic Evidence in the Kennedy Assassination," *Science*, 218 (Oct. 8, 1982), 127-133. 3) D. B. Thomas, "Echo Correlation Analysis and the Acoustic Evidence in the Kennedy Assassination Revisited." *Science & Justice* 41 (2001), 21-32. 4) Michael O'Dell, "The acoustics evidence in the Kennedy assassination." Accessed February 9, 2013, http://mcadams.posc.mu.edu/odell/. For an update on attempts to use the latest technology to uncover new evidence from the acoustics, Jefferson Morley, "The JFK Murder: Can New Technology Finally crack the case?" *Reader's Digest.* March 2005, 84-91.

53. HSCA proceedings Vol. VIII, 41.

54. Computer Science Department of the City University New York used their experts in sonar applications. M. R. Weiss and A. Aschkenasy, *An Analysis of Recorded Sounds Relating to the Assassination of John F. Kennedy* (Department of Computer Sciences, Queens College, City University of New York, 1979).

55. National Research Council, "Reexamination of Acoustic Evidence," 127-133.

56. Thomas, "Echo Correlation Analysis," 21-32.

57. George Lardner Jr., "Study Backs Theory of Grassy Knoll: New Report Says Second Gunman Fired at Kennedy," *Washington Post*, March 26, 2001, A03.

58. O'Dell, "The acoustics evidence in the Kennedy assassination."

59. In the aftermath of Ruby's murder of Oswald, public opinion polls showed that roughly two-thirds of the public believed that Kennedy was assassinated as a result of a conspiracy. Thomas Banta, "The Kennedy Assassination: Early Thoughts and Emotions*,"* *Public Opinion Quarterly*, 28 (1964), 216-220 (discussing the myriad of emotions directly following the assassination).

60. WCR, Vol. XIII, 68 (testimony of Secret Service Agent Forrest Sorrels).

61. Posner, *Case Closed*, 399 (discussing Gerald Posner's interview with Rabbi Hillel Silverman, January 15, 1993).

62. Seth Kantor, *The Ruby Cover-Up* (New York: Kensington Publishing, 1978), 33.

63. WCR, Vol. XIV, 471-85 (testimony of Eva Grant, Jack Ruby's sister).

64. WCR, Vol. XV, 533 (testimony of Danny Patrick McCurdy); WCR, Vol. V, 203 (testimony of Jack Ruby); WCR, Vol. XIII, 68 (testimony of Forrest V. Sorrels).

65. Harold Lasswell, *Power and Personality* (New York: W. W. Norton, Inc., 1948).

66. Clarke, *Defining Danger,* 103.

67. Norman Mailer, *Oswald's Tale: An American Mystery* (New York: Random House, 1995), 780-782.

Chapter Two

Oswald as Conspirator

A conspiracy is defined as "a plan . . . by two or more persons to commit an unlawful, harmful, or treacherous act."[1] Most social scientists view conspiracies as extreme and incorrect explanations of reality.[2] However, this does not mean that conspiracies never occur. Conspiracies occur within political systems, particularly against the powerless and the disadvantaged of society. For example, in 1995, a group of Philadelphia police officers were indicted and pled guilty to manufacturing evidence against poor blacks. This called into question over one thousand prosecutions. In one instance, a grandmother was framed for selling crack cocaine and spent three years in prison. She later won a civil lawsuit against the city of Philadelphia for $1 million.[3] Conspiracies also happen on a larger scale. For example, a controversial body of literature has surfaced recently that suggests the possibility of conspiracies in the murders of major political and civil rights leaders in the 1960s.[4] This chapter attempts to apply the scientific method to determine whether Lee Harvey Oswald was involved in a conspiracy to assassinate one of the greatest political and civil rights leaders of the twentieth century, President John F. Kennedy.

THE SCIENTIFIC METHOD AND THE LOGIC OF CONSPIRACY

Science is "all knowledge gathered only by means of the scientific methodology."[5] The scientific method is based upon the collection of knowledge using our perceptions, experience, and observations to discover logical patterns in the natural world. While it can be argued that Lee Harvey Oswald was involved in the assassination based upon the physical evidence against Oswald as well as an empirical analysis of his behavior (see chapter 1), a conspiracy, including Oswald, to murder Kennedy cannot be ignored because of empirical evidence that also exists about the patterns of behavior associated within the intelligence community and the organized crime syndicate. Many scholars have argued that the scientific method cannot be applied to the study of conspiracy because much of the information in this area of study is secretive and intentionally deceptive. For instance, conspirators, such as the Central Intelligence Agency (CIA) and organized crime, use false records, fronts, and other devices to hide the phenomenon under study. In describing the counter-intuitive behavior of the intelligence community, Gerald Posner stated conspiracy theorists don't understand that, if there was a CIA plot to assassinate President Kennedy, no documents would exist.[6] Because events can be manipulated by elites, whether they are individuals or organizations, social scientists must develop new tools, or adapt their current tools of research, to understand conspiracy as a phenomenon. This chapter argues that the scientific method can be applied in a limited sense to the study of the JFK assassination, even if a conspiracy existed. How? It is well documented that observable patterns of misinformation and lies are common practice within the intelligence community and the world of organized crime. If individuals, organizations, or institutions maintain a history of deceptive behavior, one must draw the conclusion that such a pattern of behavior is logical, explainable, and predictable. Hence, the scientific method is compatible as a tool for understanding conspiracy if it is understood that deceptive behavior is logical within the context of an organization's history.

By using the scientific method, an attempt will be made to answer the following questions related to the assassination of President John F. Kennedy: 1) Does empirical evidence indicate a larger conspiracy to assassinate President Kennedy as suggested by the House Select Committee on Assassinations (HSCA) in 1979?[7] If so, what forces were behind the conspiracy? 2) Did Oswald's pattern of behavior make him vulnerable to those individuals, organizations, or institutions that exhibited a pattern of deception and misinformation in their manipulation of events? (i.e., Is there a connection between the empirical analysis of Oswald's behavior and the behavior demonstrated by the intelligence community and/or organized crime?) Any evidence connecting Oswald to an empirical pattern of deceptive behavior demonstrated by the intelligence community and/or organized crime strengthens the argument for conspiracy in the assassination of Kennedy.

THE CENTRAL INTELLIGENCE AGENCY

Since the National Security Act of 1947 consolidated power in the military-industrial complex, the U.S. government repeatedly has engaged in deception and misinformation regarding its activities at home and abroad.[8] C. Wright Mills was referring to the military-industrial complex when he coined the term, the power elite, in the 1950s. The power elite are recognized within political science as a phenomenon where organizations with great resources become involved in criminal activity and subsequent cover-ups.[9] This holds true, particularly for the CIA. In 1954, the CIA orchestrated the removal of President Jacobo Guzman, a leftist, from power in Guatemala while the U.S. government lied to the American people about its involvement. In 1960, Francis Gary Powers, a CIA pilot flying a U-2 spy plane over Soviet airspace, had his plane shot down by the Soviet Union. While the U.S. government had been using spy planes since the 1950s, U.S. officials refused to take responsibility for the incident and claimed that Soviet air space had not been violated by the United States.[10] A year later, in 1961, the CIA orchestrated an invasion of Cuba at the Bay of Pigs, but Adlai Stevenson, U.S. Ambassador to the United Nations, lied to the United Nations and the American public when he said that the United States had not provided any assistance in the operation.[11] In 1964, President Lyndon Johnson deliberately misled the Congress and the public regarding the Gulf of Tonkin incident in order to escalate the U.S. involvement in Vietnam.[12] President Johnson indicated that U.S. ships had been fired upon when, in fact, it was never confirmed. President Johnson also secretly funded "volunteers" from Asia to fight in Vietnam but he neglected to mention that the U.S. government had paid Thailand and the Philippines $200 million each for the use of their "volunteers." President Nixon also lied about U.S. involvement in Southeast Asia when he told the American public that the United States was not involved militarily in Cambodia. In fact, the United States had conducted thousands of bombings in Cambodia at the time of Nixon's statement. The U.S. government also deliberately underestimated the strength of the North Vietnamese to offer the illusion that the United States was winning the Vietnam conflict.[13] In 1976, CIA director, George H. W. Bush, was quoted as saying that ". . . the CIA will not enter into any paid or contractual relationship with any full-time or part-time news correspondent accredited by any U.S. news service, newspaper, periodical, radio, or television network or station."[14] At the time of Bush's announcement, the CIA employed almost 100 members of U.S. media organizations and journalists. As recently as 2003, in the build-up to war with Iraq, the U.S. government's intelligence community manipulated information to justify a major military operation in Iraq.[15]

Based upon the chronology of events listed above, it is evident that the CIA has demonstrated a pattern of misinformation and deception over the years. The CIA was involved in almost a thousand foreign interventions in a period of two decades during the Cold War according to a Senate investigation committee.[16] This included paramilitary operations, the overthrow of foreign governments, and assassination plots. From 1960–1965, the CIA planned several plots to assassinate Fidel Castro and, in 1975, the CIA also planned to assassinate Patrice Lumumba, the first and only elected prime minister of the Congo in 1960. Lumumba had demanded that Belgium end its colonial rule over the Congo by withdrawing Belgian troops from the Congo. Belgium had been exploiting the mineral-rich southern area of the Congo for forty years. Lumumba expelled Belgian diplomats and called for the United Nations to intervene. Because Lumumba had received military assistance from the Soviet Union in his battle with the Belgium government over their colonial rule of the Congo, the CIA devised a plot to kill Lumumba by using poisonous toothpaste.[17] It has been argued that the order for the murder of Lumumba came directly from President Eisenhower. The CIA plot to assassinate Lumumba was never carried out because the man allegedly in charge of the Lumumba assassination, Larry Devlin, the CIA station chief in Leopoldville, threw the poisonous tube of toothpaste in the Congo River. The U.S. government has also been linked to the assassinations of world leaders in the Dominican Republic (Rafael Trujillo), South Vietnam (Ngo Dinh Diem), and Chile (General Rene Schneider).[18]

It was inevitable that the U.S. government's use of disinformation, propaganda, and assassinations in foreign nations would carry over into the domestic arena. Presidential scholars have expressed serious concern that presidents have consolidated power in the modern era which has allowed for the domination of foreign policy which, in turn, has led to a domination of the domestic policy arena.[19] In 1979, the HSCA concluded that the assassination of President John F. Kennedy was probably the result of a conspiracy. Because only circumstantial evidence exists implicating the CIA in the assassination of President Kennedy, the HSCA refused to conclude that any government agencies were involved in the assassination. However, in the aftermath of the assassinations, it has been suggested by scholars that the CIA killed President Kennedy because he refused to continue intelligence operations against Cuba after the assassination attempts on Castro and the Bay of Pigs fiasco. Coincidentally, a number of government officials involved in the Bay of Pigs invasion and the CIA-Mafia plots to assassinate Fidel Castro have been connected to the Kennedy assassination and may even have been in Dallas, Texas, on November 22, 1963. CIA agents, E. Howard Hunt and Frank Sturgis, serve perhaps as the best example of individuals who were involved in the Bay of Pigs and the numerous attempts to murder Castro. Both men also were alleged to have been associates of Lee Harvey Oswald and were involved in a deliberate attempt to mislead investigators about the identity of Oswald in the aftermath of the assassination.[20] In 1972, Hunt and Sturgis were arrested for breaking into the Democratic National Headquarters based at the Watergate Hotel in Washington, D.C.

In addition to the frustration that the CIA felt toward Kennedy concerning the Cuban problem, it has been speculated that the CIA and the military were also angered by Kennedy's decision to withdraw troops from Vietnam and his desire to end the Cold War with the Soviet Union. Ultimately, the evidence that the CIA or any other government agency was involved in the assassination is circumstantial at best. However, at the very least, there is strong evidence that government agencies, such as the Federal Bureau of Investigation (FBI), CIA, and other government agencies, participated in a cover-up after the assassination by deliberately withholding information and misleading investigators to protect their organizations.[21]

Another example of deception by the U.S. government is the domestic surveillance of its citizens by the CIA, FBI, and National Security Agency (NSA) in recent times. From 1967-1973, the NSA followed the communications of thousands of U.S. citizens and organizations as well as foreign nationals and groups.[22] From 1953-1973, roughly one-quarter of a million letters were opened and copied by the CIA within the United States. William Colby, Director of the CIA from 1973-1976, testified to Congress that the CIA opened the mail of private citizens and also noted that the CIA maintained secret files with information on thousands of Americans.[23] Foreign embassies and controversial groups such as the Ku Klux Klan, the Socialist Workers Party, and the American Communist Party have also been subject to harassment by the U.S. government using warrantless searches and raids.[24] The illegal surveillance of Martin Luther King, Jr. is another troubling example of the government's use of counterintelligence and surveillance in an attempt to discredit and destroy a political leader.[25] In addition to their conclusion that President Kennedy was probably assassinated as a result of a conspiracy, the HSCA also concluded that Martin Luther King was also probably assassinated as the result of a conspiracy. King had become a powerful and charismatic figure who frightened segments of the federal government because of his staunch opposition to the Vietnam War as well as his alleged connection to the American Communist Party.

After the events of September 11, 2001, the U.S. intelligence community was harshly criticized for failing to thwart the terrorist attacks on America carried out by Islamic fundamentalists.[26] As a result of the 9-11 attacks, the U.S. government has increased its domestic surveillance of the American public at an alarming rate. An expert analysis detailing the history of the NSA has established that data on the American public are currently being mined and used in a disturbing manner.[27]

There also exists documented evidence that the U.S. government used its own citizens as guinea pigs in experiments. For example, the CIA administered LSD to various people without their knowledge to monitor their reaction to the hallucinogen. In 1953, a CIA official slipped LSD into the drinks of government scientists without their knowledge resulting in the death of one man,[28] and the CIA also hired prostitutes in San Francisco to administer drugs to their customers.[29] The CIA developed a pattern of testing such drugs on various people who were powerless against the resources of the U.S. government. Besides the administration of the LSD, human subjects also were used illegally and unethically by the U.S. government to test their exposure to X-rays, biological agents, radiation, poisonous bacteria, nuclear bomb tests, and other potentially dangerous chemicals.[30]

The documented evidence above illustrates that the U.S. government has, at times, been involved in criminal activity as well as attempts to conceal such activity. Because the U.S. government maintains vast financial resources, it has been able to manipulate events to serve its political and economic interests at home and abroad. While this evidence does not prove a conspiracy in the assassination of President Kennedy, it creates the real possibility that the intelligence community might have been connected to the assassination in some manner.

ORGANIZED CRIME SYNDICATE

The world of organized crime maintains its own pattern of deception and misinformation in carrying out illegal activities.[31] In addition, it is troubling to note that the U.S. government has worked in conjunction with the Mafia over the years in clandestine operations. The connection between organized crime and the U.S. government actually began during World War II when Mafia figures in control of the docks in New York were used by naval intelligence to protect against any infiltration by German submarines. The U.S. government discovered that underworld Mafia figures and their employees (such as pimps, prostitutes, and drug dealers) could act as counterintelligence units for the American government. Later, in the early 1960s, the CIA hired the Mafia for assassination attempts against Fidel Castro. The fact that the Director of the FBI, J. Edgar Hoover, in the 1960s deliberately misled the public by stating that organized crime did not exist in the United States provides circumstantial evidence that the government may have been protecting its sources and operations connected to the underworld. The Mafia also had ties to President Nixon and the Watergate burglars during the early 1970s. As noted above, the same names involved in the Bay of Pigs invasion and the CIA-Mafia plots to assassinate Castro in the 1960s also surfaced in the Watergate and Iran-Contra scandals in the 1970s and 1980s.[32]

Using its own airline, Air America, the CIA worked in conjunction with organized crime figures transporting illegal drugs such as heroin throughout Southeast Asia in an area called the Golden Triangle. Organized crime also has provided a great deal of financial assistance to politicians at the local, state, and national levels over the years. In sum, there has been a close relationship, at times, between the organized crime syndicate and political elites. This has led scholars, such as C. Wright Mills, to coin the term "higher immorality" in describing the systematic corruption and the pervasiveness of organized crime both politically and economically in American society.[33]

The HSCA in 1979 concluded that organized crime probably was the source of the conspiracy to murder President John F. Kennedy. The HSCA tentatively concluded that Kennedy was assassinated by the Marcello crime family of New Orleans led by Carlos Marcello and the Traficante family of Tampa, Florida, led by Santos Traficante.[34] The HSCA determined that the Mafia bosses had "the means, motive, and opportunity" to assassinate the president. Some conspiracy theorists have argued that Carlos Marcello ordered the murder of President Kennedy because Attorney General Robert Kennedy had ordered the deportation of Marcello to Guatemala.[35] It has also been argued that Marcello instructed a family associate, Jack Ruby, to murder the alleged assassin of Kennedy, Lee Harvey Oswald. In general, the Kennedy brothers made enemies with powerful elements of the organized crime syndicate by declaring an all-out war against the Mafia. The HSCA also suggested that anti-Castro activists may have assisted organized crime in the assassination. Some researchers have even speculated that presidential candidate, Robert F. Kennedy, was also assassinated by the Mafia in 1968. It has been established that thirteen shots were fired at Robert Kennedy on June 5, 1968, at the Ambassador Hotel in Los Angeles, California. Sirhan Sirhan, the alleged assassin, had only an eight-shot revolver. The fatal shots that killed Robert Kennedy evidently came from behind, but Sirhan Sirhan stood in front of Kennedy. Examinations also produced evidence that two separate .22 caliber guns were used in the assassination. Most importantly, Sirhan did have a connection to organized crime. He had worked on a horse-breeding farm run by an ex-convict named Frank Donneroummus. Mickey Cohen was the owner of the farm and he was connected to Carlos Marcello as well as other organized crime figures named in the Kennedy assassination.[36]

It is evident that the intelligence agencies of the U.S. government and/or the world of organized crime had the motive and opportunity to commit the assassination of President Kennedy given their patterns of behavior. Therefore, it is necessary to attempt to bridge the gap between the circumstantial and real evidence before drawing a conclusion. The following section evaluates the evidence that might connect Lee Harvey Oswald's pattern of behavior to those patterns of behavior associated with the intelligence community and organized crime.

THE EVIDENCE FOR CONSPIRACY

Oswald maintained a long list of associates connected to the world of intelligence and/or organized crime. Oswald's movements and contacts throughout his life provide for great mystery and intrigue. The members of the Warren Commission simply concluded that a series of coincidences accounted for Oswald's mysterious behavior and associations.[37] But, was it merely a coincidence that Oswald maintained such a wide variety of contacts with intelligence community and organized crime figures? Was Oswald simply obsessed with the politics of the era, specifically Kennedy, Castro, Russia and Cuba, to the point where he simply placed himself within controversial and explosive situations by chance? The following section examines the evidence for conspiracy in the assassination of President John F. Kennedy.

PHYSICAL EVIDENCE

The acoustical analysis of the gunshots fired during the assassination at Dealey Plaza provides strong evidence that a conspiracy existed in the murder of President Kennedy.[38] As noted in chapter 1, the Dallas police were using two radio channels for communication purposes and, most likely, recorded the shots fired in Dealey Plaza on November 22, 1963. In 1979, the HSCA hired two independent laboratories to analyze the acoustic evidence found on the Dallas Police Department radio recordings and concluded that, while shots were fired from the Texas School Book Depository (TSBD), at least one shot was fired from the grassy knoll area.[39] Hence, the HSCA concluded that there existed a 95 percent probability that shots were fired at the president's motorcade from two different locations. Therefore, the HSCA concluded that the assassination of President Kennedy was probably the result of a conspiracy. While the National Research Council (NRC), part of the National Academy of Sciences, reviewed the acoustical evidence and concluded, in 1982, that the noises on the radio recordings were most likely random,[40] D. B. Thomas published an article in a peer-reviewed journal from Britain in 2001 and concluded that the probability for a grassy knoll shot was actually set at 97.3 percent. Hence, even if Lee Harvey Oswald fired his rifle from the TSBD, scientific evidence suggests the strong probability that a second shooter also fired a shot from the grassy knoll area.

David Lifton also claims to have discovered physical evidence proving the existence of a conspiracy in the Kennedy assassination based upon a meticulous examination of the Warren Commission Report as well as interviews conducted with various medical and security personnel who attended to the president's body in Dallas and at the Bethesda Naval Hospital in Maryland.[41] Lifton argues that the president's head wounds were altered to give the false impression that Kennedy was shot from the rear and to conceal the fact that shots were actually fired at the president from a direction in front of the motorcade. Based upon interviews with the medical staff at Parkland Hospital in Dallas and Bethesda Naval Hospital, Lifton maintains that surgery most likely was performed on the president's head after the president's body left Dallas but prior to its arrival for the official autopsy at Bethesda Naval Hospital. Apparently, the Dallas medical staff reported that the president had an entry wound in the front of his head and an exit wound in the back of his head, while the Bethesda medical staff concluded that Kennedy possessed a large exit wound in the front of his head. In support of his theory, Lifton points to a FBI report produced by two agents, James Sibert and Francis O'Neill, who observed the autopsy of the president's body at Bethesda Naval Hospital. Prior to the autopsy, Sibert and O'Neil observed the president's body upon its arrival at Bethesda and noted that a tracheotomy had been done on the president and surgery on the head had also been performed, specifically on the area near the top of the skull. While a tracheotomy had been performed in Dallas in a desperate attempt to save the president's life, there had not been any surgery conducted on the president's head according to the medical staff at Parkland Hospital. Hence, Lifton concludes that the president's head wounds were altered, thus proving the existence of a conspiracy in the assassination.

While Lifton does not name specific conspirators involved in the altering of the head wounds, he theorized that the president's body was most likely removed from its original bronze casket and placed in a plain metal casket during Air Force One's flight from Dallas to Andrews Air Force Base. After Air Force One arrived at Andrews, Lifton argues that the plain metal casket containing Kennedy's body was taken off of Air Force One and flown by helicopter to Walter Reed Medical Center where surgery was conducted on the head area to make it appear as if Kennedy had been shot from behind. The implication of Lifton's research points toward a conspiracy involving powerful forces inside the government altering the president's body prior to the official autopsy at Bethesda. In order for such a covert operation to succeed, Lifton concludes that a number of Secret Service personnel and other government officials would have been required to participate in the conspiracy. According to Lifton, the Secret Service had to be involved because they controlled all aspects of the president's trip to Dallas, specifically the planning of the trip, the security detail in Dealey Plaza, and the speed and route of the motorcade. In addition, the Secret Service had custody of the president's body, his clothes, the bullets, and the limousine. Finally, the Secret Service had in its possession the X-rays and photographs produced at Bethesda Naval Hospital.

THE CIRCUMSTANTIAL EVIDENCE

In 1955, at the age of 15, Lee Harvey Oswald served in the Civil Air Patrol (CAP) under the direction of his instructor, David Ferrie. Ferrie maintained a variety of contacts within the world of intelligence and organized crime. Many conspiracy theorists point to Oswald's relationship with Ferrie as evidence that Oswald was being recruited into intelligence operations at this time.[42] There also is evidence to suggest that Oswald was in contact with Ferrie after he returned to the United States from the Soviet Union in 1962. Ferrie supposedly was hired as the private pilot for New Orleans crime boss, Carlos Marcello and, according to an unconfirmed report cited by the HSCA, flew Marcello back to the United States in 1961 after he was deported to Guatemala by Attorney General Robert Kennedy. In addition, Ferrie was known to have worked closely with anti-Castro Cuban organizations planning a second attempt, after the Bay of Pigs, to overthrow the Castro regime in Cuba. As noted above, some researchers have speculated that Ferrie was ordered by Carlos Marcello to have Jack Ruby murder Lee Harvey Oswald in the aftermath of the Kennedy assassination. Ruby made numerous telephone calls to associates of Carlos Marcello and Santos Traficante in the months leading up to the assassination of Kennedy and the murder of Oswald. In fact, the Warren Commission was suspicious of Ruby's telephone calls from September 1963 until November 22, 1963, which it itemized in detail in its final report.[43]

Ferrie was questioned extensively by District Attorney Jim Garrison of New Orleans who began investigating the Kennedy assassination in 1967. Based largely upon information that he received from Ferrie, Garrison eventually brought charges against Clay Shaw, a wealthy businessman with CIA connections, for conspiring to murder President Kennedy. Ferrie and Shaw allegedly were seen with Oswald at a voter registration drive for African Americans in Clinton, New Orleans during the late summer or early fall of 1963.

Oswald's defection to the Soviet Union in 1959 is another mystery that has not been understood completely by researchers. Prior to his defection to the Soviet Union, Oswald served three years in the Marines from 1956–1959 and was stationed at a top-secret airbase in Atsugi, Japan where he worked as a radar operator monitoring the U-2 spy plane. The Atsugi base in Japan contained a large facility used by the CIA. Oswald was given a security clearance of "confidential" and many researchers maintain that Oswald began working as a CIA operative during his time in Japan by providing disinformation to Japanese women posing as KGB agents. Oswald supposedly frequented an expensive nightclub called the Queen Bee in Japan where 100 of the most beautiful women in Tokyo would often attempt to gather information from American military personnel, usually officers and pilots. While Oswald was only a first class private in the Marines and could not afford an evening at the Queen Bee, it has been alleged that he was given money to spend at the Queen Bee by the CIA to spread disinformation to the Japanese Communists.[44] Interestingly, one of Oswald's fellow Marines, Gerry Patrick Hemming, who was also stationed in Japan, said he believed that Oswald was recruited by the CIA. Hemming, who claimed to have been recruited in Japan by the CIA as well, said that he and Oswald had conversations that suggested Oswald was a CIA recruit. It has been theorized that, once Oswald was recruited by the CIA in Japan, he was then asked to infiltrate the Soviet Union as a spy. James Wilcott, a CIA finance officer, testified before the HSCA that, based upon his conversations with CIA personnel, he believed Oswald served as a CIA spy during his time in Japan and was later sent to the Soviet Union on a clandestine operation. Coincidentally, the Office of Naval Intelligence (ONI) sponsored a secret defector program in the late 1950s where young men in the military with above average intelligence would feign disillusionment with the United States and defect to the Soviet Union. This "phony" defector program was an intelligence operation designed to provide information for the U.S. government about life in the Soviet Union. Robert E. Webster, a Navy man, defected to the Soviet Union and returned to the United States at approximately the same time frame as Oswald. It has been speculated that Webster was part of the same phony defector program.

Further evidence of Oswald's intelligence training is based upon the fact that he was administered a Russian language examination during his time in the Marines.[45] District Attorney Jim Garrison claimed the language examination was evidence that Oswald received intelligence training while in the military. In fact, Warren Commission members were told two months after the Kennedy assassination that Oswald also studied at the Monterey School of the Army, which today is known as the Defense Language Institute where the U.S. government provides language training at an accelerated rate.

The Warren Commission report provided a detailed account of Oswald's financial transactions throughout his life to determine if he received any financial support regarding his travel to the Soviet Union. The results of the Commission's investigation were that Oswald did not receive any such support. Hence, while it appears that Oswald supposedly did not receive any financial assistance in his travels to and from the Soviet Union, the State Department oddly provided a small loan to Oswald at his request to finance a portion of his trip home. After returning to the United States in 1962 with his Russian wife and infant child, Oswald repaid the small loan to the State Department.

Oswald's time spent in the Soviet Union also raised suspicions that he may have been recruited by Soviet intelligence and returned to the United States to assassinate Kennedy. Some authors suggest that Oswald may have been provided with a cover, or a legend, by Soviet intelligence.[46] A legend in the intelligence world is "an operational plan for a cover, or a cover itself, depending upon the mission." Oswald did maintain a personal diary of his time spent in the Soviet Union and the Russian government released various files of information throughout the 1990s but, for the most part, very little is known about Oswald and his activities in the Soviet Union. Hence, it is necessary to speculate whether the Soviet Union provided him with a fictional history in order to deceive the United States. In 1964, a Soviet defector to the United States, Yuri Nosenko, may have been used "to allay suspicions that the Soviets had anything to do with the assassination of Kennedy and to cover for Soviet 'moles,' or agents deep within U.S. intelligence."[47] Nosenko claimed to be the KGB agent in charge of Oswald during his time in Russia. While the Warren Commission entertained the counterintelligence possibilities of the Nosenko defection in relation to the Kennedy assassination, they refused to address the issue formally within their final report. (Chapter 5 explores the theory that a "Russian Oswald" may have been responsible for the assassination.)

After his return to the United States in 1962, Oswald was monitored closely by the CIA and FBI. The CIA maintained surveillance on Oswald by opening his mail as well as his mother's mail at various times. Many researchers are suspicious of the fact that the CIA possessed a 201 file on Oswald which indicates that he probably was connected to intelligence operations in some fashion. Victor Marchetti, who served as the executive assistant to the CIA's deputy director was quoted as saying, "Basically, if Oswald had a 201 file, he was an agent."[48] A CIA agent who trained anti-Castro-Cubans, Bradley Ayers, stated that a 201 file meant that Oswald was probably employed full-time as a contract agent for the CIA or he was working on some type of intelligence project for the CIA. Finally, Patrick McGarvey, a former CIA agent, maintained that if a 201 file existed on Oswald, then he was employed by the CIA as a professional agent.

The FBI occasionally sent agents to question Oswald and his wife which has caused investigators to speculate that he may have been working as an informant for the FBI. Because Oswald attempted to infiltrate an anti-Castro organization while simultaneously acting overtly pro-Castro by passing out "Fair Play for Cuba" leaflets in New Orleans during the summer of 1963, it is possible that he was being used by government agencies to collect information about radical groups associated with the anti-Castro movement, such as Alpha 66 and the Student Revolutionary Directorate, also known as the DRE.[49] Oswald mysteriously stamped the address "544 Camp Street" on his pro-Castro leaflets which led directly to the offices of Guy Banister, a former FBI agent, with connections to naval intelligence, who was working as a private detective in New Orleans. It was widely acknowledged that Banister was a staunch anti-Castro activist who supplied weapons to the anti-Castro Cuban movement.

During this time period, Oswald also was supposedly seen in the company of David Atlee Phillips, a CIA operative who later became the Chief of the Western Hemisphere Division. Phillips served as the director of CIA propaganda for the Bay of Pigs Operation in 1961 and also served as the third ranking official of CIA operations in Mexico City at the time of Oswald's visit to the Cuban and Russian embassies in September of 1963. Antonio Veciana, the founder of a radical anti-Castro group known as Alpha 66, told author Gaeton Fonzi that he saw Phillips in the company of Oswald several times. However, Phillips used the alias "Maurice Bishop" whenever he conducted intelligence business with Veciana.[50]

After his return to the United States, Oswald also developed an odd and interesting friendship with a wealthy man named George de Mohrenschildt. There is little doubt that de Mohrenschildt had ties to the U.S. intelligence community. De Mohrenschildt, a Russian émigré to the United States, was an oil geologist who had diverse business interests across the world. He was fifty-one years old when he met Oswald and his wife, Marina, through a group of Russian friends in the Dallas area. The older and handsome de Mohrenschildt, who was quite charming, established a close friendship with Oswald who was only twenty-two years old at the time and very introverted. Some researchers have suggested that de Mohrenschildt, as instructed by the CIA, wittingly, or unwittingly, directed Oswald and his movements leading up to the assassination.[51]

Interestingly, after Oswald was arrested by authorities for the assassination of President Kennedy, a notebook with the word "microdots" was found among Oswald's belongings as well as a small Minox camera.[52] The word "microdots" is regarded as a photographic technique in the world of the intelligence community where a large amount of information can be reduced to a small dot. The small Minox camera was discovered by Dallas Police among Oswald's effects at the home of Michael and Ruth Paine in Irving, Texas, where his wife, Marina, had been living. The Minox camera was made in Germany and was roughly three inches long. It was commonly used in the intelligence world by both sides during World War II. In 1963, the camera was still considered to be spy equipment and was not available to the public.

Perhaps the best piece of circumstantial evidence connecting the intelligence community to the Kennedy assassination involved a CIA document released in 1977 and discovered by researcher Mary Ferrell. According to the document, a French mercenary by the name of Jean Rene Souetre was in Dallas, Texas, on November 22, 1963, and was expelled by U.S. authorities 18 hours after the Kennedy assassination to either Mexico or Canada. Souetre was part of an organization composed of French military officers who had been exiled from France. Souetre allegedly had been part of a number of plots to assassinate the president of France, Charles de Gaulle, because of de Gaulle's decision to support independence for Algeria, a colony of France. Conspiracy theorists point to the fact that the Senate Intelligence Committee in 1975 documented the suspected use of French mercenaries by the CIA in assassination plots against foreign leaders. During the HSCA hearings in 1979, the CIA admitted that they were afraid of such mercenaries who often times developed assassination plans of their own. Hence, Souetre was not the type of individual who the CIA wanted to see deported from Dallas, Texas, only hours after the assassination.[53] As with any information released by the CIA concerning the Kennedy assassination, it is always possible that the document pertaining to Souetre was part of a disinformation campaign to divert the attention of investigators away from the actual conspiracy. Interestingly, the Souetre document was released just as the HSCA was beginning its inquest into the Kennedy assassination in the late 1970s.

The information above provides only circumstantial evidence that may connect Oswald to a conspiracy to assassinate President Kennedy. Oswald's associations with a myriad of characters in the world of intelligence and organized crime cannot definitively be used to establish a conspiracy in the assassination of Kennedy. Two well-respected authors, Gerald Posner and Vincent Bugliosi, provide comprehensive analyses of the Kennedy assassination and both argue strongly that no concrete evidence exists to prove a conspiracy in the murder of President Kennedy.[54] However, the information above raises new questions and provides fertile ground for new hypotheses that may increase our knowledge as more information is released by the U.S. and Russian governments in the future. According to the National Archives, nearly all of the records and documents related to the Kennedy assassination have been released to the public. However, those records and documents that have not been released in full or in part will be released in 2017 unless certified as justifiably closed by the president of the United States.[55]

TESTIMONIES THAT FORETOLD OF THE ASSASSINATION

Additional evidence that points toward a conspiracy in the assassination of President John F. Kennedy involves information and testimony from persons who foretold of the event. From March to November 1963, the intelligence section of the Secret Service received information concerning over 400 possible threats to the safety and security of President Kennedy.[56] The Secret Service judged approximately one-fifth of these threats to be politically motivated. The HSCA deemed three of these threats to be serious in nature. The first threat judged to be serious against Kennedy in 1963 was a single postcard that vaguely warned of the assassination of the president while riding in a motorcade. Because of this threat, President Kennedy was given additional protection during a March 1963 trip to Chicago.

The second threat that the HSCA found serious involved the city of Chicago and an individual named Thomas Arthur Vallee. Vallee, an outspoken critic of Kennedy, allegedly had secured a number of weapons and had requested time off from his place of employment for the president's planned visit to Chicago on November 2, 1963. President Kennedy's trip to Chicago for a parade and a college football game between Army and Air Force was cancelled and Vallee was arrested while in the possession of a rifle, a handgun, and a few thousand rounds of ammunition. He was strangely released almost immediately after his arrest. Interestingly, Vallee had a background that paralleled that of Lee Harvey Oswald which has led some conspiracy theorists to speculate that Vallee was to have been the "fall guy" in a Chicago assassination plot. Oswald and Valle both served in the Marines and both were politically active. While Oswald was connected to pro-communist groups, Vallee was linked to radical conservative groups, such as the John Birch Society. Vallee had a documented history of mental illness and was considered to be a marksman with a rifle.

On that same day, November 2, 1963, it appears that another plot to assassinate Kennedy in Chicago was received by the FBI via a teletype message. The message stated that a four-man team with high-powered rifles would attempt to assassinate Kennedy. Abraham Bolden, a Secret Service agent in the Chicago office, alleged that the FBI relayed the message to the Secret Service Office. Bolden stated that at least one member of the assassination team had a Spanish-sounding name. The HSCA could not confirm Bolden's allegations but the FBI was never questioned about the existence of the teletype message and attempts by the Secret Service to investigate the matter were blocked by President Johnson's appointment of the Warren Commission which gave the FBI primary responsibility for any such investigation. After the Kennedy assassination in Dallas, the Chicago Secret Service received credible information about a group in Chicago that may have had possible ties to the murder of Kennedy. Homer S. Echevarria, a Cuban exile, who was critical of Kennedy's foreign policy toward Cuba, had stated that his group had sufficient finances and would secure military arms as soon "as we (or they) take care of Kennedy."[57] Although there was speculation that the group might have connections to organized crime, the FBI concluded that Echevarria's group was not likely to be involved in illegal activity, even though they had ties to the more militant anti-Castro groups within the United States.

The third and probably most significant threat identified by the HSCA occurred about two weeks prior to the assassination. William Somersett, a Miami police informant, tape recorded Joseph Milteer's foretelling of the assassination of Kennedy.[58] Milteer, a wealthy right-wing extremist, was the leader of an ultra-conservative group known as the National States' Rights Party. On November 9, 1963, Milteer outlined for Somersett the plan of assassinating Kennedy by using a high-powered rifle from a tall building with an innocent man being picked up off the streets by police immediately afterward. Somersett stated that Milteer called him the day of the assassination to inform him that he had been in Dealey Plaza to witness the assassination. A researcher in Texas, Jack White, claims to have located a photograph of someone resembling Milteer near the Texas School Book Depository on the day of the assassination. After the FBI questioned Milteer and the HSCA investigated the matter, it could not be confirmed whether Milteer was in Dealey Plaza at the time of the assassination.

Richard Case Nagell, a decorated Korean War veteran, provided one of the more interesting and bizarre tales of someone who claimed to have foreknowledge of the Kennedy assassination. In 1957, Nagell reportedly was employed as a military counter-intelligence officer with the U.S. Army in Tokyo. At this time, Nagell was supposedly in charge of classified military files and also performed a role as an informant for the CIA. In November 1957, Nagell claimed that he and Oswald worked together on a CIA operation to persuade a Russian colonel to defect to the United States. The two men were also allegedly seen together at the Queen Bee, a Tokyo nightclub where the most beautiful women in Japan served as hostesses. According to Nagell, the Queen Bee served as a prime location for Russian intelligence activities.[59]

In 1962, Nagell continued his intelligence work as an undercover agent in Mexico City where he was supervised by a CIA officer, named "Robert Graham." Graham encouraged Nagell to infiltrate a Russian intelligence agency after the Soviets offered Nagell an assignment connected to the Cuban Missile Crisis. At this time, Nagell also was instructed by Graham to gain access to Alpha 66, a militant group of Cuban exiles whose members sought the overthrow of Fidel Castro. Graham asked Nagell to find out if any members of Alpha 66 were planning an assassination attempt on President John F. Kennedy as revenge for Kennedy's promise to the Soviets after the Cuban Missile Crisis that the United States would not invade Cuba. In exchange for Kennedy's promise not to overthrow Castro, the Soviets removed their nuclear missiles from Cuba.[60]

Nagell reported to Graham that two members of Alpha 66 pretending to be intelligence agents for Castro had recruited Oswald into a plot to assassinate Kennedy under the pretext that Oswald would be hailed as a hero by Castro and his military officers if he successfully carried out the assassination. Graham then supposedly ordered Nagell to eliminate Oswald in order to prevent the assassination. When Nagell refused to carry out the murder of Oswald, Graham revealed that he was a double agent working for both the CIA and Soviet intelligence and attempted to blackmail Nagell into carrying out the murder. If Nagell refused to carry out the assassination of Oswald, then Graham said that he would report to the FBI that Nagell was employed by Soviet intelligence. Graham was alleged to have told Nagell that the Soviets wanted Oswald eliminated because they feared that, if Oswald assassinated Kennedy, it would have been an international embarrassment for the Soviet Union. Even though Oswald would not be acting on behalf of the Soviets, the fact that Oswald had lived in Russia for over two years might implicate them by association.[61]

Instead of eliminating Oswald, Nagell said that he fired a Colt .45 revolver twice at the ceiling inside a bank in El Paso, Texas, on September 20, 1963, for the sole purpose of getting arrested. Nagell feared that he was being set up as the patsy in the assassination of Kennedy and his arrest prevented him from being near Dallas on November 22, 1963. Because Nagell was in custody at the time of the assassination, he maintained that he was provided with an alibi to protect himself from being framed in the plot to murder the president. According to Jim Bundren, the El Paso police officer who made the arrest, Nagell was quoted as saying, "Well, I'm glad you caught me. I really don't want to be in Dallas."[62]

Nagell made a number of claims that he possessed evidence to support his story. He was alleged to have sent a letter by way of registered mail to the FBI on September 17, 1963, three days prior to his arrest in El Paso. In the letter, Nagell said that he informed J. Edgar Hoover that Oswald and other co-conspirators were planning the assassination of Kennedy. While the FBI denied ever receiving such a letter from Nagell, he claimed to be in possession of the receipt for the letter. In addition to the letter, Nagell stated that he secretly made a tape recording in late August 1963 of four persons discussing the plot to assassinate Kennedy. Finally, Nagell said that, in mid-September 1963, he had a Polaroid photograph taken of himself in the company of Oswald in New Orleans to prove the existence of his relationship with the alleged assassin.[63]

Based upon information received from Nagell, author Dick Russell documented three separate assassination plots planned against Kennedy by members of Alpha 66 in 1962-1963. The first assassination plot involved a plan to set off a bomb in Miami, Florida, where Kennedy gave a speech on December 29, 1962. Kennedy gave the speech in the Orange Bowl to roughly 40,000 people as well as a brigade of 1,113 Cuban exiles who had just been released from prison in Cuba. The Cuban exiles had participated in the disastrous Bay of Pigs operation in April 1961 and had been captured and imprisoned by Castro. While Kennedy was able to secure the release of the prisoners in exchange for $53 million in medical drugs and equipment, the members of Alpha 66 were incensed at Kennedy for his failure to provide U.S. military support during the Bay of Pigs invasion as well as for his promise not to invade Cuba in exchange for the Soviet missiles being removed from Cuba. According to Nagell, the first plot never moved past the talking stage.[64]

A second plot also supposedly included members of Alpha 66 in Los Angeles where a leftist, Vaughn Marlowe ("the original Oswald"), would be recruited and framed for the assassination. According to Nagell, the second assassination plot was scheduled for June 1963, when President Kennedy would be visiting Los Angeles to attend a showing of the movie *PT-109* at the Beverly Hills Hotel. The *PT-109* film documented the story of Kennedy's wartime heroics during World War II.[65]

Nagell maintained that this second assassination plot was a more serious plan than the Miami plot. Vaughn Marlowe, whose real name was Vaughn Snipes, was going to be recruited as the shooter by two members of Alpha 66. The two members went by the names of "Leopoldo" and "Angel" and were the same two men who later would allegedly visit Silvia Odio with a "Leon Oswald" in late September 1963. Nagell supposedly was in Los Angeles during the time when the second assassination plot was being discussed and he claimed to be conducting surveillance for either the CIA or Soviet intelligence on Marlowe, Leopoldo, and Angel.[66]

Vaughn Marlowe's life bore an eerie resemblance to that of Lee Harvey Oswald. Similar to Oswald, Marlowe had served in the military as a veteran of the Korean War and was considered a good shot with a rifle. By the early 1960s, Marlowe had become a militant supporter of communism as the executive officer of the Fair Play for Cuba Committee (FPCC) in Los Angeles and was connected to a variety of left-wing organizations such as the Socialist Workers Party, American Civil Liberties Union, and the Congress for Racial Equality. As with Oswald, Marlowe visited the Cuban Embassy in Mexico City as part of his duties with the FPCC in the summer of 1962 and was known to use a pseudonym. Ultimately, the second assassination plot never materialized but Nagell claimed that it did proceed past the talking stage, even though the Cuban exiles never contacted Marlowe. In 1967, Marlowe told Jim Garrison that he was aware that Nagell was checking him out in the spring of 1963 but never understood why he was under surveillance.[67]

The third assassination attempt against Kennedy was scheduled to occur in late September 1963 in Washington, D.C. The story behind this assassination attempt was allegedly revealed in coded form using pseudonyms in a 1976 novel entitled *Betrayal* written by Robert Morrow, a CIA contract agent.[68] Morrow, who referred to Richard Case Nagell as "Richard Carson Fillmore" in the novel, spins a tale of Nagell being given an assignment by a CIA case officer, Tracy Barnes. The assignment involved Nagell infiltrating a paramilitary camp near New Orleans where Cuban exiles were being trained for another possible invasion of Cuba. Nagell was instructed to pose as a mercenary soldier and uncover who was in charge of running the camp. In addition, Nagell was asked to penetrate a group led by David Ferrie and Guy Banister to determine whether Lee Harvey Oswald was operating as an FBI informant.[69]

Apparently, in the performance of his duties as an undercover operative, Nagell was able to learn about the third assassination plot scheduled for late September and he even claimed to possess proof of the conspiracy by way of a tape recording. Nagell secretly made the recording between August 23 and

27, 1963, wherein four persons met to discuss the assassination of Kennedy. The four people in attendance at the meeting were Oswald, Angel, Nagell, and an unidentified person. During the meeting, a Cuban exile by the name of Sergio Arcacha-Smith was discussed as well as an individual whose cover name was "Raul." The cover name of "Raul" was assumed to be that of David Atlee Phillips who was in charge of the CIA's Cuban Operation desk in Washington, D.C. in August 1963. From August 23 to August 27, 1963, the whereabouts of Lee Harvey Oswald are unknown. However, interestingly, Oswald wrote several letters to various leftist organizations, such as the U.S. Communist Party and the Socialist Workers Party, during the last days of August 1963 indicating that he and his family would be moving to the Baltimore-Washington Area, the exact location of the assassination plot against Kennedy.[70]

Other interesting stories related to the foretelling of the assassination involved two mafia crime bosses, Carlos Marcello of New Orleans and Santos Traficante, Jr. of Tampa.[71] According to Edward Becker, a Las Vegas promoter who testified before the HSCA, Marcello supposedly uttered a Sicilian curse against the Kennedy brothers in the presence of Becker in September 1962 at Marcello's estate in New Orleans. Marcello said "Livarsi na petra di la scarpa," which in Italian means "take the stone out of my shoe."[72] Becker added that Marcello discussed the assassination of Kennedy and how a "nut" would be used for the job. Marcello had been fighting the Kennedy administration which had deported him to Guatemala in the spring of 1961.

Two FBI informants also provided fascinating stories that intimated the involvement of the Marcello crime syndicate in the assassination of President Kennedy.[73] In March or April of 1963, Eugene De Laparra was working as an FBI informant in New Orleans at the Lounnor Restaurant which was controlled by the Marcello establishment. De Laparra supposedly overheard a conversation between the owner of the restaurant, Ben Tregle, and two of his associates. The conversation focused on an advertisement in a detective magazine for a foreign-made rifle and Tregle commented that it "would be a nice rifle to buy to get the president."[74] He added that "[s]omebody will kill Kennedy when he comes down south."[75] De Laparra also told the FBI that he heard Anthony Marcello, the brother of Carlos Marcello, announce to Tregle and others in the restaurant that "[t]he word is out to get the Kennedy family."[76]

A second informant, known only as SV T-1, witnessed a separate incident during the same time period at the Town & Country Motel and Restaurant in New Orleans which was owned and operated by Carlos Marcello. SV T-1 allegedly saw the owner of the restaurant, Joseph Poretto, seated with a young man at one of the tables in the restaurant. Poretto proceeded to pass a large sum of cash under the table to the young man. It was not until after the assassination of Kennedy that SV T-1 saw photographs of the accused assassin and realized that the young man at the Town & Country Restaurant who received the large sum of money from Poretto was, without a doubt, Lee Harvey Oswald. SV T-1 reported his story to the police and FBI, not knowing that Poretto was a high-ranking member of Marcello's crime syndicate or that Marcello owned the Town & Country Motel and Restaurant. Interestingly, Lee Harvey Oswald's uncle, Charles "Dutz" Murret, worked as a bookie for Carlos Marcello and Oswald lived with and worked for his uncle in New Orleans during the spring and summer of 1963 when these events supposedly occurred. Oswald's mother, Marguerite, also associated with two underworld figures directly connected to Marcello.[77] Marguerite Oswald was friendly with Sam Termine, who worked as a chauffeur for Marcello and also provided security for the crime boss. A second associate of Marguerite Oswald connected to Marcello was Clem Sehrt, who she had known from childhood. Sehrt, a New Orleans attorney, helped Lee Harvey Oswald enlist in the Marines, even though he was underage, by altering his birth certificate at the request of Marguerite. The investigation by the HSCA in 1979 concluded that Carlos Marcello was probably behind the murder of President Kennedy because there were simply too many connections and coincidences between Marcello and the assassination.[78]

Santos Traficante, Jr., was another organized crime figure who perhaps foretold of the Kennedy assassination.[79] Traficante inherited his father's organized crime business in the 1950s and controlled narcotics trafficking and gambling casinos in Havana under the regime of Fulgencio Batista, the Cuban dictator who supported U.S. economic interests. Robert Blakey, chief counsel for the HSCA, described Traficante as the "undisputed Mafia boss in Havana."[80] However, after Fidel Castro's revolution in 1959, American organized crime was expelled from Cuba and the narcotics and gambling operations came to an abrupt end with Traficante confined to a prison in Havana. The CIA and Mafia then joined forces to attempt an overthrow of Castro in April of 1961 with the Bay of Pigs invasion and also attempted to assassinate Castro on multiple occasions. In addition to Traficante, other organized crime figures involved in the assassination plots against Castro were Frank Sturgis (later arrested as one of the Watergate burglars), Robert Maheu, Johnny Roselli, and Sam Giancana. The failure of the Bay of Pigs and President Kennedy's refusal to support a second invasion of Cuba, known as *Operation Mongoose*, infuriated Traficante.[81] In September 1962, Traficante met with a wealthy Cuban exile named Jose Aleman in a Miami hotel and complained about the way that the Kennedy administration was cracking down on the Teamsters Union and Jimmy Hoffa who had a close relationship with organized crime.[82] According to evidence collected by the HSCA, Traficante informed Aleman that Kennedy was going to be "hit" prior to the 1964 presidential election and Jimmy Hoffa would play a critical role in the "elimination" of Kennedy. Unbeknownst to Traficante, Aleman was a FBI informant and immediately reported the conversation to federal agents who dismissed his story. When Aleman testified before the HSCA, he provided only a vague recollection of the conversation and simply told the committee members that Traficante was referring to the idea that Kennedy was going to get "hit" by Republican votes in 1964. During his testimony, Aleman admitted that he feared for his safety.

Silvia Odio also foretold of the Kennedy assassination in her story that she received a visit from Oswald and two Cubans in late September of 1963. As noted in chapter 1, Odio's family was part of an anti-Castro organization that was forced to leave their homeland in Cuba after Fidel Castro's revolution in 1959. Odio suspected that Oswald and the two Cubans were pro-Castro Cubans attempting to obtain information from her. They presented themselves as members of an anti-Castro group called JURE, which stands for Junta Revolucionara Cubana or Cuban Revolutionary Council. JURE was created in 1963 as a leftist group of Cuban exiles opposed to Fidel Castro. Odio told the visitors to leave, but the next day she received a telephone call from one of the Cubans, known to her as Leopoldo. Leopoldo asked her what she thought about Oswald and he told her that Oswald was an ex-Marine who was "kind of nuts." Leopoldo then mentioned to Odio that Oswald said that somebody should kill President Kennedy because he failed to provide military support for the Cuban exiles during the Bay of Pigs invasion.

The Warren Commission discounted Odio's testimony because she had been under psychiatric care for emotional distress at the time and the HSCA entered her testimony into the record without acknowledging her credibility. However, Odio continues to maintain that she is positive that Oswald visited her with the two Cubans and her story rings true given Oswald's behavior in New Orleans during the summer of 1963 when he was arrested in a dispute with anti-Castro Cubans after attempting to infiltrate their organization.[83] Her story confirms a pattern of behavior wherein Oswald concealed his pro-Castro sentiments and disguised himself as an anti-Castro activist in an attempt to gain information. Researchers have used Odio's story to confirm Oswald's role as an intelligence operative and/or an FBI informant. Others maintain that Oswald was either part of a conspiracy to assassinate Kennedy or he was being set up as the patsy.

A final forecast of the assassination involved an airtel message sent from FBI headquarters to all of its offices on November 17, 1963, warning of an attempt to assassinate President Kennedy during his trip to Dallas on November 22–23, 1963.[84] The message revealed that a militant revolutionary group was behind the assassination attempt. Some researchers intimate that Oswald, as a FBI informant, may have been the source of the message because he visited the FBI offices in Dallas on November 12, 1963, and delivered a written note for FBI agent James Hosty. However, as noted in the previous chapter, it is most likely that Oswald wanted to confront Hosty who recently had visited and questioned Oswald's wife, Marina.

CONCLUSION

This chapter has detailed the patterns of behavior demonstrated historically by the intelligence community and the organized crime syndicate within the United States in the post–World War II era. It has argued that Oswald clearly was a person placed within the milieu of the intelligence community and organized crime which often overlapped during this time period in places such as New Orleans, Louisiana, where Oswald grew up and spent a good portion of his adult life.[85] By applying the scientific method in a limited manner, this chapter has posited that a real possibility existed that Oswald may have been part of a larger conspiracy to assassinate President Kennedy based upon the physical and circumstantial evidence presented as well as testimonials that foretold of the assassination.

NOTES

1. *Random House Webster's College Dictionary* (New York: Random House, 1997), 282-283.
2. David Simon, *Elite Deviance* (Needham Heights, Mass.: Allyn & Bacon, 1999), 306.
3. David Shipler, "Living under Suspicion," *New York Times*, February 7, 1997, A33.
4. Anthony Summers, *Conspiracy* (New York: McGraw-Hill, 1980); Mark Lane, *Plausible Denial: Was the CIA Involved in the Assassination of JFK?* (New York: Thunder's Mouth Press, 1991) and Ray and Mary La Fontaine, *Oswald Talked: The New Evidence in the JFK Assassination* (Gretna, La.: Pelican Publishing Company, Inc., 1996).
5. Chava Frankfort-Nachmias and David Nachmias, *Research Methods in the Social Sciences* (New York: Macmillan, 2000), 3.
6. Scott Shane, "CIA Is Still Cagey about Oswald Mystery," *New York Times*, October 16, 2009, Accessed February 12, 2013, http://www.nytimes.com/2009/10/17/us/17inquire.html?pagewanted=all&_r=0.
7. *Investigation of the Assassination of President John F. Kennedy: Hearing Before the House, Select Committee on Assassinations* (HSCA), 95th Congress (1979) [House Select Committee on Assassinations, herein HSCA)].
8. David Wise, *The Politics of Lying: Government Deception, Secrecy and Power* (New York: Random House, 1973).
9. C. Wright Mills, *The Power Elite* (New York: Oxford University Press, 1956).
10. Harold Berman, *The Trial of the U-2* (Chicago: Translation World Publishers, 1960).
11. Peter Kornbluh, *Bay of Pigs Declassified: The Secret CIA Report on the Invasion of Cuba* (New York: New Press, 1998).
12. "The Phantom Battle That Led to War," *U.S. News and World Report*, July 23, 1984, 56-67.
13. Daniel Ellsberg, *Secrets: A Memoir of Vietnam and the Pentagon Papers* (New York: Penguin Books, 2003).
14. David Corn, "The Same Old Dirty Tricks," *The Nation,* August 27, 1988, 158.
15. Bob Woodward, *State of Denial: Bush at War Part III* (New York: Simon and Schuster, 2006).

16. J. Roebuck and S. C. Weeber, *Political Crime in the United States: Analyzing Crime by and Against Government* (New York: Praeger, 1978), 82.

17. "CIA Murder Plots Weighing the Damage to U.S.," *U.S. News and World Report*, 1 (December 1975), 13-15.

18. "The CIA's Hit-List," *Newsweek*, 1 (December 1975), 28-32.

19. Arthur M. Schlesinger, *The Imperial Presidency* (New York: Houghton Mifflin Co., 2004).

20. Peter Dale Scott, "From Dallas to Watergate," in *Government by Gunplay: Assassination Conspiracies from Dallas to Today*, eds. Sid Blumenthal and Harvey Yazijian (New York: Signet, 1976), 113-129.

21. Simon, *Elite Deviance*, 308.

22. "Project Minaret," *Newsweek*, 10 (Nov. 1975), 31-32.

23. "Who's Chipping Away at Your Privacy," *U.S. News and World Report*, 31 (March 1975), 18.

24. "The FBI's 'Black-Bag' Boys," *Newsweek*, 28 (July 1975), 18, 21.

25. "The Crusade to Topple King," *Time* 1 (December 1975), 11-12.

26. Amy Zegart, *Spying Blind: The CIA, FBI, and the Origins of 9/11* (Princeton, N.J.: Princeton University Press, 2007).

27. James Bamford, *The Shadow Factory: The NSA from 9/11 to the Eavesdropping on America* (New York: Random House, 2009).

28. W. H. Bowart, *Operation Mind Control: Our Government's War against Its People* (New York: Dell Publishing, 1978), 87-91.

29. Maia Szalavitz, "The Legacy of the CIA's Secret LSD Experiments on America." *Time: Health & Family*, March 23, 2012, accessed January 2, 2013, http://healthland.time.com/2012/03/23/the-legacy-of-the-cias-secret-lsd-experiments-on-america/.

30. Simon, *Elite Deviance*, 256-258; Jill Lawrence, "Americans Served as Guinea Pigs for Radiation Testing," *Fort Collins Coloradoan*, 25 (October 1986): A-10.

31. Jay Albanese, *Organized Crime in Our Times* (Newark, N.J.: Matthew Bender & Co., Inc. 2010).

32. J. Ridgeway and K. Jacobs, "Onward Christian Soldiers," *Village Voice*, 17 (March 1987), 32ff.

33. Simon, *Elite Deviance*, 50-96.

34. John Davis, *Mafia Kingfish: Carlos Marcello and the Assassination of John F. Kennedy* (New York: McGraw-Hill, 1989).

35. Jim Marrs, *Crossfire: The Plot That Killed Kennedy* (New York: Carroll & Graf, 1989), 165.

36. Michael Martinez and Brad Johnson, "RFK Assassination Witness Tells CNN: There Was a Second Shooter, CNN: Justice," accessed June 4, 2013, http://www.cnn.com/2012/04/28/justice/california-rfk-second-gun/.

37. *Investigation of the Assassination of President John F. Kennedy: Hearing before the President's Commission on the Assassination of President Kennedy*. 88th Congress (1964) [Warren Commission Report here in WCR].

38. D. B. Thomas, "Echo Correlation Analysis and the Acoustic Evidence in the Kennedy Assassination Revisited" *Science & Justice* 41 (2001), 21-32.

39. J. E. Barger, et al., *Analysis of Recorded Sounds Relating to the Assassination of John F. Kennedy* (Cambridge, Mass.: Bolt, Baranek & Newman Inc., 1979); M. R. Weiss and A. Ashkenasy, *An Analysis of Recorded Sounds Relating to the Assassination of John F. Kennedy* (Department of Computer Sciences, Queens College, City University of New York, 1979).

40. Committee on Ballistic Acoustics, National Research Council, "Reexamination of Acoustic Evidence in the Kennedy Assassination," *Science*, Oct. 8, 1982.

41. David Lifton, *Best Evidence: Disguise and Deception in the Assassination of John F. Kennedy* (New York: Carroll & Graf Publishers, 1988).

42. Jim Garrison, *On the Trail of the Assassins* (New York: Sheridan Square Press, 1988).

43. WCR, Warren Commission Exhibit No. 2303 (25 H at 237-245).

44. Jim Marrs, *Crossfire*, 103-104.

45. Garrison, *On the Trail of the Assassins*, 53-54.

46. Jay Edward Epstein, *Legend: The Secret World of Lee Harvey Oswald* (New York: Reader's Digest Press, 1978).
47. Marrs, *Crossfire,* 131.
48. Marrs, *Crossfire,* 192.
49. Ray and Mary La Fontaine, *Oswald Talked: The New Evidence in the JFK Assassination* (Gretna, La.: Pelican Publishing Company, Inc., 1996), 152-155.
50. Gaeton Fonzi, *The Last Investigation* (New York: Thunder's Mouth Press, 1993).
51. Bruce C. Adamson, *Oswald's Closest Friend: The George de Mohrenschildt Story* (Santa Cruz, Calif.: Self-published, 2001).
52. Marrs, *Crossfire,* 190.
53. Russell, *The Man Who Knew Too Much*, 352-354.
54. Vincent Bugliosi, *Reclaiming History: The Assassination of President John F. Kennedy* (New York: W. W. Norton & Co., 2007); Gerald Posner, *Case Closed: Lee Harvey Oswald and the Assassination of JFK* (New York: Random House, 1993).
55. *JFK Assassination Records*, accessed January 3, 2013, http://www.archives.gov/research/jfk/faqs.html#sealed.
56. The intelligence section of the Secret Service Office is called the Protective Research Section. Charles A. Crenshaw with Jens Hansen and J. Gary Shaw, *JFK: Conspiracy of Silence* (New York: Signet, 1992), 36-40.
57. Ibid., 39.
58. T. Mack Durham, *The Innocent Man Script: Cui Bono-To Whose Advantage?* (Lincoln, Neb.: Writer's Showcase, 2000), 502.
59. Dave Reitzes, "Truth or Dare: The Lives and Lies of Richard Case Nagell," accessed June 21, 2013, http://mcadams.posc.mu.edu/nagell3.htm.
60. Ibid.
61. Ibid.
62. Dick Russell, *The Man Who Knew Too Much* (New York: Carroll and Graf, 1992), 3.
63. Reitzes, "Truth or Dare."
64. Russell, *The Man Who Knew Too Much*, 165.
65. Ibid., 210.
66. Ibid., 219.
67. Ibid., 210-218.
68. Robert Morrow, *Betrayal: A Reconstruction of Certain Clandestine Events from the Bay of Pigs to the Assassination of John F. Kennedy* (Chicago: Henry Regnery, 1976).
69. Russell, *The Man Who Knew Too Much*, 264.
70. Ibid., 275-276.
71. Marrs, *Crossfire,* at 164-171.
72. Ibid., 165
73. Davis, *Mafia Kingfish,* 118-122.
74. Ibid., 119.
75. Ibid.
76. Ibid., 120.
77. *Id.* at 126-127.
78. Simon, *Elite Deviance,* 306.
79. Scott M. Deitch, *The Silent Don: The Criminal Underworld of Santos Traficante* (Fort Lee, N.J.: Barricade Books, Inc., 2009).
80. Marrs, *Crossfire,* 168.
81. Don Bohni, *The Castro Obsession: U.S. Covert Operations against Cuba, 1959-1965* (Dulles, Va.: Potomac Books, Inc., 2006).
82. Lamar Waldron and Thom Hartmann, *Ultimate Sacrifice: John and Robert Kennedy, the Plan for a Coup in Cuba, and the Murder of JFK* (New York: Carroll & Graf, 2005), 434-437, 768-769.
83. Marrs, *Crossfire,* 147-155.
84. Garrison, *On the Trail of the Assassins*, 256-259.
85. Peter Scott, *Deep Politics and the Death of JFK* (Berkeley: University of California Press, 1993).

Chapter Three

Oswald as Patsy and Hero

According to some conspiracy theorists, Lee Harvey Oswald was a courageous figure serving his country perhaps attempting to prevent the assassination of President John F. Kennedy.[1] Oswald's suspected connections to the Central Intelligence Agency (CIA), the Federal Bureau of Investigation (FBI), and the Office of Naval Intelligence (ONI) provide circumstantial evidence that Oswald was employed in some manner by the U.S. intelligence community during, and perhaps after, his military service in the Marine Corps. In 1977, a CIA "201" file on Lee Harvey Oswald was discovered. Many researchers with knowledge of CIA activities maintain that a 201 file indicates that Oswald was employed in some fashion by the CIA. Victor Marchetti who served as an assistant to a deputy director in the CIA was quoted as saying: ". . . if Oswald had a '201' file, he was an agent."[2] Oswald also had in his possession a Department of Defense identification card at the time of his arrest. The identification card was the same type of card carried by CIA contract agent Francis Gary Powers.[3]

In his capacity as an alleged government informant and/or contract intelligence agent, it has been argued that Oswald infiltrated an extremist organization, or rogue element within an intelligence agency, planning the assassination and was subsequently framed by this group who had uncovered his role as a low-level informant. It is also possible that organized crime figures may have worked in conjunction with such an extremist group or intelligence agency, to frame Oswald. Organized crime figures, such as Carlos Marcello of New Orleans, Sam Giancana of Chicago, Johnny Roselli of Los Angeles, and Santos Traficante of Miami wanted President Kennedy eliminated because Attorney General Robert Kennedy had aggressively increased the prosecution of Mafia leaders. The Kennedy administration's prosecution of the Mafia coincided with the fact that organized crime figures were working closely with U.S. intelligence agencies on various illegal activities such as political assassinations, counter-intelligence propaganda, and attempts to overthrow foreign governments opposed to American interests abroad. In particular, the Mafia sought the overthrow of Fidel Castro, the communist leader of Cuba, to restore their organized crime operations in Havana. Organized crime also worked closely with the CIA in various attempts to assassinate Castro. Between 1960 and 1965, the CIA tried to assassinate Castro at least eight times. In one such attempt, the CIA attempted to apply a lethal toxin to his cigars. In another attempt, the CIA hired organized crime figures to poison him.[4]

COMMUNISM AND THE MARINES: WAS OSWALD A COUNTER-INTELLIGENCE OPERATIVE?

As a young boy, Oswald's favorite television show was called *I Led Three Lives*.[5] This television program was based upon an anti-communist government spy involved in intelligence operations. Oswald watched the television show every week and also watched the re-runs regularly. The television show ran from 1953-1956 and was based on the life of Herbert Philbrick who worked for the FBI in the 1940s and successfully infiltrated the U.S. Communist Party. Philbrick narrated all of the 117 episodes and was a consultant on the set of the show. Interestingly, J. Edgar Hoover, Director of the FBI, approved all of the scripts for the show. Oswald also enjoyed reading spy stories such as the James Bond novels written by Ian Fleming. Oswald's childhood easily fits the profile of persons who were recruited for intelligence assignments because he was an intelligent loner who was fascinated by spy stories.

At the age of fifteen in 1955, Oswald joined the Civilian Air Patrol (CAP) where he met David Ferrie who was connected with right-wing extremist groups, intelligence agencies, and organized crime figures involved in the sale of weaponry and the military training of Cuban refugees for such anti-Castro operations as the Bay of Pigs and Operation Mongoose. After the assassination of President Kennedy, Ferrie denied ever knowing Oswald but, during the investigation of Oswald's background, the evidence demonstrated otherwise. For example, a 1955 photograph surfaced of Oswald and Ferrie together during a CAP meeting in Alexandria, Louisiana, and, after Oswald's arrest as a suspect in the Kennedy assassination, a library card was found in his possession with Ferrie's name on it.[6]

In October 1956, Oswald joined the Marines signing an enlistment contract for three years. He was stationed at various bases across the United States and trained as an aviation electronics operator. In September 1957, Oswald was transferred to a military base in Atsugi, Japan. It has been revealed that this military base was used as a testing ground for the secret U-2 spy plane being developed by the United States. Oswald worked as a radar operator at this military installation and some have questioned whether he may have developed connections with military intelligence at Atsugi, a base renowned for its CIA facilities. Oswald was treated for contracting gonorrhea while serving in Japan and his military records strangely note that he contracted this disease as part of his military duties. Oswald was known to frequent an upper-class gentlemen's nightclub in Japan called the Queen Bee. It is puzzling to many researchers that Oswald frequented this establishment because it was the type of place where military officers with higher salaries would enjoy entertainment. An evening at the Queen Bee could cost military officers and pilots as much as $100. Oswald's take home salary at this time was $85 a month. Jay Edward Epstein stated that U-2 pilots often frequented the Queen Bee and the Japanese hostesses often attempted to secure information from U.S. military personnel. Oswald clearly could not afford this type of entertainment given his lower salary, however, he was often seen with very attractive Japanese women who were employed at the Queen Bee. Conspiracy theorists have speculated that Oswald was trying to obtain information from these women by dating them and/or perhaps engaging in sexual intercourse. Oswald allegedly dated one attractive woman from the Queen Bee which puzzled other Marines in his unit who didn't understand why she would be interested in Oswald. The ONI suspected that Oswald may have been receiving money from someone at the Queen Bee.[7]

In addition to his activities at the Queen Bee, Oswald allegedly was in contact with Japanese Communists during his military service at Atsugi. Oswald supposedly admitted to meeting with an organization of Communists during his military service in Japan and Warren Commission lawyers, W. David Slawson and William T. Coleman Jr., stated in a classified document that Oswald may have come into contact with Communist agents during his time in Japan.[8]

After his service at Atsugi, Oswald was stationed in El Toro, California, and continued his fascination with Communism and the Soviet Union by reading Russian newspapers which he purchased on his furlough trips into town. While serving in the Marines, Oswald supposedly began to teach himself the Russian language and became semi-proficient at the language. Oswald requested a military examination to test his linguistic abilities and his performance on the examination revealed that he answered two more questions right than wrong. Oswald's education in the Russian language provides evidence for many conspiracy theorists who have suggested that Oswald was being trained by military intelligence for an undercover operation. In addition to learning the Russian language, Oswald acted overtly Marxist perhaps establishing credibility as a Communist and laying the groundwork for his defection to the Soviet Union.[9]

In August of 1959, Oswald applied for an early hardship discharge from the military to care for his ailing mother who had been injured when a jar fell on her nose. The military uncharacteristically allowed him to leave two months ahead of the end of his three-year commitment which caused some researchers to suggest that his discharge was simply an intelligence cover to send Oswald on his first intelligence mission abroad. In order to obtain a passport, Oswald applied for admission to study at the Albert Schweitzer College in Switzerland, but he never arrived for classes. Instead, after Oswald stayed with his mother for a few days, he left on a steamboat for Europe with the intent of defecting to the Soviet Union through Helsinki, Finland. Coincidentally, in the late 1950s, the ONI had a "fake-defector" program wherein young men serving in the military were recruited to defect to a foreign country for the purpose of gathering information about life in a closed society, such as the Soviet Union. The ONI used roughly forty young men who gave the appearance of having come from poverty and also were instructed to feign disillusionment with American life. At this time, the U.S. government conducted an investigation in order to attempt to identify the real defectors from the fake defectors. Oswald seemingly fit the profile of these so-called "fake-defectors" as a young man serving in the military with above-average intelligence from a lower-income family.[10]

OSWALD IN THE SOVIET UNION

On October 16, 1959, Oswald entered the Soviet Union on a six-day student tourist visa and applied for Soviet citizenship. When Oswald was denied by Soviet officials and told to leave the country, he attempted suicide by slitting his left wrist. Some have speculated that Oswald's attempted suicide was a ploy to manipulate the Soviet authorities into granting him citizenship or residency in the country. Oswald was treated for a superficial wound at a local hospital and released. A few days after his release from the hospital, Oswald entered the U.S. Embassy in Moscow on October 31, 1959, and indicated that he wanted to renounce his U.S. citizenship in order to become a citizen of the Soviet Union. Oswald also indicated that he planned to provide U.S. military intelligence to the Soviets based upon his work as a radar operator on the U-2 spy plane project. Soon after this incident, the Soviets shot down a U-2 spy plane being flown by a pilot named Francis Gary Powers. Some researchers, including Francis Gary Powers himself, have speculated that Oswald may have given the Soviets enough information as a former radar operator to shoot down the U-2 spy plane which seemingly was untouchable as it hovered over the Soviet Union at altitudes of 80,000 feet. Oswald's dramatic behavior at the embassy may have been another ploy to convince the Soviets of his sincerity in wanting to become a Soviet citizen.

In fact, U.S. officials at the embassy noted that his statements seemed rehearsed as if he was acting out a part. If Oswald was attempting to manipulate the Soviet authorities with an attempted suicide and dramatic show of support for the Soviets, it worked. He was given a residence permit for persons without citizenship and he was moved to far off Minsk and given a stipend from the Red Cross (a Russian agency), an apartment, and employment at a local radio factory. Oswald was assigned a job at the Belorussian Radio and Television Factory as a metalworker. In addition to Oswald, there were more than five thousand workers employed at the factory.[11]

While living in Minsk, Oswald dated various Russian women and eventually married Marina Prusakova, the niece of a Lieutenant Colonel in the KGB. It has been postulated that Marina attended a trade union dance at the request of her uncle for the specific purpose of meeting Oswald to gain information about him. Clearly, the Soviets were concerned that Oswald might be a spy sent by the United States to gather information about the Soviet Union. Interestingly, when Marina was introduced to Oswald, she mistakenly thought that he was from a Baltic state because his Russian language was excellent. During their time together in the Soviet Union, Oswald and his wife, Marina, were closely monitored by Soviet authorities. Their apartment was constantly under electronic surveillance and Oswald was closely followed in his travels around Minsk. Obviously, the Soviets were suspicious that Oswald might be a phony defector. In fact, Oswald's tour guides and translators who accompanied him during his initial days in the Soviet Union were regularly providing information about Oswald to the KGB.[12]

OSWALD'S RETURN TO THE UNITED STATES

In February of 1961, Oswald decided that he no longer wanted to live in the Soviet Union and he began correspondence with both U.S. and Soviet authorities in an attempt to reenter the United States with his pregnant wife. Because Oswald was permitted to leave the Soviet Union in 1962 with his Russian wife and child and the fact that the U.S. authorities agreed not to prosecute him upon his return, conspiracy theorists have maintained that Oswald utilized intelligence connections to gain re-entry into the United States. Interestingly, the U.S. Embassy never processed the paperwork to dissolve Oswald's American citizenship which left the door open for his return to the United States and the State Department even loaned Oswald $346 to finance his travels from the Soviet Union to the United States.[13]

Prior to his return to the United States, Oswald wrote a letter on January 30, 1962, to the Secretary of the Navy, John Connally, challenging his military status which had been changed from an honorable discharge to undesirable discharge.[14] In the letter to Connally, Oswald also wrote that his decision to enter the Soviet Union was "fully sanctioned" by the U.S. Embassy. Is it possible that Oswald was hinting at his role as a "fake-defector" in order to manipulate Connally into changing his status? Whatever the case, the obvious question was how Oswald persuaded both U.S. and Soviet authorities to allow his return to the United States considering that he had promised in October of 1959 to turn over U.S. military secrets to the Soviets and he also was leaving the Soviet Union with a Russian citizen who happened to be the family member of a KGB officer.

The Oswalds arrived in the United States in June of 1962 and initially stayed with Oswald's brother, Robert, in Fort Worth, Texas. Soon after his return, Oswald hired a public stenographer, Pauline Bates, to record his notes about his experience in the Soviet Union. Oswald hired Bates to type fifty pages of his manuscript which he had titled, *The Collective*. However, Bates only typed ten pages of the manuscript because Oswald ran out of money. Oswald told Bates that a Russian petroleum engineer, Peter Gregory, was going to assist Oswald in getting his manuscript published.[15] During this time, Oswald also was interviewed twice by the FBI in the summer of 1962 and continued his interest in communism and socialism by subscribing to *The Worker*, a newspaper published by the U.S. Communist Party. He also wrote to the Socialist Workers Party inquiring about membership in the organization.[16]

After a brief stint working for a welding company in Fort Worth, Oswald was hired by a photographic firm, Jaggers-Chiles-Stovall Co., in Dallas on October 12, 1962, where he began work as a photoprint trainee at $1.35 per hour. Oswald had been referred to Jaggers-Chiles-Stovall Co. by Helen Cunningham of the Texas Employment Commission after he performed well on examinations revealing an aptitude for clerical work. Interestingly, Jaggers-Chiles-Stovall had a contract to produce maps for the U.S. Army. The fact that Oswald was openly behaving as a communist while simultaneously working for a firm connected to the U.S. military has caused researchers to speculate that Oswald remained connected in some fashion to military intelligence. For example, Jim Garrison stated that Oswald had access to "classified materials" while employed at Jaggers.[17] Anthony Summers also noted that Oswald wrote the term "microdots" next to the Jaggers's listing on page 44 of his address book. Oswald's address book contained an entry that read "Jaggers-Chiles-Stovall Typography 522 Browder RI 15501 microdots."[18] "Microdots" is a term associated with a spy technique that uses photography to reduce a large amount of information to a very small dot. In moving to Dallas to work for the Jaggers-Chiles-Stovall Company, Oswald began a pattern of separating himself periodically from his wife and child. While many interpret Oswald's behavior as that of an antisocial loner and disconnected Marxist, the significant amount of time that Oswald spent alone away from his family also can be interpreted as the behavior of a low-level informant collecting information or performing minor tasks for intelligence agencies.

THE ASSASSINATION ATTEMPT ON GENERAL EDWIN WALKER

In the early months of 1963, Oswald ordered a pistol from Seaport Traders using an alias, "Alex Hidell," and also ordered a Mannlicher-Carcano rifle from Klein's Sporting Goods based out of Chicago using the same alias. At this time, Oswald also began surveillance on the Dallas home of General Edwin Walker, a right-wing extremist, who had led pro-segregation rallies at various colleges and universities in the South and eventually became involved in a legal dispute that went all of the way to the U.S. Supreme Court when he sued the Associated Press (AP) for comments that he instigated riots against integration of the races on the campus of the University of Mississippi. In a famous ruling concerning libel law, the U.S. Supreme Court ruled against Walker stating that the AP was not guilty of actual malice, or reckless disregard, in their news stories about Walker.[19]

In addition to his controversial position regarding segregation, General Walker had been reprimanded by the U.S. military for attempting to indoctrinate troops with his radical views based on the philosophy of the John Birch Society. The John Birch Society is considered an extremist political group in the United States that supports limited power for the federal government as well as an intense opposition to communism. President John F. Kennedy ordered Secretary of Defense Robert McNamara to relieve General Walker as commanding officer of the 24th Army Infantry Division under NATO in Germany. Walker was relieved from his duties because he had been distributing John Birch Society literature to his troops. After an investigation was conducted, Walker resigned from the Army on November 2, 1961.[20]

Oswald's behavior of ordering weapons by using an alias as well as photographing and monitoring the home of an extremist military officer perhaps suggests that Oswald was carrying out an intelligence assignment. On April 10, 1963, an assassination attempt was made on General Walker when one rifle shot was fired at him from an alley near his home. The assassin barely missed Walker as the general sat at a desk inside his home preparing his taxes. According to Marina Oswald, Oswald confessed to his wife that he fired the rifle shot. Researchers have speculated that Oswald may have been under instructions to eliminate Walker or perhaps he was simply involved in the assassination attempt with other low-level operatives. Witnesses recalled seeing more than one person fleeing the alley near Walker's home after the rifle shot was fired. Eyewitness testimony suggests that Oswald may not have acted alone in the assassination attempt on Walker. Walter Coleman, a fourteen year-old neighbor of General Walker, informed police that, after he heard a shot fired, he saw some men leaving the scene in a Ford automobile. In addition, two other witnesses recalled that there was suspicious activity around Walker's home prior to the assassination attempt. On April 6, 1963, four days prior to the shooting, Robert Surrey, an assistant to Walker, saw two men loitering around the house and peering into the windows. Another of Walker's assistants, Max Claunch, said that he thought that he witnessed a Cuban man driving around the home of General Walker repeatedly on April 8, 1963, two nights before the shooting.[21]

While Marina Oswald testified to the Warren Commission that Oswald confessed to her about trying to assassinate General Walker, he may have embellished his role in the assassination attempt to impress his young wife who often belittled him by speaking about her former lovers. Throughout his life, Oswald demonstrated a pattern of deceiving others by exaggerating his role in events and he repeatedly lied about his personal background on employment applications to present himself as an important person. Hence, it is difficult to determine whether Oswald was truthful to his wife about anything based upon his behavioral pattern of lying and exaggerating about himself.[22]

Whatever the case, it was not uncommon during the 1960s, 1970s, and 1980s for rogue elements of the military intelligence agencies to be implicated in the political assassinations of controversial leaders abroad such as Fidel Castro of Cuba, Ngo Dinh Diem of South Vietnam, General Rene Schneider of Chile, Patrice Lumumba of Zaire, and Shiite Muslim leader, Sheihk Mohammad Hussein Fadlallah, of Lebanon. During this time period, the CIA was involved in nine hundred foreign operations where the agency engaged in paramilitary operations, manipulation and propaganda as well as political assassinations.[23] In the domestic arena, some researchers have hypothesized that the U.S. government, specifically elements of the CIA and FBI, may have played a role in the assassination of civil rights leader, Martin Luther King. General Walker was clearly an embarrassment to the U.S. military and his assassination perhaps would have been welcomed by some military intelligence operatives.

OSWALD AND GEORGE DE MOHRENSCHILDT

While living in Dallas, Texas, Lee and Marina Oswald were introduced to a community of Russians who had emigrated to the United States. The Russians expressed an interest in the Oswalds mainly because they hoped to hear about conditions in their Soviet homeland. Peter Gregory, a petroleum engineer who taught the Russian language at the Fort Worth Public Library, arranged a meeting between the Oswalds and the Russian émigrés. Oswald had hoped that Gregory would write a recommendation for him so he could become a translator. It was during this time that Oswald was befriended by George de Mohrenschildt, a person with intelligence connections. De Mohrenschildt and Lee Harvey Oswald struck up an odd friendship because Oswald was not formally educated with a lower-class background, while de Mohrenschildt was well-educated and a wealthy oil baron connected to high society. De Mohrenschildt led a strange and mysterious life traveling around the world to exotic places and many researchers argue that de Mohrenschildt was possibly Oswald's "handler" in terms of his intelligence assignments. After the assassination attempt on Walker, de Mohrenschildt coincidentally joked with Oswald by asking him how he could have missed Walker with the rifle shot. Interestingly, researchers have confirmed that de Mohrenschildt was employed by the CIA. In 1978, de Mohrenschildt was scheduled to testify before the House Select Committee on Assassinations (HSCA) but, the day before his scheduled testimony, he supposedly committed suicide in his Florida home by shooting himself with a rifle.[24]

OSWALD IN NEW ORLEANS: MARCELLO, FAIR PLAY FOR CUBA, AND THE ANTI-CASTRO CUBANS

In the spring of 1963, Oswald moved from Dallas to New Orleans because he had lost his job with Jaggers-Chiles-Stovall and his wife also was concerned that the authorities would connect him to the assassination attempt on General Walker. Hence, Oswald was again separated from his wife and child. During this time period, Lee Harvey Oswald lived with and worked part-time as a runner for his uncle, Charles "Dutz" Murret, who was employed as a midlevel bookie with Carlos Marcello, the organized crime leader of New Orleans. It is likely that Marcello was aware of Oswald's defection to the Soviet Union and his "pro-communist" activities in New Orleans during this period. Marcello and other organized crime figures supposedly had been plotting against President Kennedy and Attorney General Robert Kennedy because of the Justice Department's aggressive prosecution of Mafia leaders. As noted above, organized crime also shared a mutual interest with rogue elements of the intelligence community and anti-Castro exiles incensed at Kennedy's refusal to attempt a second overthrow of Fidel Castro after the failure of the Bay of Pigs. Some researchers have gone as far as suggesting that Oswald may have been paid by Marcello to engage in "pro-Castro" activities during the spring and summer of 1963 to frame him for the Kennedy assassination which could, in turn, be used to blame pro-Castro forces for the murder of the American president.[25]

In April of 1963, Oswald wrote to the Fair Play for Cuba Committee (FPCC) requesting information and also seeking to establish a chapter of the FPCC in New Orleans. Also, during this time, Oswald gained employment with the William Reily Coffee Co. in New Orleans as a maintenance man earning $1.50 per hour. Oswald was hired to grease and oil the fittings in the company's machinery. The Reily Coffee Co. allegedly had a reputation as a front for intelligence operations and the owner of the company, William Reily, was renowned throughout New Orleans as an intense supporter of the anti-Castro movement. Reily used his company as a front to raise money for the Crusade to Free Cuba Committee. As with Oswald's employment at Jaggers-Chiles-Stovall where the photography firm had a contract to produce maps for the U.S. military, it seemed odd that Oswald, an alleged Marxist, would gain employment at the Reily Coffee Company.[26]

There is also some circumstantial evidence that Oswald was in contact with officials from the FBI during his time at Reily. The Crescent City Garage was located in the neighborhood of the Reily Coffee Company and the owner of the garage, Adrian Alba, stated that he saw a FBI agent hand an envelope to Oswald which he put under his shirt and Alba claimed that the agent also spoke with Oswald on another occasion. Interestingly, the Alba garage provided automobile service to the Secret Service and the FBI.[27]

After being fired from the Reily Coffee Company on July 19, 1963, Oswald supposedly informed Adrian Alba, the owner of a garage next door to the Reily Coffee Company, that he would be leaving Reily to begin employment at the Chrysler Aerospace Division at the National Aeronautics and Space Administration (NASA). Oswald supposedly told Alba that he had "found his pot at the end of the rainbow."[28] While Oswald never worked for NASA, almost everyone that he worked with at the Reily Coffee Company was eventually transferred to NASA on the eastern side of New Orleans. Conspiracy theorists have argued that Oswald may have been part of a government intelligence operation with the other employees from Reily or perhaps these individuals were given government employment to make them unavailable to any investigative commissions after the assassination. Interestingly, none of Oswald's fellow employees at Reily testified before the Warren Commission.[29]

During the summer of 1963 in New Orleans, Oswald apparently was seen in the company of David Ferrie who, as stated earlier, had served as Oswald's leader in the CAP and maintained a plethora of connections to the intelligence community and organized crime. Supposedly, Oswald, Ferrie, and an unidentified man made an appearance at a voter registration rally in Clinton, Louisiana.[30] The three individuals stood out because they arrived in a Cadillac and Oswald took his place in the registration line as the only white person among numerous African Americans. The unidentified man with Ferrie and Oswald was believed to have been either Guy Banister or Clay Shaw. Guy Banister was one of David Ferrie's close associates, a former FBI agent who was employed with the ONI, and allegedly the leader of a radical paramilitary group called the Minutemen of Louisiana. Clay Shaw has been the subject of much conspiratorial discussion because he ran the International Trade Mart in New Orleans in the early 1960s, and District Attorney Jim Garrison attempted to prosecute Shaw for his conspiratorial role in the assassination of President Kennedy. While Shaw was acquitted in the only trial to bring charges of conspiracy in the Kennedy assassination, the CIA acknowledged after Shaw's death in 1974 that he had been employed as a contract agent for their agency. In fact, Victor Marchetti was told by former CIA director, Richard Helms, that Clay Shaw and David Ferrie both had been employed by the CIA.[31] Clay Shaw frequently used the alias "Clay Bertrand" and this name appeared in the Warren Commission Report as someone who tried to secure an attorney for Oswald after he was charged with the murders of President Kennedy and Dallas police officer, J. D. Tippit.[32]

In the early 1960s, Clay Shaw was known to frequent the offices of Guy Banister who, at this time, worked as a private investigator in New Orleans. The address of Banister's investigative office, 544 Camp Street, was stamped on pro-Castro leaflets that Oswald distributed on the streets of New Orleans in August 1963. This strange coincidence has caused some conspiracy theorists to maintain that Oswald was possibly employed by Banister, Shaw, the CIA, and/or the FBI as an informant or low-level operative. In the summer of 1963, Oswald set up the New Orleans chapter of the FPCC possibly as a front to infiltrate pro-Castro groups and gather information for Banister, other right-wing operatives, or organized crime leaders, such as Marcello, who were staunchly anti-Castro. Ray and Mary La Fontaine have argued that Oswald may have been used by Banister to create the FPCC as an anti-Castro propaganda operation.[33] Because Oswald was viewed as a "kook" who had defected to the Soviet Union, Banister and others perhaps saw the FPCC organization in New Orleans as a way to damage more fully the image of Castro and communism in Cuba.

However, the La Fontaines also have argued that Oswald simultaneously may have been attempting to infiltrate the offices of Banister to gather information for the U.S. government, either the CIA or FBI. Banister had strong connections with a host of anti-Castro exile organizations, such as the Student Revolutionary Directorate (DRE), and he participated in gunrunning activities as well as military camps in support of the anti-Castro exiles. In 1961, the DRE was an independent organization but worked in coordination with the CIA during the Bay of Pigs invasion. After the Bay of Pigs fiasco, the Kennedy administration clamped down on such anti-Castro activities in favor of a policy of neutrality toward Cuba, however, the DRE continued its work for the CIA under a secret code name, AMSPELL, with its members on the CIA payroll. In the summer of 1963, an anti-Castro arms camp just north of Lake Pontchartrain was raided by the FBI and, coincidentally, Oswald was in nearby New Orleans at this time. The La Fontaines and others have speculated that Oswald may have provided the information to the FBI about AM-

SPELL because Banister had been a major supporter of such military operations involving persons from the CIA, Mafia, and Cuban exile groups who wanted to overthrow Castro. From this perspective, Oswald created the FPCC, a nonexistent organization, in order to add to his "legend" as a Marxist, while concomitantly spying on right-wing operatives. A legend in the intelligence world is an operational plan for a cover based largely upon the mission at hand. Was it conceivable that Oswald was operating as a double agent in the spirit of his favorite television show, *I Led Three Lives*? If true, Oswald had placed himself in a precarious spot because it was likely that his role as an informant would have been uncovered by Banister or someone associated with the Mafia-CIA-Cuban exile camps. If Oswald had been revealed as the FBI informant for the arms camp near Lake Pontchartrain, Oswald may have become a target for revenge.[34]

Further evidence of Oswald's "double agent" role was possibly revealed in his FPCC leaflet campaign where he also chose to antagonize a member of the DRE, Carlos Bringuier. On August 8, 1963, Oswald approached Bringuier and offered his services as a former Marine to assist in any military action against Fidel Castro. When Bringuier was told the following day that Oswald was passing out pro-Castro leaflets on the streets of New Orleans, Bringuier and one of his associates confronted Oswald and the police arrested Oswald after a scuffle between the two men. Bringuier obviously felt betrayed because Oswald had been deceptive in presenting himself as an anti-Castro activist. Many individuals who observed the scuffle, however, remarked that it appeared to have been a staged event.[35]

During his brief time in jail, Oswald met with a FBI agent, John Quigley.[36] Quigley interviewed Oswald on August 10, 1963, but later destroyed his notes from the meeting. Interestingly, William Walter, a security clerk employed in the New Orleans FBI office, testified before the House Select Committee on Assassinations that Quigley asked Walter to conduct a file check on Oswald. Walter conducted the check and discovered a security and informant file on Oswald within the New Orleans FBI office. Quigley later testified that only a security file existed on Oswald, not an informant file. Interestingly, Walter also testified before the HSCA that, while he was on night duty at the FBI office in New Orleans, he saw the infamous teletype on November 17, 1963, warning of an assassination attempt on President Kennedy.[37]

As a result of his fight with the Cuban exiles and his arrest, Oswald was given considerable press coverage and participated in a radio interview on August 17, 1963, with Bill Stuckey from WDSU of New Orleans. On August 21, 1963, WDSU asked Oswald to return for a second radio interview including a debate with Bringuier about Marxism and U.S. foreign policy toward Cuba. During the second interview, Oswald may have accidentally revealed that he had been working closely with the U.S. government during his stay in the Soviet Union. When Oswald was asked how he supported himself in the Soviet Union, he replied that ". . . I worked in Russia . . . I was . . . under the protection of the American government. . . . "[38] Oswald quickly corrected himself by stating that he "was not under the protection of the American government."[39] But, some researchers have speculated that Oswald perhaps unveiled an intelligence connection with this comment.[40]

While Oswald appeared to be operating as a double agent during the summer of 1963, researchers have further speculated that Oswald also may have been laying the groundwork to gain publicity and establish himself as a pro-Castro activist in order to gain entry into Cuba on yet another counter-intelligence mission as a "fake-defector" to another communist society. On August 12, 1963, Oswald wrote the FPCC informing the pro-Castro group of the extensive press coverage of his arrest seemingly to establish credibility as a pro-communist revolutionary.

In September of 1963, Oswald supposedly took a trip to Dallas with two Cubans to visit Silvia Odio, a Cuban refugee whose father was imprisoned in Havana for speaking out publicly against Fidel Castro.[41] As described in chapters 1 and 2, Odio tells a story which, if true, paints a portrait of individuals attempting to frame Oswald for the assassination of President Kennedy. Odio stated that the two Cubans and Oswald arrived at her home seeking assistance for their anti-Castro movement. Odio was suspicious of the three visitors and said that Oswald was introduced to her as "Leon Oswald," an ex-Marine. Odio cautiously ended the conversation but one of the Cubans contacted her by telephone the next day asking about her impressions of "Leon Oswald." The Cuban indicated that Oswald had criticized Cuban exiles in the United States for not being more outraged at President Kennedy for the Bay of Pigs fiasco. He also informed Odio that Oswald said that the Cubans should have killed Kennedy by now. Then, he told Odio that Oswald was thinking about assassinating Kennedy himself.[42] Similar to Oswald's attempt to infiltrate Bringuier and the anti-Castro exiles, it is possible that Oswald had infiltrated another anti-Castro group who happened to visit Odio. Perhaps "Leopoldo" and other anti-Castro Cubans had learned that Oswald was an informant and started laying the groundwork for framing Oswald by planting the assassination story with Odio.

Silvia Odio relayed the story in a letter to her father in Cuba who responded that she should be suspicious of anyone trying to gain information from her because someone could be trying to deceive her by presenting themselves as friends of her father when, in fact, they might be pro-Castro sympathizers. On November 22, 1963, the day of the Kennedy assassination, Odio fainted when she saw the television coverage of Oswald because she remembered him from the late-night visit with the two Cubans. She was taken to a hospital and spoke with her sister about the pre-assassination visit from the three suspicious individuals. Conspiracy theorists have maintained that her story hints at a conspiracy and cover-up and cannot be resolved within the lone-gunman theory. Robert Groden and Harrison Livingstone have maintained that Odio "is among the strongest witnesses to conspiracy" in the assassination of President Kennedy.[43]

Silvia Odio has never attempted to profit financially from her story and has never changed her story over time. Some authors have pointed to her history of receiving psychological counseling in an attempt to destroy her credibility but, otherwise, she remains one of the strongest testaments of a conspiracy to assassinate Kennedy as well as the real possibility that someone, or some organization, was trying to frame Oswald for the murder. Odio's story points to the possibility that Oswald was being set-up to take the fall for the assassination. It is unknown whether Oswald was accompanied on his visit to Odio's home with pro-Castro Cubans posing as anti-Castro Cuban exiles or whether, in fact, he had infiltrated a right-wing anti-Castro group whose members visited Odio to obtain genuine support from the daughter of an anti-Castro leader imprisoned in Cuba. Odio supposedly learned later from a source in New Orleans that Oswald was working as a "double agent" attempting to infiltrate both anti-Castro and pro-Castro organizations.[44] There is also the possibility that Oswald did not accompany the two Cubans who visited Odio on the evening in question. It simply could have been an individual who resembled Oswald in order to frame him for the assassination.

OSWALD'S TRIP TO MEXICO CITY

During the fall of 1963 from September 26 to October 3, Oswald took a trip to Mexico City which suggests that he may have been given another intelligence assignment at this time. Oswald traveled by bus and arrived in Mexico City at 10:00 am on Friday, September 27, 1963. He stayed in Mexico City until the morning of Wednesday, October 3, 1963, when he boarded a bus destined for Texas. Interestingly, Oswald should not have been allowed to leave the country given the controversy surrounding his recent defection to Russia and return to the United States, however, the State Department quickly issued Oswald a passport and claimed later that it was a clerical error. The passport issued immediately before Oswald's was suspiciously that of a CIA agent, William Gaudet. Oswald may have traveled with (or was closely watched by) this CIA agent on his trip to Mexico City. It is worth noting that on September 17, 1963, ten days prior to Oswald's trip to Mexico City, he obtained a fifteen-day tourist visa from the Mexican Consulate in New Orleans. The number of Oswald's tourist card was 24085. After the assassination, the FBI listed Oswald's tourist card number as 24084 and later corrected the error. When the CIA released a study of Oswald's tourist card in

1976, the numbers 24082, 24083, 24085, 24086 and 24087 were listed but the number 24084 was mysteriously lost. Interestingly, the number 24084 belonged to none other than William Gaudet, who had filed for a tourist card in front of Oswald. Gaudet admitted that he had been employed by the CIA and also stated that he had seen Oswald in the company of Guy Banister in New Orleans. Gaudet's CIA files revealed that he had been a contact for the New Orleans office of the CIA. In an interview with Anthony Summers, Gaudet stated, "I think (Oswald) was a patsy. I think he was set up on purpose."[45]

During Oswald's five-day stay in Mexico City, he visited the Russian and Cuban embassies in a desperate attempt to gain an entrance visa to Cuba. Oswald told officials at both embassies that he wanted to travel to the Soviet Union through Cuba but was told that he could not obtain a visa to Cuba until he had obtained a Russian visa which would take four months. As noted above, most researchers speculate that Oswald had no intention of traveling to the Soviet Union and that he would have stayed in Cuba as part of an intelligence mission. Lamar Waldron and Thom Hartmann argue that the purpose of Oswald's trip to Mexico City was designed for Oswald to gain entrance into Cuba as part of an intelligence operation to lay the groundwork for the overthrow of Fidel Castro. They also contend that the secret intelligence operation to overthrow Castro, which was scheduled for December in 1963, was infiltrated by the Mafia who, in turn, framed Oswald for the Kennedy assassination because his cover as a communist sympathizer made Oswald the perfect patsy. Mafia leaders, Carlos Marcello, Santos Traficante, and Johnny Roselli, may well have infiltrated the Kennedy administration's secret plan to overthrow Castro through their intelligence contacts, namely David Atlee Phillips and David Morales, who had previously worked in conjunction with the Mafia leaders on assassination plots aimed at Castro. As a result, the U.S. government would have been forced to cover up the truth behind the Kennedy assassination because a comprehensive investigation would have revealed such CIA-Mafia intelligence operations.[46]

The Russian officials who met with Oswald reported that, at one point in their conversation, Oswald began to cry and broke down emotionally stating that he feared for his life. One of the Russian officials confiscated a handgun and bullets from Oswald during his emotional breakdown. While the U.S. government maintained video surveillance of the Russian and Cuban embassies, they could not produce any actual photographs or footage of Oswald entering or leaving the embassies. Instead, U.S. officials reported that, during Oswald's visits to both embassies, the surveillance equipment at the Soviet Embassy had been turned off and the equipment at the Cuban Embassy had malfunctioned. A photograph supposedly of Oswald was eventually released by the United States but the person in the photograph was obviously not Oswald. Instead, the photograph showed a male somewhat older than Oswald with a larger build. Because of the confusion and complexity surrounding Oswald's trip to Mexico City, it remains an unsolved mystery whether Oswald, an impostor posing as Oswald, or both Oswald and his impostor traveled to Mexico City and visited the Russian and Cuban embassies.[47]

John Newman has researched Oswald's trip to Mexico City extensively and has argued that the Mexico City trip was a CIA disinformation campaign that unwittingly made Oswald vulnerable to being set up because it connected him to the Russians and Cubans immediately prior to the assassination of Kennedy. Newman suggests that intelligence files indicate that Oswald was being guided in some fashion by the intelligence community during his trip to and from Mexico City. Newman's analysis shows that the CIA had a "keen operational interest" in the activities of Oswald during his trip to Mexico City. Specifically, the CIA drastically changed its intelligence file on Oswald a week after he left for Mexico City by creating a new file to replace his previous 201 file. The new operational file on Oswald contained information about his FPCC activities, while the old 201 file was kept separate and would later include surveillance of Oswald's trip to Mexico City. It is Newman's contention that these two separate files form a "smoking file" that prove Oswald was involved in very sensitive operations with the CIA. Newman speculates that Oswald may have been involved in anti-Cuban operations for the CIA, specifically a CIA plan to sabotage FPCC activities in foreign countries or providing disinformation to embarrass the FPCC.[48]

Newman also puts forward the idea that Oswald may not have even made the trip to Mexico City. The only proof of Oswald's visits to the Russian and Cuban embassies came from an employee of the Cuban Embassy, Silvia Duran, and CIA officials who provided surveillance of the Russian Embassy. Strangely, the CIA ordered the Mexican police to arrest Silvia Duran the day after the assassination of Kennedy. The CIA did not want Duran providing any information to leftist factions of the Mexican government. The extent to which the CIA tried to control this situation has caused researchers to speculate that the CIA was desperate to prove that Oswald had gone to the Cuban Embassy when, in fact, it was an impostor posing as Oswald. Silvia Duran was later rearrested when she tried to discuss Oswald's visit to the Cuban Embassy. After her second arrest by Mexican officials, Duran refused to discuss the situation again until Anthony Summers showed her films of Oswald to which she replied, ". . . the man on the film is not like the man I saw here in Mexico City."[49] In 1978, Eusebio Azcue, counsel for the Cuban Embassy, told the HSCA that he was certain that the man who visited the Cuban Embassy was not Oswald. Newman has argued that an alleged sexual affair between Oswald and Duran may have been employed as disinformation by the CIA in the aftermath of the Kennedy assassination to connect Oswald, the alleged assassin, with Cuban intelligence.[50]

If an impostor posing as Oswald was used by the CIA, it would have allowed someone to frame Oswald for the assassination and concomitantly link him to the Soviets and Cubans. By placing Oswald, or his impostor, in Mexico City eight weeks before the assassination of Kennedy, it is theorized that the CIA immersed Oswald in a mysterious world of espionage and counterespionage. Newman's suspicions are based upon the fact that the CIA mysteriously had no photographic evidence of Oswald's five visits to the two embassies even though "Mexico City . . . was one of the most surveilled spots on the planet"[51] in the fall of 1963 and also because evidence exists that several telephone calls to the Soviet Embassy in Mexico City were probably made by an impostor posing as Oswald. For instance, the first telephone call supposedly made by Oswald upon his arrival in Mexico City on September 27, 1963, was recorded by the CIA station in Mexico City. The conversation was oddly in Spanish and the translator did not indicate that Oswald's Spanish was spoken with an accent or was less than fluent. Another telephone call supposedly made by Oswald from the Cuban Embassy to the Russian Embassy was judged to have been made by an impostor who was incoherent.[52] Researchers have speculated the CIA withheld and manipulated information about Oswald's visit to Mexico City from investigators because either the CIA, or a rogue element thereof, had a role in the assassination of Kennedy or the CIA was embarrassed that it allowed one of its operatives, Oswald, to be compromised and subsequently framed for the assassination. An example of such manipulation perhaps occurred in January 1964 when the CIA submitted information to the Warren Commission members that Oswald had been in contact with Valery Kostikov, a KGB agent, during one of his visits to the Russian Embassy in Mexico City. The CIA informed the Commission that Kostikov was in charge of "assassination and sabotage" as part of Department 13 of Soviet intelligence. Conspiracy theorists have speculated that the CIA used Oswald's contact with Kostikov to frighten the Commission members and, in turn, stop them from seeking information about Oswald's trip to Mexico City.[53]

The CIA officer in charge of operations in Mexico City in September 1963 was David Atlee Phillips.[54] Phillips was renowned for his counterintelligence skills throughout Latin and South America. Phillips played a major role in establishing CIA fronts in Cuba and recruiting informants to spy on Castro in order to gain intelligence about communist organizations. Antonio Veciana, the leader of a militant group of anti-Castro Cubans called Alpha 66, stated that he saw Oswald in the presence of David Atlee Phillips. Veciana knew Phillips according to his undercover name, "Maurice Bishop." If Veciana's story is accurate, it is possible that Oswald was working with Phillips at the time of his visit to Mexico City. Oswald's emotional breakdown at the Soviet Embassy in Mexico City may have occurred because of his intuition that something had gone wrong in his role as an informant for

Phillips. Oswald may have sensed that his life was in danger or that he was being "sheep-dipped" by the CIA, or a rogue element of the organization, to take the blame for a criminal act. The term "sheep-dipping" is used to describe the process of preparing an innocent person for their role as a patsy by planting false incriminating evidence prior to an event.

In the early 1970s, Phillips was instrumental in leading an intelligence task force to stop the election of a socialist, Salvador Allende, as president of Chile. Phillips retired in 1975 at the same time that the media was uncovering illegal activities of the intelligence agencies which inspired the formation of the Church Committee in the U.S. Senate and the most extensive investigation of clandestine operations in American history.

WAS OSWALD FRAMED FOR THE ASSASSINATION OF PRESIDENT KENNEDY?

In early October of 1963, Oswald returned to Fort Worth, Texas, where his wife, Marina, and two children were staying with a friend, Ruth Paine. Ruth Paine had become separated from her husband, Michael, and began a close friendship with Marina. Ruth Paine allowed Marina to live with her in Fort Worth in exchange for Marina assisting with the housework and helping her to learn the Russian language.[55] After returning from his mysterious trip to Mexico City, Oswald was again unemployed so Ruth Paine informed Oswald that a neighbor, Buell Frazier, might be able to assist Oswald in gaining employment at the Texas School Book Depository (TSBD) in Dallas. Oswald was interviewed by the manager of the TSBD, Roy Truly, and hired to fill textbook orders at $1.25 per hour. On October 7, 1963, Oswald rented a room in Dallas from a landlady, Mary Bledsoe, who quickly evicted Oswald after a week because he spoke on the telephone in a foreign language which made her uncomfortable. Because Oswald often spoke in a foreign language on the telephone and made his initial landlady in Dallas suspicious and uncomfortable, conspiracy theorists have asserted that this provides more evidence of Oswald becoming involved in clandestine activities and perhaps assuming a more active role as an informant.

After his eviction, Oswald then rented a room at 1026 North Beckley in Dallas. He lived at this residence during the work week but would then travel to Fort Worth with Buell Frazier on Friday to spend the weekend with his family at the Paine residence. Oswald did not own an automobile and never obtained a driver's license throughout his life. Ruth Paine gave Oswald some driving lessons during the fall of 1963 but she noted that he was "pretty unskilled" operating a motor vehicle.[56] While residing in Dallas at 1026 North Beckley, Oswald informed his landlady that his name was O. H. Lee, another alias which provides more speculation about his role as an informant.

There has been some speculation that Oswald's alias may have simply been a reversal of his name but it is also possible that he was trying to emulate V. T. Lee who was the president of the FPCC. Oswald apparently was fearful that the FBI, or some other agency, had been monitoring his activities which would have been consistent with his emotional breakdown in Mexico City when he indicated to officials at the Soviet Embassy that he feared for his life. When FBI agent James Hosty stopped by the Paine residence to speak with Oswald but instead had a conversation with Marina, she recorded the license plate number of Hosty's vehicle as Oswald had instructed her to do in the case of a visit by the FBI. It is possible that Oswald wanted the license plate number because it was commonplace for FBI informants to meet with their intelligence contacts in a parked vehicle.

After Marina informed Oswald that Hosty had visited her, Oswald left a note for Hosty at the FBI office in Dallas, Texas during the time period of November 12–15, 1963. Conspiracy theorists have speculated that Oswald's note to Hosty may have been a warning about the plot to assassinate Kennedy. In fact, some researchers have argued that Oswald may have been the source of the FBI warning that was sent out as a teletype message to all of the FBI offices that an extremist right-wing group was planning the assassination of Kennedy on November 22–23, 1963. The contents of the note were never revealed because, after Jack Ruby murdered Oswald, Hosty's superiors instructed him to destroy the note. Did Hosty destroy the note because its contents might have linked Oswald to the U.S. government as an informant in some fashion? In fact, the attorney general of Texas, Waggoner Carr, told the Warren Commission in a closed session on January 22, 1964, that he uncovered evidence from the Dallas sheriff's office that Oswald had been employed by the FBI as an informant wherein he was paid $200 a month for roughly one year prior to the assassination. Carr said he obtained the evidence that Oswald was an FBI informant from Allan Sweatt who was employed with the Dallas sheriff's office as chief of the criminal division. Other investigators claim that Henry Wade, the district attorney for Dallas, was Carr's source about Oswald's status as an informant who was assigned Informant Number S-179.[57]

On Thursday, November 21, 1963, Oswald broke his pattern of visiting his family on Friday for the weekend and instead arrived on Thursday evening. Oswald told Buell Frazier that he needed a ride to Irving on Thursday "to get some curtain rods" for his apartment at 1026 North Beckley. Oswald arrived on Thursday because he was trying to reconcile with Marina who was angry that he had used the alias, O. H. Lee, to rent the rooming house at 1026 North Beckley. Marina had discovered Oswald's use of the alias when she telephoned Oswald on Monday, November 18th, but the landlady informed her that no one by the name of Lee Oswald lived at 1026 North Beckley. Hence, on the Friday morning of November 22, 1963, it was necessary for

Oswald to drive to work with Buell Frazier from Fort Worth to Dallas. Oswald left behind all of his money, $170 in cash, and his wedding ring in a Russian tea cup for his wife.[58] While some researchers interpret Oswald's behavior as a sign that he was trying to make his wife feel guilty for not reconciling with him, others note that Oswald had his Marine Corps ring and bracelet as well as a form of identification from the Department of Defense on his person as he left for work.[59] Researchers have speculated that Oswald may have been given an intelligence assignment related to preventing the Kennedy assassination. Is it possible perhaps that Oswald left for work on this Friday morning with the intent of performing an assignment for the U. S. government in some capacity?

In addition to those personal effects related to the U.S. military, Oswald also carried a small package with him and placed it in the backseat of Frazier's automobile. When Frazier inquired about the package, Oswald reminded him that it contained the curtain rods for his rooming house at 1026 North Beckley. Conspiracy theorists speculate that the package was too small to contain Oswald's disassembled Mannlicher-Carcano rifle, especially given the fact that Buell Frazier estimated the package to be 27 inches long and the disassembled rifle would have been 35 inches long.[60] Other researchers have surmised that Oswald may have been asked by his handlers to bring his rifle to the TSBD and perhaps the CIA, or Dallas Police Department, planted the rifle as part of the set-up to frame Oswald for the assassination.

A former CIA operative, Robert Morrow, stated that he was ordered by a CIA supervisor to purchase four Mannlicher-Carcano rifles which he believes were delivered to the Dallas Police Department on the day of the Kennedy assassination. Morrow argues that Oswald was framed by Clay Shaw, Guy Banister, and Jack Ruby along with CIA operatives and anti-Castro Cubans.[61] Moreover, the ammunition found on the sixth floor of the Texas School Book Depository (TSBD) was manufactured by Western Cartridge Corporation of Illinois as part of a defense contract for the U.S. government. The United States Marine Corps purchased millions of rounds of this ammunition in the 1950s which oddly couldn't be fired by any of their weapons. A FBI document revealed that the ammunition was purchased for use by the CIA in intelligence operations.[62] As discussed in chapter 2, Morrow was the source for the assassination plot against Kennedy scheduled for late September 1963, in Washington, DC. The plot was allegedly devised by members of Alpha 66, a militant anti-Castro organization funded by the CIA. Morrow uses code names in his novel, *Betrayal*, in describing how a counter-intelligence operative, Richard Case Nagell, stumbled upon the plot wherein Oswald was recruited as a shooter in the assassination and ultimately framed by members of Alpha 66 who had presented themselves to Oswald as intelligence agents acting on behalf of Castro. Hence, Nagell maintained that Oswald was indeed a patsy set up by the Cuban exiles, but he is not cast as a hero attempting to prevent the assassination but, instead, as a co-conspirator and willing participant in the assassination.[63]

Immediately after the assassination on November 22, 1963, the Dallas homicide unit added more confusion to the mystery of the rifle when it initially issued a statement that a 7.65 Mauser rifle was found on the sixth floor near the sniper's lair but then it was apparently "lost." Seymour Weitzman, a Dallas police officer considered to be an expert on weapons, identified the rifle to Dallas police Chief Will Fritz as a 7.65 Mauser. Deputy Sheriff Roger Craig stated that he observed the word "Mauser" marked on the rifle. Deputy Sheriff Eugene Boone signed a sworn affidavit that the rifle was a Mauser and, finally, as late as midnight on November 22, 1963, the Dallas District Attorney, Henry Wade, informed the media that a Mauser rifle was recovered from the sixth floor of the TSBD.[64]

In regard to Oswald's whereabouts at the time of the assassination, Oswald was seen on the sixth floor by four employees of the TSBD, specifically Bonnie Ray Williams, Billy Lovelady, Danny Acre, and Jack Dougherty, prior to the arrival of the presidential motorcade but witnesses within Dealey Plaza provided conflicting reports about how many persons were seen near the windows of the sixth floor. For instance, an elderly African American man was seen in the sixth floor window by Arnold Rowland and his wife, Barbara. A blond-haired man with a rifle was spotted on one of the top floors of the TSBD by Carolyn Walthers. On one of the top floors of the building, Toney Henderson witnessed a dark-haired man with a second man who was either Hispanic or African American. Amos Eunis saw a dark-skinned man with a bald head on the sixth floor with a rifle and, finally, Richard Randolph Carr saw a white man on the sixth floor but on the opposite side of the building where Oswald was supposedly located. Based upon the observations of all of these witnesses, conspiracy theorists conclude that at least three men were on the sixth floor of the Depository and none of them bore a resemblance to Oswald.[65] Howard Brennan, supposedly the only person who actually witnessed Oswald firing the Mannlicher-Carcano rifle, provided a vague description of Oswald, at best, and initially failed to select Oswald from a police lineup. Interestingly, Carolyn Arnold, a secretary to the vice-president of the TSBD, allegedly saw Oswald in the second floor lunchroom at 12:15 pm only fifteen minutes prior to the motorcade passing in front of the TSBD. If Arnold's recollection is accurate, it would have been almost impossible for Oswald to move into position on the sixth floor in only fifteen minutes and fire three shots at the motorcade. Arnold supposedly gave two statements to the FBI. In the first statement, she said that Oswald was on the first floor in the hallway and, in the second statement, she apparently denied seeing Oswald. Arnold claims that she was misquoted by the FBI.

After the shots were fired at President Kennedy's motorcade at approximately 12:30 pm, Marrion Baker, a Dallas police officer who was part of the motorcade, left his motorcycle and stormed into the TSBD. Accompanied by Roy Truly, the manager of the TSBD, Officer Baker drew his revolver and confronted Oswald who was drinking a Coke on the second floor of the TSBD where Arnold stated that she saw Oswald fifteen minutes prior to the assassination. Skeptics have maintained that it would have been impossible for Oswald to fire three shots at Kennedy, hide his rifle, walk, or run, across the sixth floor of the TSBD, and then proceed down four flights of stairs to the second floor lunchroom where he was located drinking a Coke. Moreover, five employees of the TSBD walked down the stairs from the fourth and fifth floors after the final shot was fired at President Kennedy but none of the five saw Oswald descending from the sixth floor. The five employees were Junior Jarman, Bonnie Ray Williams, Harold Norman, Sandra Stykes, and Victoria Adams. Jarman, Williams, and Norman walked down the stairs from the fifth floor, while Styles and Adams descended from the fourth floor with none of the five persons witnessing Oswald. Oswald also showed no sign that he was out of breath or in a panic which would have been expected if he was the assailant who had just assassinated a U.S. president, hurried down four flights of stairs in less than a minute, and then faced a confrontation with a Dallas police officer on the second floor. Roy Truly, the manager of the TSBD, stated Officer Baker's gun "appeared to be almost touching the middle portion of Oswald's body."[66] However, Oswald "didn't seem to be excited or overly afraid of anything. He might have been a bit startled like I might have been if somebody confronted me."[67]

Oliver Stone's movie, *JFK*, based upon Jim Garrison and Mark Lane's interpretation of the assassination, presents an argument that Oswald fled the TSBD perhaps aware that he was being framed for the assassination.[68] Oswald boarded a bus but, when the bus stalled in traffic, he hailed a taxi cab to the 500 block of North Beckley. Oswald may have been in a panic because this was the only known instance in his lifetime that he hailed a taxi cab. Conspiracy theorists assert that this provides circumstantial evidence that Oswald was desperate to flee the scene because he had come to the realization that he was being framed for the assassination. When Oswald entered his rooming house at 1026 North Beckley, his landlady indicated that a Dallas police car pulled up to the residence and honked its horn twice. Conspiracy theorists have suggested that this was a signal being sent to Oswald by the Dallas police force renowned for its corruption and violence as an organization in the early 1960s. Speculation exists that a rogue element of the Dallas Police Department perhaps controlled by the CIA may have been hired to eliminate Oswald. After retrieving a beige jacket and pistol from his rooming house at North Beckley, Oswald waited curbside for a bus. After becoming impatient, Oswald began walking and was supposedly confronted by a Dallas patrolman, J. D. Tippit. Oswald allegedly shot Tippit numerous times and then fled on foot. Some researchers have alleged that Tippit may have been hired to eliminate Oswald or perhaps Oswald mistakenly feared that Tippit was part of the conspiratorial plot and he seemingly shot and killed Tippit in self-defense.[69] Others have argued that Oswald could not have committed the murder simply because Tippit was shot between 1:06 pm and 1:10 pm and Oswald was seen by his landlady at 1:04 pm standing at the bus stop approximately one mile from the Tippit shooting. Interestingly, eyewitness reports indicated that Oswald may not have fired the shots at Tippit. A number of witnesses reported conflicting stories of two assailants, or an assailant that did not match Oswald's description. Prior to the shooting, Acquilla Clemons stated that she saw two men standing near the patrol car of Officer Tippit. Mr. and Mrs. Frank Wright confirmed Clemons's testimony. FBI Director J. Edgar Hoover instructed his agents to disregard Clemons and Mr. and Mrs. Wright in their investigation.[70]

In addition to the timeline and eyewitness problems, the chain of evidence proved to be troublesome because the shell casings found at the murder scene and the bullets in Tippit's body raised reasonable doubt that Oswald was the murderer. Dallas police officer, J. M. Poe, scratched his initials on two of the cartridge shells and Sergeant W. E. Barnes also placed his initials on the same cartridges which was standard operating procedure in the law enforcement field. However, neither officer could identify the two shells positively when presented with the cartridges by the Warren Commission. The FBI crime lab also supposedly could not connect any of the four bullets found in Tippit's body to Oswald's .38 revolver.[71]

Soon after the murder of Tippit, Oswald entered a shoe store and was noticed by the store's manager, Johnny Calvin Brewer. After quickly leaving the shoe store, Oswald entered the Texas Movie Theater without purchasing a ticket. An employee of the theater, Julia Postal, contacted the Dallas police because she was suspicious of Oswald. Interestingly, researchers have theorized that Oswald may have planned to meet with an intelligence contact in the darkened theater, a place where intelligence informants commonly met with their superiors, or handlers. In fact, this particular theater was owned by Howard Hughes, an individual with solid connections to the CIA.[72] Dallas police descended on the theater and arrested Oswald after a scuffle where he punched a Dallas police officer, N. M. McDonald, and attempted to fire his revolver, however, the weapon did not fire when Oswald pulled the trigger. After he was handcuffed, Oswald shouted, "I am not resisting arrest. Don't hit me anymore."[73] This comment indicated that Oswald may have feared for his life perhaps realizing that he was being framed for the assassination of Kennedy and, in turn, was about to be silenced by the culprits.

After Oswald was arrested at approximately 2:00 pm, he was driven to the Dallas police headquarters. During the trip to police headquarters, Sergeant Gerald Hill recommended to Oswald that he should hide his face from news photographers. Interestingly, Oswald questioned why he should hide his face because he hadn't done anything wrong. Dallas patrolman K. E. Lyon also noted that Oswald repeatedly questioned why he was being arrested during the ride to police headquarters.[74]

While in police custody, Oswald never confessed to the murders of Kennedy or Tippit and consistently denied that he was the assassin who shot the president. Oswald was given a paraffin test and, while his hands tested positive, his right cheek tested negative. Paraffin is a white or colorless, waxy solid mixture of hydrogen and carbon. The paraffin test on Oswald involved making a cast of his hands and his right cheek. The test is based on the idea that gunpowder residue will react to the paraffin and produce a blue color in the cast. The positive finding of the paraffin test on Oswald's hands meant that he probably had fired a gun but the negative finding on his right cheek cast doubt as to whether Oswald fired a rifle. Even the paraffin test on Oswald's hands was deemed suspect because paraffin reacts to substances other than gunpowder such as tobacco, cosmetics, and various food products.

After the paraffin test, Oswald was made available to the media for a press conference. The reporters shouted questions at Oswald and took photographs creating a very chaotic and circus-like atmosphere.[75] In front of a parade of media, Oswald maintained his innocence and also added that he was, in fact, a patsy. On one occasion when reporters shouted questions at Oswald asking whether he shot the president, he hollered, "I don't know what kind of dispatches you people have been given. I have not committed any act of violence."[76] When Henry Wade, the district attorney, responded to a reporter's question that Oswald belonged to the "Free Cuba Committee," Jack Ruby, a Dallas nightclub owner, corrected Wade by stating that it was called the "Fair Play for Cuba Committee." Ruby, somehow, had gained access to the press conference probably through his contacts with the Dallas police and continued to stalk Oswald throughout his short time in custody. Interestingly, Ruby was spotted by a Dallas news reporter, Seth Kantor, at Parkland Hospital immediately after Kennedy was shot and he also was alleged to have been seated in the Texas Theater at the time of Oswald's arrest. George J. Applin was supposedly seated in the theater at the time of Oswald's arrest and he told the *Dallas Morning News* in 1979 that Ruby was seated in the back row of the theater when police confronted Oswald. A witness in Dealey Plaza, Julie Ann Mercer, also provided a connection between Ruby and Oswald when she claimed to have seen the two men together with a rifle near the Triple Underpass shortly before the assassination. Finally, a photograph of Jack Ruby was allegedly shown to Oswald's mother, Marguerite, on Saturday, November 23, 1963, the day before Ruby shot and killed Oswald. If such eyewitness accounts are accurate, then Ruby was most likely involved in the conspiracy to assassinate Kennedy and frame Oswald from the outset.[77]

When Oswald was visited by his brother, Robert, in his jail cell on Saturday, November 23, he instructed his brother not to develop "any opinion on the so-called evidence" presented against him.[78] It has been suggested that Oswald already was aware that his Mannlicher-Carcano rifle and three shell casings found in the TSBD were going to be used to frame him for the assassination. Interestingly, the famous photograph of Oswald holding the Mannlicher-Carcano rifle which was eventually published in *Life* magazine also provided circumstantial evidence that Oswald may have been framed for the assassination. After police investigators showed the photograph to Oswald, he claimed that the photograph was a composite and his head had been superimposed onto the body of another person.[79]

It is also worth questioning the legitimacy of the alleged palm print of Oswald found on the Mannlicher–Carcano rifle by the Dallas Police Department. Initially, the Dallas police failed to find any prints on the rifle based upon a review of Dallas radio broadcasts from Friday evening, November 22. Two Dallas newsmen, Joe Long and Gary DeLaune, were in touch with Dallas police detectives and reported that no fingerprints had been found on the rifle obtained from the TSBD. On Saturday, November 23, Captain Will Fritz of the Dallas police also reported that Oswald's prints were not found on the rifle. The weapon was received by the FBI on Saturday, November 23, where FBI fingerprint expert Sebastian Latona examined the rifle and concluded that latent prints found on the rifle were of no value. However, on Friday, November 29, the Dallas police sent a palm print to the FBI and claimed it had been lifted from the barrel of the rifle on November 22, 1963. Conspiracy theorists speculate that the palm print may have been lifted from Oswald while his body was at the morgue on Sunday, November 24.[80] Interestingly, the FBI sent the rifle back to Dallas on Sunday, November 24 and, on the same day, a team of FBI agents spent a significant amount of time inside the morgue with a camera and crime lab kit.[81] Jack Moseley, a writer for the *Fort Worth Press* at this time, stated that Oswald was being fingerprinted by the FBI agents while his body was at the morgue. Paul Groody, the director of Miller's Funeral Home who embalmed Oswald's body, confirmed a post-mortem fingerprinting had been done on Oswald. The Warren Commission Report contains a fingerprint card for Oswald dated Monday, November 25, and it is intriguing that the card arrived at FBI headquarters on November 29, the exact date that the palm print was received by the FBI.[82]

While the president's head wounds and the ballistics evidence were important pieces of evidence used to prove that Oswald was the assassin, David Lifton argues that Oswald was framed based upon an alteration of the president's body and the fabrication of ballistics evidence. As discussed in chapter 2, Lifton notes that the Parkland Hospital medical staff in Dallas testified that President Kennedy possessed an entry wound in the front of his head and a 2 inch by 2 inch exit wound in the rear of his head. However, the medical personnel conducting the official autopsy at Bethesda Naval Hospital in Maryland reported that the president had a large exit wound in the front of his head. Therefore, Lifton maintains that surgery must have been performed on the president's head to make it appear as if the president had been shot from the TSBD. By altering the president's head wound, the conspirators sought to frame Lee Harvey Oswald for the assassination and eliminate any evidence that shots were fired from the front of the president's motorcade. Lifton also maintains conspirators created a sniper's nest on the sixth floor of the TSBD where Oswald's rifle and shell casings were planted. Finally, Lifton raises interesting questions about the two bullet fragments supposedly confiscated from inside the presidential limousine and a third "magic" bullet suspiciously discovered on a stretcher at Parkland Hospital. Lifton surmises that the bullets were probably fired from the Mannlicher-Carcano rifle prior to the assassination and planted to link Oswald to the rifle and the ballistics evidence. Lifton concludes that high ranking government officials most likely carried out the assassination with assistance from members of the Secret Service. Secret Service personnel controlled the president's body on Air Force One and also were responsible for providing the ballistics evidence which linked Oswald's rifle to the assassination.[83] In short, the unnamed conspirators altered and fabricated evidence in order to make Oswald the patsy in the assassination of President Kennedy.

THE SILENCING OF LEE HARVEY OSWALD

The murder of Oswald by Jack Ruby occurred within forty-eight hours of the assassination in the presence of over forty law enforcement officers in the basement of the Dallas Police Department and convinced a majority of people that the Kennedy assassination was the result of a conspiracy and the elimination of Oswald was part of the cover-up. Public opinion polls at the time showed that two-thirds of the American public believed that the assassination was the result of a conspiracy. Jack Ruby had connections with organized crime and telephone records indicated several calls between Ruby and organized crime figures in the months leading up to the assassination of Kennedy and the murder of Oswald. Ruby allegedly was in contact with the top aides of Carlos Marcello, the Mafia leader in New Orleans, and Santos Traficante, the organized crime leader in Miami as well as Teamsters president, Jimmy Hoffa. Ruby also may have been employed at one time by the CIA and/or FBI as an informant. Ruby allegedly took mysterious trips to Cuba in the late 1950s possibly to gather information for the U.S. government or to visit Traficante, who was being held in prison by Castro in Havana.[84] It was commonplace for intelligence agencies at the national level and/or organized crime figures to exert control over local law enforcement in the

1960s and, therefore, it would have been fairly easy for some member of the Dallas police force to provide Ruby with access to the basement of the police department where Oswald was scheduled to be transferred from the city jail to the county jail.[85] It was imperative that Oswald be eliminated because he was being transferred from the city jail to the county jail and outside the jurisdiction of the Dallas city police where organized crime and/or a rogue element of an intelligence agency might lose access to Oswald. Of course, it also would have been necessary to eliminate Oswald before he began to talk specifically about who might have framed him and what forces were behind the assassination.

David Ferrie, an individual with a wide array of contacts within the intelligence community and organized crime, allegedly was ordered by Carlos Marcello to have Ruby murder Oswald. As noted above, Marcello was the leader of the organized crime syndicate in New Orleans and employed Oswald's uncle, Charles "Dutz" Murret. Oswald's mother also associated with underworld figures connected to the Marcello organization. During the spring and summer of 1963, when Oswald was living with and working for his uncle in New Orleans, it has been speculated that Marcello discovered the perfect patsy to take the fall for the assassination. According to the testimony of FBI informants, Marcello had told associates in early 1963 that a plot to assassinate Kennedy was in development and the Mafia boss was looking for a "nut" to frame for the "job." Interestingly, one FBI informant, known only as SV T-1, witnessed a person resembling Oswald receive a "wad of money" at the Town & Country Restaurant in New Orleans in the spring of 1963. This particular establishment was owned and operated by the Marcello crime organization.[86]

Marcello and other organized crime figures had worked closely with members of the intelligence community as well as anti-Castro exiles to overthrow Fidel Castro. Two theories have taken center stage regarding the Mafia's role in the assassination. The first theory focuses on the secret negotiations during the Cuban Missile Crisis in October 1962, where President Kennedy supposedly promised the Soviet Union that the United States would end any attempt to oust Castro in exchange for the removal of Soviet nuclear missiles from Cuba.[87] Therefore, it has been argued that rouge elements of the Mafia combined forces with the intelligence community and Cuban exiles to eliminate Kennedy for his betrayal and, in the process, blame the assassination on Oswald, a communist supporter of Fidel Castro. A second theory maintains that President John F. Kennedy continued to pursue efforts to overthrow Fidel Castro and allegedly offered U.S. military support to the Chief of the Cuban Army, Juan Almeida, who agreed to participate in the coup which was scheduled for December 1, 1963. However, three Mafia bosses, Marcello, Sam Giancana, and Johnny Roselli, who had been targeted by Attorney General Robert F. Kennedy, used their connections in the CIA to change the objective of the intelligence operation from a plot to overthrow Castro to the assassination of Kennedy and the framing of Oswald. This obviously resulted in cover-ups by Attorney General Robert Kennedy and President Lyndon Johnson, who feared the exposure of the planned coup and a possible nuclear war with the Russians.[88]

CONCLUSION

In conclusion, conspiracy theorists, such as Jim Garrison, Mark Lane, and Anthony Summers, have argued that Lee Harvey Oswald was framed for the assassination of President Kennedy. After Oswald supposedly was recruited by an intelligence agency during his time spent in the Marines, he then may have faked a defection to the Soviet Union to gather information about life in the Soviet Union. After his return from the Soviet Union, Oswald may have been assigned by the intelligence community as a low-level operative or by the FBI as an informant to gather evidence about pro-Castro and anti-Castro groups in New Orleans. Oswald's childhood desire to lead the life of a "double agent" may have been realized by assisting the government in the fight against communism and perhaps even the protection of the president. In the process of performing his duties for the U.S. government, Oswald may have unwittingly placed himself within the milieu of the intelligence community and organized crime becoming vulnerable to sinister forces plotting the assassination.

NOTES

1. Mark Lane, *Plausible Denial: Was the CIA Involved in the Assassination of JFK?* (New York: Thunder's Mouth Press, 1991).
2. Jim Marrs, *Crossfire: The Plot That Killed Kennedy* (New York: Carroll & Graf, 1989), 191–196.
3. Ray and Mary La Fontaine, *Oswald Talked: The New Evidence in the JFK Assassination* (Gretna, La.: Pelican Publishing Company, Inc., 1996), 88–89.
4. David Simon, *Elite Deviance* (Needham Heights, Mass.: Allyn & Bacon, 1999), 260.
5. Herbert Philbrick, *I Led Three Lives: Citizen, "Communist," Counterspy* (New York: McGraw-Hill Book Co., 1952).
6. Marrs, *Crossfire,* 99–100.
7. Jay Edward Epstein, *Legend: The Secret World of Lee Harvey Oswald* (New York: Reader's Digest Press, 1978), 71–72.
8. Marrs, *Crossfire,* 103.
9. Ibid., 189–190.
10. Ibid., 116–117.
11. Posner, *Case Closed: Lee Harvey Oswald and the Assassination of JFK* (New York: Random House, 1993), 52–57.
12. Norman Mailer, *Oswald's Tale: An American Mystery* (New York: Random House, 1995).
13. Garrison, *On the Trail of the Assassins* (New York: Sheridan Square Press, 1988), 57–58.

14. Diane Holloway, *The Mind of Oswald* (Victoria, B.C.: Trafford Publishing, 2000).
15. Ibid., 119.
16. Posner, *Case Closed*, 79–91.
17. Garrison, *On the Trail of the Assassins*, 60.
18. Summers, *Conspiracy*, 201–203.
19. *Associated Press v. Walker* 388 U. S. 130 (1967).
20. Posner, *Case Closed*, 98–105.
21. Marrs, *Crossfire*, 255–265.
22. Holloway, *The Mind of Oswald*, 225–232.
23. James A. Nathan and James K. Oliver, *Foreign Policy Making and the American Political System* (Baltimore: Johns Hopkins University Press, 1994); Julian Roebuck and Stanley Weeber, *Political Crime in the United States: Analyzing Crime by and against Government* (New York: Praeger Publishers, 1978), 82.
24. Posner, *Case Closed*, 83–118.
25. John Davis, *Mafia Kingfish: Carlos Marcello and the Assassination of John F. Kennedy* (New York: McGraw-Hill, 1989), 121–136.
26. Ibid.
27. Summers, *Conspiracy*, 283.
28. Ibid., 284.
29. Garrison, *On the Trail of the Assassins*, 134–135.
30. Gaeton Fonzi, *The Last Investigation* (New York: Thunder's Mouth Press, 1993), 140–141.
31. Victor Marchetti and John D. Marks, *The CIA and the Cult of Intelligence* (New York: Alfred Knopf, 1974).
32. Testimony of Frederick O'Sullivan, WCR, vol. III, 326–335.
33. La Fontaine, *Oswald Talked*, 183.
34. Ibid., 183–184.
35. Marrs, *Crossfire*, 146.
36. *Id.* at 154–155.
37. Marrs, *Crossfire*, 228.
38. Holloway, *The Mind of Oswald, 182.*
39. Ibid.
40. Garrison, *On the Trail of the Assassins*, 159–161.
41. Sylvia Meagher, *Accessories After the Fact: The Warren Commission, the Authorities, and the Report* (New York: Vintage, 1992), 376.
42. Sylvia Odio's Testimony, WCR, vol. XI, 368–373.
43. Robert Groden and Harrison Livingstone, *High Treason: The Assassination of President John F. Kennedy and the New Evidence of Conspiracy* (New York: Conservatory Press, 1989), 399.
44. LaFontaine, *Oswald Talked*, 360.
45. Summers, *Conspiracy*, 346–347.
46. Waldron and Hartmann, *Ultimate Sacrifice*, 561–580.
47. John Newman, *Oswald and the CIA* (New York: Carroll & Graf, 1995), 352-362.
48. Ibid. at 394.
49. Marrs, *Crossfire*, 195.
50. Newman, *Oswald and the CIA*, 352–391.
51. Ibid., 352.
52. Edwin Lopez, "Report on Lee Harvey Oswald's Trip to Mexico City," *HSCA* (1979), 248.
53. Marrs, *Crossfire*, 193.
54. Fonzi, *The Last Investigation*, 157–160.
55. Priscilla Johnson McMillan, *Marina and Lee* (New York: Harper & Row, 1977), 344–347, 381–405.
56. Posner, *Case Closed*, 200.
57. Marrs, *Crossfire*, 231.
58. Posner, *Case Closed*, 220–225.

59. LaFontaine, *Oswald Talked,* 65–90.
60. Marrs, *Crossfire,* 41–42.
61. Robert Morrow, *Betrayal: A Reconstruction of Certain Clandestine Events from the Bay of Pigs to the Assassination of John F. Kennedy* (Chicago: Chicago Henry Regnery Co., 1976).
62. Marrs, *Crossfire,* 200–202.
63. Dick Russell, *The Man Who Knew Too Much* (New York: Carroll & Graf, 1992), 275–276.
64. Garrison, *On the Trail of the Assassins,* 235.
65. Garrison, *On the Trail of the Assassins,* 105–112.
66. David Lifton, *Best Evidence: Disguise and Deception in the Assassination of John F. Kennedy* (New York: Carroll & Graf, 1980), 350–351.
67. Ibid.
68. Oliver Stone and Zachary Sklar, *JFK: The Book of Film* (New York: Applause Books, 1992), 167–169.
69. Henry Hurt, *Reasonable Doubt: An Investigation into the Assassination of John F. Kennedy* (New York: Henry Holt & Co., 1985), 158.
70. Garrison, *On the Trail of the Assassins,* 226–229.
71. Ibid., 231–234.
72. Peter Harry Brown and Pat H. Broeske, *Howard Hughes: The Untold Story* (Cambridge, Mass.: Da Capo Press, 2004), 276–277.
73. Testimony of M. N. McDonald, WCR, vol. III, 300.
74. Lifton, *Best Evidence,* 352.
75. Posner, *Case Closed,* 348–350.
76. Lifton, *Best Evidence,* 352.
77. Marrs, *Crossfire,* 352, 402–414.
78. Lifton, *Best Evidence,* 352.
79. Ibid., 352–355.
80. Ibid., 354–355.
81. Jack Moseley, "Body of JFK Assassin Is Under Guard in FW," *Fort Worth Press,* November 25, 1963.
82. Lifton, *Best Evidence,* 355–356.
83. Ibid., 362–379.
84. William Scott Malone, "The Secret Life of Jack Ruby," *New York Times,* January 23, 1978, 46-51.
85. "CIA Link to L.A. Police Reported," *Los Angeles Herald Examiner,* January 12, 1976.
86. Davis, *Mafia Kingfish,* 119–133.
87. Irving Janis, *Groupthink: Psychological Studies of Policy Decisions and Fiascoes* (Boston: Wadsworth, 1982), 132–159.
88. Lamar Waldron and Thom Hartmann, *Ultimate Sacrifice: John and Robert Kennedy, the Plan for a Coup in Cuba, and the Murder of JFK* (New York: Carroll & Graf, 2005).

Chapter Four

Two Oswalds?

As a complement to chapters 2 and 3, this chapter documents a variety of instances where researchers have speculated about the "Two Oswalds" theory based upon alleged impersonations and various sightings of Oswald prior to the assassination which may suggest Oswald was involved in a conspiracy to assassinate President Kennedy or perhaps he was being framed by ominous forces. Conspiracy theorists raised the issue of Oswald impersonators and unusual or unlikely sightings of Oswald almost immediately after he became the key suspect in the assassination of President Kennedy. The Warren Commission dismissed the possible impersonations and sightings of Oswald as instances of mistaken identity or deliberate attempts to mislead investigators.

LEO SAUVAGE AND THE "FOREIGN RIFLE"

Leo Sauvage, a correspondent in New York for a Paris newspaper, *Le Figaro*, was the first person to suggest that Oswald may have been impersonated in an attempt to frame him for the assassination.[1] In an article published in *Commentary* in March 1964, Sauvage raised interesting questions about the presumption of guilt made against Oswald by the Dallas police, the FBI, and the news media.

In Sauvage's discussion of Oswald's Italian Mannlicher–Carcano rifle, he referenced a *Dallas Morning News* article from December 6, 1963, in which four witnesses apparently saw Oswald practicing with the Italian rifle at a gun range, the *Grand Prairie Sportsdrome*, located near Dallas. The four customers at the gun range supposedly saw Oswald practicing with a foreign rifle which contained a telescopic sight on the two weekends preceding the assassination of President Kennedy. The four customers claimed that Oswald demonstrated a keen expertise with the rifle and also drew attention to himself by shooting at other people's targets. The witnesses also remembered Oswald arriving at the gun range behind the wheel of an automobile.

Sauvage noted serious problems with the story told by the four customers at the gun range. For example, Oswald was known to spend his weekends preceding the assassination with his wife, Marina, and their two children at the home of Ruth Paine in Irving, Texas. Furthermore, Oswald did not possess an automobile or even a driver's license, although Ruth Paine was attempting to teach him how to drive an automobile. Therefore, Sauvage concluded that the four customers were probably mistaken in their identification of Oswald. But, it has been implied that perhaps someone was impersonating Oswald at the gun range in an attempt to frame Oswald as an assassin who practiced regularly with his foreign rifle and was capable of firing accurately at the presidential motorcade within a short period of time.[2]

In referencing a separate story about Oswald's rifle, Sauvage suggests more directly that someone may have been trying to plant evidence against Oswald prior to the assassination. Dial Duwayne Ryder, a gunsmith and service manager at the *Irving Sports Shop*, stated that he had mounted a telescopic sight on a rifle for Oswald during the first weeks of November 1963. Ryder came forward with his story to investigators on November 28, 1963, six days after the assassination. Ryder did not specifically remember Oswald but he produced a repair ticket with Oswald's name on it. The work order form revealed that the customer paid $6.00 for three holes to be drilled into the rifle at $1.50 per hole and an additional $1.50 was charged for aligning the barrel of the rifle with the sight. The problem with Ryder's story was that Oswald's Mannlicher-Carcano rifle, which he purchased through the mail from a sporting goods firm in Chicago, had only two holes for the sight and already had a telescopic sight mounted on it. Sauvage was critical of investigators who failed to examine a number of possibilities concerning whether Oswald had a second rifle, whether there was a different person also named Oswald who had ordered the repairs on the rifle, or whether someone was trying to plant evidence in an attempt to implicate Oswald in the assassination.

Another Oswald sighting connected to the incident involving Dial Ryder and the *Irving Sports Shop* occurred during the first week of November 1963. Mrs. Edith Whitworth, the manager of a furniture store in Irving, Texas, supposedly had a conversation with Oswald where she mentioned the *Irving Sports Shop* to him. Whitworth and her friend, Mrs. Gertrude Hunter, told a reporter for a British newspaper that Oswald visited the used-furniture store on November 6 or 7, 1963. Oswald inquired about a firing pin for his rifle because, apparently, the furniture store had a sign in its front window which advertised for a gunsmith who previously had worked in the building. They directed Oswald to the *Irving Sports Shop* which was within walking distance of the furniture store. The two women, Whitworth and Hunter, stated that Oswald was with his wife and two children and spoke a foreign language to his wife. The two women testified at the Warren Commission hearings and identified Lee and Marina Oswald from photographs shown by the legal counsel for the commission. Conspiracy theorists have argued that the person at the furniture store must have been an impersonator because Oswald was at work at the Texas School Book Depository (TSBD) on November 6 and 7, 1963. In addition, the two women at the furniture store mentioned that Oswald drove his family away in an automobile which was impossible because Marina told the Warren Commission that Oswald, who did not have a driver's license, had never driven the family in an automobile. Furthermore, Marina told investigators that she had never visited the furniture store in Irving.

"THE NORTH DAKOTA IMPERSONATOR"

Another fascinating and bizarre theory concerning an Oswald impersonator involved a letter written to President Lyndon Johnson in December 1963, by a woman named Alma Cole. She alleged that her son, William Timmer, had a friendship with a person claiming to be Oswald during the summer of 1953 in Stanley, North Dakota. This impersonation of Oswald supposedly began when the real Oswald was thirteen years of age and most likely living in New York City with his mother, Marguerite. Timmer told his mother that Oswald had moved to North Dakota from New York City, enjoyed reading books on communism, and also planned to murder the president someday.[3]

John Armstrong, a conspiracy theorist and a leading supporter of the North Dakota impersonation story, maintains that the real Oswald was not in North Dakota in 1953 but instead was being impersonated by someone who went by the name of "Harvey Oswald." The confusing and illogical theory asserts that Lee Harvey Oswald and "Harvey Oswald," a young man from Eastern Europe who spoke Russian, had their identities merged as part of a CIA project. It was "Harvey Oswald" who successfully defected to the Soviet Union in 1959 and eventually carried out the Kennedy assassination on behalf of the CIA or some other intelligence agency.[4] Therefore, "Harvey Oswald" committed the assassination, was set up as the patsy, and was subsequently killed by Jack Ruby. In essence, the real Oswald might still be alive today according to the "North Dakota" theory.

Armstrong cited two instances where "Harvey Oswald" supposedly told interviewers that he moved from New York to North Dakota at one stage in his early life. The first instance occurred when "Harvey Oswald" was interviewed by UPI reporter Aline Mosby in Moscow on November 14, 1959. The second instance cited by Armstrong involved Oswald's arrest in New

Orleans in the summer of 1963 when "Harvey Oswald" told Lieutenant Frank Martello that he had lived in North Dakota for a short period of time.

In December of 1963, one month after the assassination of President Kennedy, the FBI actually investigated the possibility that someone was impersonating Oswald during the summer of 1953 by interviewing a number of people in Stanley, North Dakota, a small town of roughly eight hundred people. None of the persons interviewed confirmed the presence of someone claiming to be Oswald in North Dakota. In regard to Aline Mosby's interview with Oswald in Moscow, Mosby claimed that she simply made a typographical error while she was typing up the interview and mistakenly typed "North Dakota" when she really meant to type "New Orleans."[5] Mosby's original notes of the interview which have been included in the Warren Commission report confirmed that Oswald told her that he and his mother moved from New York City to New Orleans, not North Dakota. An examination of the transcripts of Lieutenant Martello's interview as well as Martello's testimony before the Warren Commission produced no mention of North Dakota. Finally, Oswald's older brother, Robert, told the FBI that Oswald never lived in North Dakota during his lifetime.[6]

THE ATTEMPTED PURCHASE OF TRUCKS FOR THE FRIENDS OF DEMOCRATIC CUBA

On January 20, 1961, Lee Harvey Oswald was living in Minsk, Russia, when someone using his name entered the Bolton Ford Dealership in New Orleans and inquired about purchasing ten trucks for an anti-Castro organization, Friends of Democratic Cuba.[7] One version of the story had an Oswald impersonator apparently in the company of a Hispanic man. The two men spoke briefly with Oscar Deslatte, the assistant manager of truck sales at the dealership. The Hispanic man introduced himself as "Joseph Moore," while the impersonator claimed that his last name was "Oswald" and he would be paying for the trucks.

A second version of the story has a white man identifying himself as "Joseph Moore" who was accompanied by a Hispanic man. Moore claimed that a person by the name of "Oswald" would be paying for the ten trucks on behalf of the Friends of Democratic Cuba and asked that the last name "Oswald" be placed on the price quote sheet. Eventually, the sale of the ten trucks was not made after a negotiation between Deslatte and the two men.

Deslatte reported the story to the FBI on November 25, 1963, three days after the assassination of President Kennedy, but he was unable to identify Oswald based upon photographs shown to him by the FBI. Deslatte, however, did produce the price quote sheet for FBI investigators with the date listed as "January 20, 1961" and the last name "Oswald" listed in the upper right corner of the sheet. In May 1967, Jim Garrison, the district attorney for New Orleans, interviewed Deslatte about his encounter with the two men. Deslatte failed to remember the incident, although his supervisor at the dealership, Fred Sewell, told investigators that he remembered Oswald who used his first name "Lee" and was in the company of a Hispanic man.

Interestingly, the Friends of Democratic Cuba was an organization created in January 1961 and included Guy Banister as one of its board of directors. Banister was someone who would work closely with Oswald in the summer of 1963 after Oswald's return from the Soviet Union. Oswald and Banister supposedly shared an office at 544 Camp Street in New Orleans and may have been involved together in intelligence, or counterintelligence, operations related to anti-Castro and pro-Castro groups. The anti-Castro organization also consisted of Gerard F. Tujague who served as its vice-president. Oswald worked for Tujague's shipping company in New Orleans as a messenger boy at the age of sixteen for roughly three months, from November 1955 until January 1956.

Conspiracy theorists, such as Jim Garrison, have speculated that intelligence agents may have been using Oswald's name to purchase vehicles in preparation for the Bay of Pigs invasion of Cuba which occurred in April 1961.[8] Although a specific connection to the Bay of Pigs event is far-fetched and nearly impossible to prove, the story of the truck purchases conveyed by Deslatte creates the distinct possibility that Oswald's name was being used by individuals involved with a political group interested in a democratic revolution in Cuba. It is difficult to imagine that Oswald was being set up to take the fall for the assassination as President Kennedy was being sworn into office in 1961. But, the fact that Oswald's name surfaced in connection with an anti-Castro organization in 1961 and Oswald, later on, attempted to infiltrate pro-Castro and anti-Castro groups in the summer of 1963 clearly raises the possibility of a set–up because he was immersed in the milieu of New Orleans with its political radicals and organized crime figures interested in the overthrow of Cuba by way of intelligence operations, gun running, and political assassinations.

OSWALD AND THE WISCONSIN BARBER

In the spring of 1963, John Abbott, a barber in Sparta, Wisconsin claimed to have given a haircut to Lee Harvey Oswald.[9] Abbott reported his story to the FBI on November 30, 1963, roughly one week after the assassination. Abbott stated that Oswald told him that he was in town to visit a friend's mother who lived in Sparta. Oswald said his friend was named Philip Hemstock who supposedly was a drinking buddy of Oswald's from Dallas. Abbott also relayed to authorities that Oswald mentioned he was currently blackmailing a nightclub owner in Texas and planned to use the money from the blackmail scheme to purchase a gun and exact revenge against the United States.

The FBI interviewed the mother of Philip Hemstock who told investigators that she never received such a visit from a friend of her son. According to his mother, Hemstock did not live in Dallas but resided in Victorville, California. Abbott supposedly had a reputation for telling exaggerated stories according to the chief of police in Sparta and the local sheriff who questioned whether Abbott was mentally stable. Abbott's story appeared to be a sensationalized attempt to connect Oswald and Ruby in the immediate aftermath of the Kennedy assassination and the murder of Oswald by Ruby.

OSWALD AT U.S. SELECTIVE SERVICE HEADQUARTERS

Toward the end of September in 1963, Oswald supposedly made a trip to the U.S. Selective Service Headquarters in Austin, Texas.[10] On September 25, 1963, Oswald allegedly spoke with Jesse Skrivanek, an employee of the Selective Service, about how to correct his dishonorable discharge from the Marines. Skrivanek took Oswald to meet with Mrs. Lee Dannelly, the assistant chief of the Administrative Division of the Selective Service. Oswald informed Dannelly that his name was "Harvey Oswald" and he was registered with the Selective Service in Florida. He then stated that he had been referred to the Selective Service by Governor John Connally's offices in Austin, Texas. Dannelly told Oswald that she could not assist him but provided information for Oswald concerning how to correct his military status. On December 30, 1963, Dannelly relayed her story to the FBI about Oswald's visit.

Conspiracy theorists and researchers have maintained that Oswald was being impersonated by someone at the Selective Service headquarters because, on September 25, 1963, it is known that Oswald was either in New Orleans or en route to Mexico City. The FBI attempted to confirm Dannelly's story but the only corroboration of Dannelly's story came from a waitress who worked at a coffee shop near the Selective Service offices. The waitress, Florence Norman, claimed to have served several cups of coffee to Oswald on the day of his visit to Dannelly's office. However, an FBI investigation into the waitress's story revealed that she was not working on the day of Oswald's alleged visit to the Selective Service offices in Austin. In addition, the other employees at the coffee shop did not remember Oswald or anyone by the name of Oswald frequenting the coffee shop at any time prior to the assassination.[11] An inspection of the records from Governor Connally's office in Austin also produced no evidence that Oswald visited the governor's office in the six–month period prior to his alleged visit to the Selective Service headquarters.[12] While it is possible that Dannelly had an encounter with a person by the name of Oswald (as there were fifteen Oswalds in the Selective Service files in Austin), the Warren Commission concluded that Dannelly most likely used information about Oswald from news reports and perhaps subconsciously created the encounter with Oswald in her own mind.

OSWALD AND MRS. LOVELL PENN'S COW PASTURE

On October 6, 1963, Mrs. Lovell T. Penn of Dallas, Texas, claimed that three men were standing in a cow pasture on her farm and one of the men was firing a rifle.[13] When she told the men that she was going to contact the police, they left the cow pasture in an automobile. Mrs. Penn wrote down the license plate number of the automobile but then disposed of the number.

Mrs. Penn reported the incident to the FBI on December 2, 1963, and later claimed that the man shooting the rifle could have been Lee Harvey Oswald. Penn also found a spent shell fired from the rifle and it was identified as a Mannlicher–Carcano cartridge case. An FBI investigation of the incident concluded that the man firing the rifle in the cow pasture was not Oswald. The conclusion was based upon the fact that Mrs. Penn did not mention Oswald until her second interview with the FBI and also ballistics tests showed that the spent shell could not have been fired from Oswald's Mannlicher–Carcano.

OSWALD AND THE DALLAS CAR SALESMAN

One of the more credible sightings, or impersonations, of Lee Harvey Oswald occurred on Saturday, November 9, 1963, at a car dealership in downtown Dallas, Texas.[14] A car salesman by the name of Albert Guy Bogard reported to the FBI and also testified before the Warren Commission that Oswald entered the Lincoln Mercury dealership and introduced himself to Bogard as "Lee Oswald." Oswald asked to test-drive a Mercury Comet and took Bogard on a ride at speeds up to 85 mph on the freeway. When they returned to the dealership, Oswald decided to purchase the Mercury Comet so Bogard prepared a customer purchase sheet and asked Oswald for $300 as a down payment on the vehicle which was priced at $3,000. However, Oswald refused to sign the purchase sheet and told Bogard that he didn't have the money for the down payment but commented that he would be coming into some money in a few weeks. Oswald also told Bogard that he lived in the Oak Cliff district in Dallas which was, in fact, true. After their conversation, Bogard wrote Oswald's name on the back of one of his business cards. Bogard eventually disposed of the business card with Oswald's name on it because he figured that Oswald would not be purchasing a car from him.

After the assassination on November 22, 1963, Bogard recognized the name of Lee Harvey Oswald when it was announced on the radio that Oswald had shot and killed President Kennedy. After watching television coverage of the assassination, Bogard also recognized Oswald as the man who had entered the showroom of the dealership a few weeks earlier.

On February 14, 1964, Bogard was administered a polygraph test by the FBI and the results revealed that he was being truthful about the story of Oswald at the car dealership.[15] In addition to the polygraph, a number of salesmen at the dealership, including Oran Brown and Eugene Wilson, corroborated Bogard's story.[16] Bogard's wife also remembered seeing the name "Oswald" written on a piece of paper at their home, although the paper was never located.

Conspiracy theorists have speculated that Oswald perhaps was going to be paid a large sum of money to assassinate President Kennedy based upon his statement at the dealership that he would be coming into some money in a few weeks. Others have argued that Oswald was being impersonated by someone in order to frame him for the assassination,[17] although it would seem illogical for the conspirators to draw attention to a "conspiracy" if they were trying to frame Oswald as the lone assassin.[18]

Lone gunman theorists, such as Gerald Posner, have argued that Oswald did not have a driver's license so it was unlikely that he was capable of driving the Mercury Comet at such a high speed. Posner also maintains that Oswald was in the company of his wife, Marina, and Ruth Paine on Saturday, November 9, 1963.[19] While Oswald did not possess a driver's license, he was being taught how to drive an automobile by Ruth Paine and she stated that by November of 1963, he had progressed to the point where he was a fairly good driver.[20] Hence, other researchers who oppose a conspiracy theory maintain that Oswald probably was the person who test-drove the car with Bogard and then simply lied when he said that he would be coming into a large sum of money in a few weeks.

OSWALD AT THE IRVING SUPERMARKET

During the first week of November 1963, Leonard E. Hutchison claimed that Lee Harvey Oswald attempted to cash a personal check for $189 at his supermarket located in Irving, Texas.[21] The supermarket was less than one mile from the residence of Ruth Paine where Marina and her children lived while Oswald worked at the TSBD in Dallas during the fall of 1963. Hutchison refused to cash the personal check because he could not cash checks greater than $25. Hutchison also recounted seeing Oswald on numerous occasions in the supermarket beginning in September 1963, where he purchased breakfast items between 7:20 am and 7:45 am. Finally, Hutchison told the FBI that Oswald, his wife, Marina, and an older woman (possibly Oswald's mother, Marguerite) entered the store on Wednesday, November 13, 1963.[22]

Since Oswald was never issued a check for $189 according to an analysis of his financial records by the Warren Commission, conspiracy theorists have argued that the man attempting to cash the check was impersonating Oswald. Moreover, it is unlikely that Oswald was at the supermarket in September 1963, because he did not begin visiting Marina at the Paine residence in Irving until the middle of October 1963 when he began his employment at the TSBD in Dallas. In regard to Oswald's visit to the supermarket on Wednesday, November 13, 1963, with his wife and an older woman, it has been established by the Warren Commission that Oswald was most likely in Dallas on this day.

The presence of Oswald at the supermarket in Irving during the days and times reported by Hutchison is further weakened by the fact that Marina told the Warren Commission that Oswald never ate breakfast.[23] Therefore, he would not have purchased breakfast items at the Hutchison supermarket in September 1963, an unlikely time for Oswald even to be in Irving as stated above. When Oswald did visit Irving on the weekends from mid-October until the latter part of November 1963 to spend time with his family at the Paine residence, he always left for Dallas on Monday mornings with Buell Wesley Frazier who gave him a ride to work. The two men always left Irving around 7:25 am in order to make it to the Texas School Book Depository for work at 8:00 am. Hence, the two men had virtually no time to stop at a supermarket for breakfast items on Monday mornings. Oswald would then stay at a rented room in Dallas until Friday evening. Finally, Marina and Marguerite Oswald were interviewed by the FBI and told authorities that they had never visited Hutchison's supermarket and had no knowledge that Oswald ever frequented the market.[24]

If Hutchison met a man who claimed to be Lee Harvey Oswald, it is quite possible that someone was impersonating Oswald, although Hutchison's story to the FBI contained many inconsistencies. The problem for conspiracy theorists concerning a "second Oswald" attempting to cash a personal check at a supermarket is to discover the purpose of an imposter involved in the fairly insignificant acts of cashing a check and purchasing breakfast food.

REDBIRD AIRPORT

Conspiracy theorists have often contemplated where Oswald was headed when he left the TSBD after the assassination. After Oswald took a taxi to his boarding house at 1026 Beckley Avenue, he retrieved a handgun and jacket. He then began walking eastward on the south side of Tenth Street where he was confronted by a Dallas police officer, J. D. Tippit, whom Oswald allegedly shot and killed. Researchers have speculated that Oswald may have been headed to Interstate 35 which was roughly seven blocks from his encounter with Officer Tippit.[25] A Secret Service investigation revealed that Oswald could have planned to catch a bus traveling east on Interstate 35 which would have taken him to the Redbird Airport about five miles away. The Redbird Airport was a small airport in the southern part of Dallas, Texas.

The manager of the Redbird Airport, Wayne January, reported to FBI detectives Kenneth Jackson and John Almon on November 29, 1963, one week after the assassination, that three people had visited the airfield in an automobile at the end of July in 1963.[26] Two of the persons exited the vehicle and approached him about renting a Cessna 310 in the next few months which they planned to fly to Mexico. The two people who spoke with January were a heavy-set man and a young lady, while a third person, a younger man, sat alone in the car. January was suspicious about the three people because he felt that they wouldn't be able to afford the price of the flight based upon their appearance and he was also concerned that they might simply hijack the plane and fly it to Cuba. January decided that he would not have allowed them to rent a plane if the three individuals ever returned to Redbird Airport. January proceeded to tell the FBI detectives that the young man seated in the automobile looked like Lee Harvey Oswald whom he had seen frequently on television in recent days.

In 1966, January told a different version of his story to Jones Harris, a conspiracy theorist. January told Harris that the three people arrived at the airport on Wednesday, November 20, 1963, two days before the assassination, and inquired about renting the Cessna 310 for November 22, 1963. The plane was to be flown to Mexico and would then be returned to Redbird Airport on Sunday, November 24, 1963. January also emphasized to Harris that he was convinced the young man seated in the automobile was Lee Harvey Oswald.

If January was correct in identifying Oswald as the young man who stayed in the vehicle, it is quite possible that the renting of the Cessna might have been part of a plan designed by Oswald's co-conspirators to fly him to Mexico or some other foreign country to escape arrest and prosecution in the United States. However, it should be noted that January's story did not surface until after Dallas authorities had already investigated all of the departures and arrivals at the Redbird Airport in the days leading up to the assassination as well as the flights scheduled for the day of the assassination. Hence, it is quite possible that January learned about the possibility of a plane being used to fly Oswald out of the country from Dallas authorities who may have even spoken with January before he told his story to the FBI. In addition, January has altered his story a number of times over the years and, therefore, has lost credibility among conspiracy theorists. For example, in 1978, January told conspiracy theorist, Anthony Summers, that Oswald was not waiting in the car but he approached January with two other persons. In 1994, January again altered his story by telling investigators that three men (not two men and a woman) had asked him about renting an airplane.

SILVIA ODIO'S STORY

Silvia Odio was a well-educated and attractive young woman from a wealthy family in Cuba. She had fled Cuba after her parents were imprisoned in 1961 because of their opposition to Fidel Castro's regime. Her parents established an anti-Castro organization known as the Movimiento Revolucionario del Pueblo (MRP) and Odio herself aligned with anti-Castro Cubans in Puerto Rico to form the Cuban Revolutionary Junta (JURE).[27]

As stated in earlier chapters, between September 25 and 27, 1963, Lee Harvey Oswald and two Cubans supposedly visited the apartment of Odio who was living in Dallas, Texas, at the time. Odio's story of the late September visit was a problem for the members of the Warren Commission because it could not be resolved and seemed to provide evidence of a conspiracy to assassinate President Kennedy. Odio stated that the two Cubans and Oswald informed her that they were involved in anti-Castro activities and were trying to raise money for operations designed to overthrow Castro. One of the Cubans introduced himself as "Leopold" and told her that the other Cuban was named "Angel" or "Angelo." He then told Odio that the white American was named "Leon Oswald." The three men then asked her to translate letters to be used to solicit funds from American businessmen. Because Odio was suspicious of the men, she told them that she did not want to get involved in their activities and asked them to leave. Prior to their departure, Annie Odio, the sister of Silvia, also claimed to have seen the three men standing in the doorway of the apartment.

A few days later, Odio received a telephone call from "Leopold" who asked her if she had any thoughts concerning the white American known to her as "Leon Oswald." "Leopold" stated that Oswald was a former Marine who was crazy and criticized the Cubans for not assassinating Kennedy after the Bay of Pigs incident. Leopold added that Oswald suggested the three of them should plan an assassination of Kennedy.

Odio and her sister were both shocked when they saw Oswald's photograph and news coverage of the assassination roughly two months after their encounter with Oswald and the two Cubans. The Warren Commission was pressured by its staff lawyers to investigate and determine the validity of Odio's story but the members were never able to disprove whether Oswald and the two Cubans visited Silvia Odio.

Initially, the Warren Commission dismissed the Odio story because of a FBI report claiming that an anti-Castro Cuban, Loran Eugene Hall, informed the FBI that he had visited Odio's apartment with two other Cubans. Hence, it appeared that Oswald could not have been one of the three men who visited Odio so the issue apparently was resolved. However, Hall's story fell apart when FBI agents interviewed the two Cubans who Hall stated were with him at Odio's residence. The two men denied that they went to Odio's home with Hall. When confronted with this information, Hall denied that he ever told the FBI that he was one of the three men to visit Odio. Interestingly, Hall had connections to Mafia leader Santos Traficante and Frank Sturgis, an anti-Castro militant with connections to the CIA and Mafia. Conspiracy theorists have speculated that Hall fabricated his story in order to throw off the Warren Commission.[28]

If Oswald actually visited Odio in late September 1963, then it is probable that he was involved in a conspiracy to assassinate Kennedy. However, if the "Leon Oswald" visiting Odio was an impersonator, then it would most likely confirm that a conspiracy to assassinate the president was in the works and the groundwork was being laid to frame Oswald.

MEXICO CITY IMPERSONATOR

Conspiracy theorists such as Jim Garrison, Gaeton Fonzi, and Jim Marrs have argued that Oswald was impersonated by someone who visited the Cuban and Soviet embassies in Mexico City in late September and early October of 1963. On the afternoon of September 26, 1963, Oswald, or someone pretending to be Oswald, entered Mexico at the city of Nuevo Laredo. Oswald then took a bus to Mexico City arriving on the morning of September 27, 1963, where he checked into the Hotel del Comerico for five nights until October 2, 1963.

During the afternoon of September 27, 1963, Oswald entered the Cuban consulate and spoke with Silvia Duran, a young woman who worked in the visa office of the Cuban Embassy. Duran processed Oswald's request for an in-transit visa to Cuba in order to gain entrance to the Soviet Union. When Duran informed Oswald that he could not obtain a Cuban visa immediately and that he first would have to obtain a Russian visa which was a lengthier process, Oswald became visibly angry and upset. Duran asked the Cuban consul, Eusebio Azcue, for assistance with Oswald and Azcue told Oswald that it would take between ten to twenty days to process his request. Oswald then proceeded to visit the Soviet Embassy in Mexico City but the Russian officials also denied him a visa and asked him to return in a month.[29]

While Duran later identified Oswald based upon a photograph as the man who entered the Cuban Embassy on September 27, 1963, Azcue testified before the House Select Committee on Assassinations (HSCA) that, when he saw the footage of Jack Ruby shooting Oswald, he was confident that the man whom he spoke with at the consulate was not Oswald. Azcue described the man claiming to be Oswald as somewhat older and thinner than Oswald.

In addition to Azcue's testimony concerning a possible impersonator, conspiracy theorists have been intrigued by a written statement from FBI Director J. Edgar Hoover in a five-page analysis of the Kennedy assassination on the day after the assassination.[30] Hoover wrote that the CIA advised him that a sensitive source reported a person claiming to be Lee Harvey Oswald visited the Soviet Embassy in Mexico City and asked whether he had received any messages. Hoover added that FBI agents who interviewed Oswald in Dallas had seen photographs and a voice recording of the individual claiming to be Oswald at the Soviet Embassy and they concluded that the individual who visited the Soviet Embassy was not Lee Harvey Oswald.

Conspiracy theorists also have questioned the fact that no photographic evidence of Oswald was ever produced from the Cuban consulate or the Soviet Embassy, even though the CIA maintained photographic surveillance of both locations during the time of Oswald's alleged visits. With two cameras monitoring the Cuban consulate and one camera providing surveillance of the Soviet Embassy, it is difficult to believe the CIA's statement that all of the cameras happened to malfunction during the time frame when Oswald supposedly visited these places. Interestingly, even though the CIA claimed that its photographic surveillance was broken, the agency eventually produced one photograph of an American male entering the Soviet Embassy who it believed to be Oswald. The photograph, which the CIA later maintained was a gaffe on its part, was not of Oswald and provided evidence for conspiracy theorists of a possible impersonator in Mexico City.[31]

Conspiracy theorists, such as John Newman, argue that Oswald was being impersonated at the Cuban consulate and Soviet Embassy in Mexico City as part of an assassination plot conducted by a rouge element within the CIA.[32] The plot would have involved Oswald being set up as the patsy for the assassination of Kennedy. Then, Oswald's connections to the Cubans and Soviets in Mexico City would, in turn, allow for the CIA to blame an international communist conspiracy for the murder of the American president.

CONCLUSION

Nearly all of the supposed impersonations or sightings of Oswald prior to the assassination were most likely based upon individuals seeking publicity in the aftermath of a dramatic event or cases of mistaken identity. It also would seem irrelevant for conspirators to impersonate Oswald in such random places as discussed above. Finally, the alleged impersonations of Oswald, at times, appear illogical. For instance, most conspiracy theorists agree that Oswald most likely made the trip to Mexico City in late September and early October of 1963.[33] But, the same conspiracy theorists also contend that someone was impersonating Oswald during the time he was in Mexico City. If conspirators wanted to blame an international communist conspiracy for the assassination by impersonating Oswald in Mexico City, it would have been unnecessary if Oswald was actually in Mexico City visiting the Cuban consulate and the Soviet Embassy.

However, the story of someone possibly using Oswald's name to purchase trucks for the Friends of Democratic Cuba and Silvia Odio's story relayed to investigators are more difficult to resolve because both accounts seem consistent with Oswald's associations during his life. The fact that someone was using Oswald's name to purchase trucks for an anti-Castro Cuban organization, a few months prior to the Bay of Pigs invasion when Oswald was living in the Soviet Union, seems plausible given Oswald's known connection to anti-Castro Cubans and Guy Banister at 544 Camp Street in New Orleans. Such an incident provides circumstantial evidence that Oswald was perhaps involved with the intelligence community in some fashion.

The Odio story is the most troubling of the Two Oswalds scenarios. Wesley Liebeler, who was an assistant counsel for the Warren Commission, and Gary Cornwell, who served as the deputy chief counsel for the HSCA, both stated that Silvia Odio's story was never fully resolved to their satisfaction. One of the most prominent critics of the conspiracy theories related to the Kennedy assassination, Vincent Bugliosi, admitted that he "was deeply troubled" by the Odio incident.[34]

Odio said that Oswald visited her in Dallas with two Cubans who claimed opposition to Fidel Castro. However, it is plausible that Oswald and the two Cubans were supporters of Castro presenting themselves as anti-Castro. While this might seem fantastic to many readers, it would be entirely consistent with Oswald's behavior of infiltrating anti-Castro organizations during his time in New Orleans. In addition, Odio's claim that the assassination of Kennedy was discussed during a telephone conversation with one of the Cubans and that Oswald's name was suggested as the possible assassin demands attention.

NOTES

1. Leo Sauvage, "The Oswald Affair," *Commentary* (March 1964), 55–65.
2. Jim Marrs, *Crossfire: The Plot That Killed Kennedy* (New York: Carroll & Graf, 1989), 544–545.
3. Vincent Bugliosi, *Reclaiming History: The Assassination of President John F. Kennedy* (New York: W. W. Norton & Co., 2007), 1021.

4. John Armstrong, *Harvey and Lee: How the CIA Framed Oswald* (Arlington, Tex.: Quasar, 2003).

5. Aline Mosby, *The View from No. 13 People's Street* (New York: Random House, 1962).

6. FBI Record 124-10010-10361, Letter from FBI Director J. Edgar Hoover to Special Agents in Charge of offices in Phoenix, Dallas, Minneapolis, December 20, 1963.

7. Bugliosi, *Reclaiming History,* 1025.

8. Jim Garrison, *On the Trail of the Assassins* (New York: Sheridan Square Press, 1988), 66-68.

9. *The Fourth Decade: A Journal of Research on the John F. Kennedy Assassination* 3 (March 1996), 35–37.

10. Gerald Posner, Case *Closed: Lee Harvey Oswald and the Assassination of JFK* (New York: Random House, 1993), 170-196.

11. *Investigation of the Assassination of President John F. Kennedy: Hearing before the President's Commission on the Assassination of President Kennedy*. 88th Congress. (1964), vol. XXIV, 735–741 [herein after WCR]. Warren Commission Exhibits 2137–2138 (FBI statements of Jesse A. Skrivanek, Lt. Col. William B. Sinclair, Lorine Shuler, and William Covington).

12. Warren Commission Exhibit 2137 (FBI statement of Larry Temple), WCR, vol. XXIV at 734.

13. Warren Commission Exhibit 2944 (FBI statement of Lovell T. Penn), WCR, XXVI, 406; Warren Commission Exhibit 2449, WCR, XXV, 588.

14. Warren Commission Testimony of Albert Guy Bogard, WCR, vol. X, 352–355.

15. Warren Commission Exhibit 3078 (FBI polygraph of Albert Guy Bogard), WCR, vol. XXVI, 682-683.

16. Ibid., 683-684.

17. Walt Brown, "You Know about Albert Guy Bogard: What about Ed Brand," *JFK/Deep Politics Quarterly*, April 1999, 15.

18. Bugliosi, *Reclaiming History,* 1033-1035.

19. Posner, *Case Closed,* 211.

20. Warren Commission Testimony of Ruth Paine, WCR, vol. II, 514.

21. Warren Commission Exhibit 2789, WCR, vol. XXVI, 178.

22. Testimony of Leonard Edwin Hutchison, WCR, vol. X, 328-330.

23. Testimony of Marina Oswald, WCR, vol. I, 70.

24. Warren Commission Exhibit 3129, WCR, vol. XXVI, 793-795.

25. Bugliosi, *Reclaiming History,* 1037.

26. Richard. H, Popkin, *The Second Oswald* (New York: Avon, 1966), 92.

27. Marrs, *Crossfire,* 150-151.

28. Ibid., 152.

29. Bugliosi, *Reclaiming History,* 1044-1048.

30. House Select Committee on Assassinations (HSCA) Record 180-10001-10126, Memorandum of J. Edgar Hoover entitled *Assassination of President John F. Kennedy, Dallas, Texas, November 22, 1963,* November 23, 1963, 4–5.

31. David Atlee Phillips, *The Night Watch: 25 Years of Peculiar Service* (New York: Antheneum, 1977), 141.

32. John Newman, "Oswald, the CIA and Mexico City: Fingerprints of Conspiracy," *Probe*, (September-October, 1999), 1-29.

33. Edwin Lopez, "Report on Lee Harvey Oswald's Trip to Mexico City," *House Select Committee on Assassinations (HSCA)*, 242-250.

34. Bugliosi, *Reclaiming History,* 1295.

Chapter Five

The "Russian" Oswald

A number of conspiracy theorists have offered the idea that, while Lee Harvey Oswald defected to the Soviet Union in 1959, he did not return to the United States in 1962. Instead, he was replaced by a Russian "look-a-like" whose mission was to enter the United States and assassinate President John F. Kennedy as part of a communist plot devised by the Soviet State Security Service (KGB).[1]

The speculation from Kennedy assassination researchers about a Russian "look-a-like" began with the defection of nineteen-year-old Lee Harvey Oswald to the Soviet Union in October of 1959.[2] In fact, U.S. government officials were immediately concerned about someone assuming Oswald's identity in the Soviet Union. On June 3, 1960, J. Edgar Hoover, Director of the Federal Bureau of Investigation (FBI) sent a memorandum to the State Department warning of the possibility that an impostor might be using Lee Harvey Oswald's birth certificate. Hoover indicated that any current information concerning Oswald that could be provided by the State Department would be valued. Hoover became troubled about a possible impostor when Oswald's mother, Marguerite, contacted her congressman and the State Department in January of 1960 to express concern that she had been unable to contact her son in the Soviet Union. On April 28, 1960, she was interviewed by the FBI and mentioned that Oswald had taken his birth certificate with him when he left the United States.[3]

When Oswald began attempting to return to the United States after nearly three years in the Soviet Union, Edward Hickey, Deputy Chief of Passport Office, wrote a letter on March 31, 1961, to the Consular Section of the State Department that also raised concerns about an impostor using Oswald's identification data. Hickey also emphasized to the U.S. Embassy that Oswald's passport should only be delivered to him in person because there was concern that an impostor might be substituted for Oswald. Again, on July 11, 1961, Secretary of State Dean Rusk sent a memorandum to the U.S. Embassy in Moscow that warned of an impostor possibly taking Oswald's place and receiving his passport. Clearly, the U.S. government wanted assurances that the person returning with Oswald's passport was, in fact, the Lee Harvey Oswald who left for the Soviet Union in 1959.[4]

The possibility of Oswald disappearing in the Soviet Union to be replaced by a Russian assassin may seem ridiculous and far-fetched to most people but, after considering the history of intelligence operations conducted by both the United States and the Soviet Union during the Cold War, the impostor scenario seems plausible.[5] Consider, for example, that the Soviets in 1940 used an impostor to assume the identity of a young Canadian by the name of Gordon Lonsdale.[6] The Soviets either abducted Lonsdale during the Russian invasion of Finland or benefited from his timely death. Whatever the case, the imposter, named Koron Melody, successfully spied for the Soviet Union in Britain after having been trained to act as a Canadian.

While the intriguing story of Gordon Lonsdale does not prove that Oswald's identity was stolen by the Soviets for the purpose of assassinating Kennedy, Oswald's defection to the Soviet Union in 1959 may have been part of an espionage operation. In fact, the Office of Naval Intelligence ran a program in the late 1950s wherein young men were cut loose as "false defectors" into the Soviet Union and Eastern Europe to gather information about life in a communist society. Two weeks prior to Oswald's defection, a U.S. citizen named Robert Webster defected to the Soviet Union and his story bears a striking resemblance to Oswald's experience. Webster served in the Navy and later was employed by the RAND Development Corporation which has a history of being involved with intelligence operations. Webster returned to the United States at the same time as Oswald and, similar to Oswald, he expressed dissatisfaction with life in the Soviet Union. Other similarities with Oswald include the fact that Webster took a common law wife and also had a child during his stay in the Soviet Union. Prior to Oswald's return to the United States in 1961, he inquired about Webster which has caused researchers to believe the two men may have been part of the same "fake defector" program.[7]

If the Soviets suspected a defector of being a U.S. intelligence agent, then the defector might be "doubled" or recruited as a KGB agent. The theory of a "Russian Oswald" posits that Oswald may have started out as a U.S. intelligence agent and then was "doubled" or recruited by the KGB. Oswald also could have come in contact with the KGB while serving in the Marines in Atsugi, Japan, as a radar operator working on the secret U-2 spy plane. While serving at the Atsugi airbase, Oswald admitted being in contact with Japanese Communists and it is possible that he may have been introduced to Soviet intelligence agents as well. In fact, during Oswald's time at Atsugi, he was often seen in the company of a Eurasian woman who, according to Oswald, was half-Russian.[8] Interestingly, upon his defection, Oswald promised to provide the Soviets with sensitive information about U.S. intelligence operations and, six months after Oswald's defection, Gary Powers's U-2 spy plane was shot down over Russia. Powers hinted that Oswald might have provided the Soviets with the proper data to shoot down the spy plane.[9] Whether the intelligence operation began with the U.S. or Soviet government, Oswald was clearly vulnerable to being used by either side or perhaps having his identity stolen by an impostor.

The Soviets also had their share of defectors to the United States in their various attempts to acquire information and supply disinformation. Yuri Nosenko is an example of an infamous defection by a Soviet official to the United States that remains a mystery to the Central Intelligence Agency (CIA).[10] In 1964, shortly after the Kennedy assassination, Nosenko defected to the United States with a claim that he had worked as a Soviet lieutenant colonel responsible for American defectors, such as Oswald. After the assassination, he stated that he personally investigated whether Oswald had a relationship with the KGB. Nosenko told the CIA that the KGB kept Oswald under close surveillance during his time in the Soviet Union and judged him to be mentally unstable. Most importantly, Nosenko concluded that the KGB had no relationship with Oswald. The CIA became bitterly divided over whether Nosenko was telling the truth or not. If Nosenko was truthful, then the Soviets would be absolved of any responsibility in the JFK assassination. If Nosenko was a false defector, then he may have been sent to provide disinformation to conceal the true relationship between Oswald and the KGB.[11]

The documented material above provides examples from a larger empirical pattern of deception on behalf of both the United States and the Soviet Union. In fact, strong evidence exists that the two superpowers had engaged in a variety of intelligence operations and false defector programs as a method of acquiring information about each other and supplying disinformation to confuse one another.

PHYSICAL EVIDENCE OF AN IMPOSTOR

The most intriguing aspect of the "Russian Oswald" theory is based upon physical discrepancies of Oswald before and after his defection to the Soviet Union. In 1945, at the age of six years old, Oswald experienced pain and discomfort behind his left ear and was diagnosed with mastoiditis. Mastoiditis usually results from a middle ear infection that spreads to the mastoid bone of the skull.[12] Oswald had an operation to remove the mastoid bone and the procedure left a mastoidectomy scar almost two inches long behind his left ear. While the scar was recorded as part of his Marine record in 1956 and 1959, the autopsy report of Oswald's body conducted by two doctors on November 24, 1963, failed to note the scar. The operation also should have produced an indentation where the bone was removed and normally the indentation would not fill in until a person reached middle age. Photographs of the twenty-four-year-old Oswald after his arrest for the assassination of Kennedy do not show a scar or indentation behind his left ear, even though he had a short haircut at the time.[13]

An analysis by a British surgeon also revealed discrepancies in scars on the left arm of Oswald before and after his defection to the Soviet Union. Based upon medical files from Oswald's Marine service in the late 1950s, three scars existed on the upper part of his left arm. However, the autopsy report of Oswald in 1963 showed only two scars with different descriptions and positions than two of the three scars from the Marine records. In addition, a vaccination scar on Oswald's arm noted in his Marine medical records was not recorded in the autopsy report.[14]

In regard to Oswald's physical height, the Warren Commission produced documents from Oswald's Marine records and passport information from October 1956 to October 1959 that showed his height to be five feet and eleven inches. After his return from the Soviet Union, Oswald consistently was listed as five feet and nine inches in height on a number of occasions from June 1962 until his arrest on November 22, 1963. This physical discrepancy would suggest that an impostor two inches shorter than Oswald had assumed his identity, unless errors were made in the measurement and observation of his height over the specified time periods.[15]

Serious questions also have been raised about Oswald's use of the Russian language.[16] When Oswald's future wife, Marina, first met him at a trade union dance in Minsk, she commented that his Russian language skills were so good that she thought he was a native Russian with a Baltic accent. At this initial meeting, Oswald also told Marina that his mother had died and that he didn't want to discuss her, even though his mother, Marguerite, was alive and well in the United States. The "Russian Oswald" theory argues that the substitution must have taken place prior to this first meeting between Lee and Marina. Interestingly, Marina had not planned to attend the dance but was persuaded to go by her uncle, Ilya Prusakova, a colonel in the Soviet Secret Police in Minsk. After Oswald's return to the United States and subsequent death, an analysis of tape recordings of Oswald's voice by language experts from Southern Methodist University surprisingly concluded that English was not his native language.[17]

A skeptic would counter that Lee Harvey Oswald's close relatives should have been able to detect whether an impostor had replaced their family member. In fact, there is evidence to suggest that his family was suspicious upon his arrival in Fort Worth, Texas, on June 14, 1962. Oswald's mother,

Marguerite, testified before the Warren Commission about physical changes in her son upon his return to the United States. She stated that he had lost some of his hair and was "very, very thin."[18] Oswald's full-blooded brother, Robert, also testified to the Warren Commission about similar changes in his brother's physical appearance. Specifically, Robert testified "that [Lee] had lost a considerable amount of hair" and his hair "had become very kinky in comparison with his naturally curly hair prior to his departure to Russia...."[19] Also, Robert Oswald noticed that Lee's complexion had changed from very fair to "rather ruddy" and that he had "picked up something of an accent."[20] Finally, Oswald's half-brother, John Pic, also testified before the Warren Commission that he barely recognized Oswald after his return from Russia. John Pic's comments paralleled those of Robert Oswald and his mother that Oswald had lost some of his hair and was thinner. However, John Pic added that Oswald's facial features had changed dramatically as well. Specifically, Pic was referring to Oswald's eyes and the shape of his face and neck. Pic was quoted as saying that "[t]he Lee Harvey Oswald that I met in November 1962, was not the same Lee Harvey Oswald that I had known ten years previously."[21] Pic was also upset because, after his return to the United States, Oswald began introducing Pic to people as his "half-brother" something that he had never done before his defection to the Soviet Union.[22]

The "Russian" Oswald theory is also supported by the fact that Oswald was anxious and nervous upon his arrival in Fort Worth, Texas, and rarely spent time with his family after his return on June 14, 1962, until his death on November 24, 1963, a period of nearly eighteen months.[23] It is worth noting that Oswald had seen his family members on only a few occasions during his service in the Marines from October 1956 until September 1959 because he was mostly stationed abroad and his family had not seen him at all since his defection, a period of nearly three years. Overall, Oswald's family had only seen him in person on a few occasions in roughly a five and a half year period. This lack of personal contact with Oswald over such an extended period of time would have provided an ideal opportunity for an impostor to deceive Oswald's family members.

Immediately after Oswald returned to the United States, he became the focus of the FBI. Oswald was interviewed twice by the FBI on June 26, 1962 and August 14, 1962 to determine if he had had any contact with Soviet intelligence and whether he posed a threat to national security. In the June 26 interview, FBI agents Tom Carter and John Fain talked with Oswald for roughly one and a half hours in Fort Worth, Texas. In the August 14 interview, Oswald was interviewed by FBI agents Fain and Arnold Brown. In both interviews, Oswald declined to discuss the reasons for defecting to the Soviet Union and also seemed uncomfortable and upset at times. After the second interview, Oswald was judged to be relatively harmless and unlikely to be a dangerous or violent threat to national security. After the second interview, Oswald's case with the FBI was listed as "closed" based upon Fain's evaluation and subsequent approval by the FBI in Washington, D.C.[24]

Oswald was interviewed a third time by the FBI after he was arrested on August 9, 1963, in New Orleans and charged with creating a public disturbance related to the Fair Play for Cuba Committee (FPCC) leaflets incident. Oswald requested that the police contact the FBI to send over an agent and Oswald sat for two hours with Special Agent John Quigley on August 10, 1963. According to Quigley, Oswald spoke mostly of the FPCC activities during the interview.[25]

In support of the "Russian Oswald" theory, the FBI agents surprisingly recorded two different heights and biographies of Oswald during the course of the three interviews from June 1962 to August 1963. In the first interview, Oswald told Agent Fain that his height was five feet and eleven inches which was the height of the original Oswald. After the second interview, Fain also recorded Oswald's height as five feet and eleven inches failing to notice that he was actually two inches shorter. However, Special Agent Quigley observed Oswald to be five feet and nine inches in height during the third interview on August 10, 1963. Hence, the FBI files contained two different heights for Oswald as a result of this discrepancy.[26]

As stated above, Oswald also appeared to offer two different biographies during the interviews. During the two interviews in 1962, Oswald stated that he had left for Russia after his discharge from the Marines and married his wife, Marina Prusakova, in Russia. Contrary to this biography, Oswald told Agent Quigley during the 1963 interview that he had lived with his mother following his discharge from the Marines and omitted the fact that he had lived in the Soviet Union. He also stated that he had married his wife in Fort Worth in March 1963 and her maiden name was "Prossa." The FBI and the Warren Commission never resolved these discrepancies in the official investigation of the assassination.[27]

Evidence that apparently damages the "Russian Oswald" theory concerns the issue of Oswald's fingerprints. Oswald had his fingerprints taken six times during his lifetime from 1956 when he joined the Marines to the day of his arrest when he was charged in the murders of Officer J. D. Tippit and President Kennedy on November 22, 1963. In each instance, the fingerprints matched those of Lee Harvey Oswald. In other words, the fingerprints of the "Marine Oswald" in 1956 matched those of the alleged assassin in 1963. Some researchers have speculated that the KGB may have substituted a forged set of fingerprints in the FBI files after Oswald's defection or that the FBI switched fingerprints in the interests of avoiding a nuclear war with the Soviets, but no solid evidence exists to support such claims.[28]

MEXICO CITY AND OSWALD'S IMPOSTOR

The "Russian Oswald" theory takes on a more sinister tone when Oswald's alleged impostor began the process of planning a trip to Mexico City in September 1963. Oswald received permission from the Mexican Consulate in New Orleans to travel to Mexico for a two-week period as an in-transit tourist. Before his departure, Oswald instructed his wife that his trip to Mexico City was to be kept secret.

Oswald arrived in Mexico City by bus on September 27, 1963, and visited the Cuban Consulate asking for a visa to visit Cuba. Oswald told the Cuban Consulate that his intent was to travel to the Soviet Union after spending a few weeks in Cuba. However, some researchers have speculated that Oswald did not intend to travel to the Soviet Union but was only trying to gain entrance into Cuba in order to receive orders from the Soviet Embassy in Havana, Cuba about the assassination and his subsequent escape out of the United States. In order to prove that he had resided previously in the Soviet Union, Oswald provided a copy of the 1959 passport from the original Oswald and his Russian work permit. He also displayed evidence that he had married a Russian woman and had supported the communist cause in the U.S. as secretary of the FPCC and as a member of the American Communist Party. In short, Oswald wanted to establish that he was a supporter of the Cuban revolution.

A woman by the name of Sylvia Duran interviewed Oswald at the Cuban Consulate and subsequently told him that his request for a visa had been denied. When Oswald became upset, Consul Eusebio Ascue was summoned and he also told Oswald that an immediate visa was out of the question because it would take several weeks to process an official request for travel to Cuba. Oswald was told that the only other alternative would be to secure approval from the Soviet Embassy for a visa to travel to Russia. A Russian visa would have allowed Oswald initially to travel to Cuba before eventually departing for the Soviet Union.[29]

After Oswald's failure to reach the Soviet Embassy in Havana supposedly to receive his instructions about the assassination, it has been argued that Oswald met with clandestine KGB agents at the Soviet Embassy in Mexico City from September 27, 1963 to October 3, 1963 to discuss the assassination of Kennedy. Specifically, there is documented evidence that Oswald met with Valery Vladimirovich Kostikov, a KGB officer in command of Department 13 known for sabotage and assassination.[30] Oswald also met with a second KGB officer connected to clandestine operations by the name of Valeri Dmitrevich Kostin who was not listed as an employee of the Soviet Embassy in Mexico City. It has been speculated that Oswald was to have met with Kostin in Havana but, when he failed to obtain permission to travel to

Cuba, Kostin was flown quickly to Mexico City. Unfortunately, the substance of the discussions between Oswald and the KGB officers is unknown.

A final clue that hints at a Russian conspiracy to assassinate Kennedy involves a letter written by Oswald to the Soviet embassy in Washington, DC on November 9, 1963.[31] In the letter, Oswald informed the Soviet Embassy of "recent events" and his "meetings" at the Soviet Embassy. Oswald also stated that his failure to obtain a visa to Cuba was limited by the fact that he could not use his "real name."[32] Finally, and perhaps most significantly, Oswald mentioned that he was not "able to reach the Soviet Embassy in Havana as planned . . . to complete our business."[33]

Proponents of the "Russian Oswald" theory assert that this letter contains conspiratorial overtones. Was Oswald using the postal system as a way to inform the Russians about the progress of the conspiracy using vague language? In fact, the postal system has been utilized routinely as a form of communication in clandestine activities. What did Oswald mean when he stated that he could not use his "real name"? Is it possible that the Russian impostor could not use his original Russian name because, although he would have been able to travel to Cuba, he would have exposed himself as an impostor to U.S. intelligence? Lastly, what type of "business" was to have been completed in the planned meeting in Havana between Oswald and the Soviet Embassy? Conspiracy theorists who argue that the KGB was responsible for the assassination maintain that the "business" involved Oswald's instructions for the assassination of Kennedy and subsequent escape from the United States.

Interestingly, U.S. government officials did not view the letter as any indication of a conspiracy. The FBI perceived the letter as an attempt by Oswald to secure a visa to Russia, while the Warren Commission simply interpreted Oswald's letter as a loner desperately trying to gain favor with the Soviets and the communist movement.

JACK RUBY: KGB AGENT?

Any theory concerning the Kennedy assassination must account for the role played by Jack Ruby. Jack Ruby's murder of Oswald can be explained in a variety of ways.[34] Ruby's actions fit easily into the "Russian Oswald" theory if he simply was distraught over the assassination of a beloved president and wanted revenge. His actions also fit if he murdered Oswald to become a hero, for financial gain, or because he was mentally unstable.

However, some researchers have tried to resolve Ruby's actions by arguing that he was a low-level KGB agent involved in the Russian conspiracy to assassinate President Kennedy.[35] These researchers have connected Ruby to Oswald through speculation that Oswald was trying to reach Ruby after the assassination because he was headed in the general direction of Ruby's apartment when he was arrested. From Ruby's apartment, it would have been a short drive to Redbird Airport where Oswald could have been flown out of the country into Mexico by any one of a number of private planes stored at the various hangars. When the escape plan failed and Oswald was apprehended by Dallas police in the Texas Theater, it has been surmised that Ruby was forced to eliminate Oswald to protect the Russian conspiracy from being revealed.

Unfortunately, there exists no real evidence to support the idea that Jack Ruby was a low-level KGB agent assisting Oswald with the assassination and his escape from Dallas. In the 1940s, Jack Ruby did work for a jeweler in Muncie, Indiana, and the jeweler, Sam Jaffe, held Communist meetings in a hall above his store.[36] It was thought that the meetings were attended by persons from Chicago, including Ruby. However, it is bizarre to extrapolate from Ruby's vague and loose connection to communists in the 1940s that he was a low-level KGB agent. This view contrasts drastically with the Jack Ruby who was seen by many as a patriot who loved his country, even though he was simultaneously viewed as a low-level member of organized crime.[37]

The murder of Oswald can be explained most effectively within the "Russian Oswald" theory by maintaining that Ruby acted independent of any conspiracy and that he had no connection to Oswald other than the fact that he became obsessed with murdering Oswald after the assassination of Kennedy. While it is intriguing to speculate about Ruby's motive for murdering Oswald, it is safe to assume that only Ruby knew the basis for his actions.

EXHUMATION OF OSWALD'S BODY

Lee Harvey Oswald was laid to rest on November 25, 1963, at Rose Hill cemetery in Fort Worth, Texas. Questions about the identity of the body buried in Oswald's grave surfaced as early as three weeks after the burial. In December 1963, Secret Service agents interviewed funeral director, Paul Groody, and questioned him about scars on Oswald's body. Groody stated that the Secret Service agents admitted they didn't know who was buried in Oswald's grave. Oswald's mother, Marguerite, requested an exhumation in 1967 based upon the scars on Oswald's body as described by the Warren Commission and because she was bothered by the drastic change in her son's appearance upon his return to the United States from Russia.[38]

Interestingly, the CIA had considered exhuming Oswald's body as early as 1964 based upon a March 13, 1964, FBI memo from J. Edgar Hoover who noted the CIA's interest in the scar on Oswald's left wrist. The CIA wanted confirmation that Oswald had tried to commit suicide by slashing his left wrist while in Russia. The CIA had grown concerned about Oswald's life in

Russia and whether it could be authenticated. The suicide attempt and his time spent in the hospital recovering may have been a cover story, or legend, provided by the Russians to allow the KGB to recruit Oswald or perhaps even substitute an impostor to assume his identity.

As a result of Oswald's letter to the Soviet Embassy in Washington wherein he stated that he couldn't use his "real name" in Mexico City, Michael Eddowes, an assassination researcher, attempted to have Oswald's body exhumed in 1979.[39] The exhumation was delayed by a legal battle between various jurisdictions and political forces.[40] Eventually, Michael Eddowes failed to gain legal authority for the exhumation based upon his status as a British citizen but he did persuade Marina Oswald to add her name to establish legal standing and she filed suit to open Oswald's grave on August 20, 1981. Finally, the exhumation occurred on October 4, 1981.[41]

Four forensic pathologists studied Oswald's remains at Baylor Medical Center in Dallas, Texas, and concluded "beyond any doubt" that the body buried in the grave was that of Lee Harvey Oswald. The findings were based upon a comparison of the corpse's teeth with the Marine Corps dental records of Oswald. The doctors also discovered a gap behind Oswald's left ear providing confirmation of the mastoid operation performed on Oswald when he was a young boy.

One would assume that the theory of "Russian Oswald" would seemingly be put to rest at this point. However, the two funeral directors, Groody and Alan Baumgartner, who prepared Oswald's body for burial in 1963 also observed the forensic examination at Baylor Medical Center in 1981. Groody and Baumgartner were perplexed that the corpse's skull was in one piece. This was inconsistent with the fact that they had performed a craniotomy on the corpse in 1963. A craniotomy is defined as a removing of the skin from the skull and cutting off the top of the skull with a bone saw.[42] The purpose of a craniotomy is to examine the brain of the deceased. Because the corpse examined in 1981 showed no evidence of a craniotomy, the funeral directors concluded that it was not the same body prepared by them for burial in 1963.[43]

Interestingly, researchers have argued that circumstantial evidence does exist that someone may have tampered with Oswald's grave prior to the exhumation in 1981. Marina Oswald informed news reporters that government officials approached her in 1964 and asked her to sign documents for an alarm system to be put in place at Oswald's grave. Marina Oswald became convinced that Oswald's body was removed from its grave based upon this suspicious request, especially since an alarm system was never installed.[44]

Paul Groody, the funeral director, also provided some interesting facts that caused many to wonder if someone had meddled with Oswald's body.[45] Groody stated that Oswald's body had been carefully embalmed and placed in a hermetically sealed coffin. The coffin was then placed in an airtight vault made of cement. Groody told news reporters that, prior to the 1981 exhumation, Oswald's body should have looked the same as it had on the day of its burial on November 25, 1963. However, when the grave was dug up on October 4, 1981, the cement vault apparently had been busted into small pieces and the airtight seal on the coffin was broken. Because the body had been exposed to air and water, it had been reduced to a skeleton. Researcher Anthony Summers interviewed a number of funeral directors who stated that it is not impossible for the seals on both the coffin and the vault to break but it would be extremely rare.[46] Proponents of the "Russian" Oswald theory have argued that someone had opened the grave prior to the exhumation in 1981 and replaced the Russian impostor's body with that of the original Lee Harvey Oswald. Is it possible that Soviet or Cuban agents received permission from Marina Oswald who wittingly, or unwittingly, allowed them to substitute the real Oswald for the Russian impostor? Marina Oswald and Michael Eddowes requested that the exhumation be videotaped and, because there is no mention of a craniotomy during the examination by the forensic pathologists, more mystery and suspicion have been added to the question of whether the body was replaced prior to the exhumation in 1981.

In 1984, the scientific community weighed in with a thorough report of the exhumation.[47] A peer-reviewed article published in the *Journal of Forensic Sciences* concluded that a craniotomy had been performed on Oswald's body during the 1963 autopsy. Evidence of the craniotomy had been concealed, however, by "decomposed mummified tissue" that had appeared to keep the skull in one piece while concomitantly covering the saw cut on the skull.[48] In other words, dead skin had coated the skull to prevent the pathologists from noticing any evidence of a craniotomy during the 1981 exhumation.

NOTES

1. Michael Eddowes, *The Oswald File* (New York: Clarkson N. Potter, 1977).
2. *Investigation of the Assassination of President John F. Kennedy: Hearing before the President's Commission on the Assassination of President Kennedy.* 88th Congress. (1964). [Warren Commission Report herein WCR] Oswald's Historic Diary, Commission Exhibit 24, VXVI.
3. WCR, vol. XVII, 702-706.
4. Eddowes, *The Oswald File*, 30.
5. Edward Jay Epstein, *Legend: The Secret World of Lee Harvey Oswald* (New York: Reader's Digest Press, 1978).
6. Eddowes, *The Oswald File,* 9.
7. Anthony Summers, *Conspiracy* (New York: McGraw-Hill, 1980), 174.
8. Summers, *Conspiracy,* 147.
9. Francis Gary Powers, *Operation Overflight: The U-2 Spy Plane Pilot Tells His Story for the First Time* (New York: Holt, Rinehart & Winston, 1970).
10. Gerald Posner, *Case Closed: Lee Harvey Oswald and the Assassination of JFK* (New York: Random House, 1993, 35–36.

11. "How the CIA Tried to Break Defector in Oswald Case," *Washington Star,* September 16, 1978.

12. Y Butbul-Aviel, et al., "Acute Mastoiditis in Children: *Pseudomonas aeruginosa* as a Leading Pathogen," *International Journal of Pediatric Otorhinolaryngology* 67 (March 2003), 277-81.

13. Eddowes, *The Oswald File,* 132-133; 211-222.

14. Ibid.

15. Eddowes, *The Oswald File,* 211-222.

16. Ibid., 28-29.

17. Gary Mack, "Who Was Really in Oswald's Grave? Parts 1-3." *Cover-ups!* (Feb.-April 1983).

18. WCR, vol. I, 147.

19. WCR, vol. I, 330.

20. Ibid., 331.

21. Jim Marrs, *Crossfire: The Plot That Killed Kennedy* (New York: Carroll & Graf, 1989), 549.

22. WCR, vol. XI, 55-59

23. Eddowes, *The Oswald File,* 36-38.

24. Ibid., 40- 44.

25. Summers, *Conspiracy,* 146.

26. Eddowes, *The Oswald File,* 61-62.

27. Ibid.

28. Ibid., 138-139.

29. Posner, *Case Closed*, 182.

30. Oleg Maximovich Nechiporenko, *Passport to Assassination: The Never-before-Told-Story of Lee Harvey Oswald by the KGB Colonel Who Knew Him* (New York: Carol Publishing, 1993).

31. WCR, vol. XVI, 33. The letter was posted on Nov. 12, 1963, because of the Veterans Day holiday.

32. Ibid.

33. WCR, vol. XVIII, 539.

34. Seth Kantor, *The Ruby Cover-Up* (New York: Kensington Publishing, 1978).

35. Eddowes, *The Oswald File,* 125-131.

36. WCR, vol. XV, 289-321 [George Fehrenbach testimony].

37. Posner, *Case Closed,* 350-403.

38. Marrs, *Crossfire,* 548.

39. Ibid., 547-548.

40. "Oswald Grave Now Battle Site," *Fort Worth Star-Telegram*, October 1, 1979.

41. Marrs, *Crossfire,* 547-550.

42. *Random House Webster's College Dictionary*, 1997, 308.

43. Marrs, *Crossfire,* 550-551.

44. Ibid.

45. Ibid., 551-552.

46. Summers, *Conspiracy,* 552.

47. Linda Norton et al., "The Exhumation and Identification of Lee Harvey Oswald," *Journal of Forensic Sciences,* 29 (1984), 19-38.

48. Ibid., 25.

Chapter Six

Critical Analysis of Oswald's Role in the Kennedy Assassination

The previous chapters have provided a substantial amount of material offering varying interpretations of Lee Harvey Oswald and his role in the assassination of President John F. Kennedy. There exists plenty of mystery concerning Oswald's life, and death, which has been the subject of much debate over the last fifty years. This chapter attempts to analyze each narrative discussed in the previous chapters within the context of significant pieces of evidence that have not been resolved by investigators and researchers, such as Silvia Odio's story about Oswald and two Cubans visiting her in September 1963, Joseph Milteer and Richard Case Nagell's separate claims that they had foreknowledge of the assassination, the acoustical evidence at the time of the assassination, David Lifton's theory concerning the alteration of the president's head wounds prior to the autopsy and the fabrication of evidence by unnamed conspirators, and, finally, the murder of Oswald by Jack Ruby. In the process of evaluating this evidence, the probability of Oswald as the lone assassin, conspirator, patsy, and hero, or Russian spy will be estimated in order to draw tentative conclusions regarding one of the most mysterious and intriguing figures in American history.

THE MOST LIKELY SCENARIO: OSWALD AS LONE ASSASSIN (75 PERCENT PROBABILITY)

As demonstrated in chapter 1, a strong probability exists that Oswald acted alone in the assassination of President Kennedy. The odds that Oswald was guilty and acted alone in the assassination are no better than 3 out of 4, or 75 percent.[1] The physical evidence against Oswald is compelling. Oswald was allegedly seen by at least one eyewitness, Howard Brennan, in the window of the sixth floor of the Texas School Book Depository (TSBD) firing a rifle at the presidential motorcade. Oswald's Mannlicher-Carcano rifle was found hidden on the sixth floor of the TSBD along with three cartridge shells. Oswald's fingerprints were also found on boxes used to create a sniper's lair on the sixth floor and his palm print was allegedly found on the butt of the rifle. Based upon the autopsy X-rays and photographs, the president's wounds indicated that he was struck by two bullets fired from the direction of the TSBD, above and behind the motorcade.[2] Oswald fled the TSBD after the assassination and most likely shot and killed a police officer, J. D. Tippit, who attempted to question Oswald. The bullets fired at Tippit matched Oswald's .38 revolver. In addition to the physical evidence, Oswald demonstrated a pattern of behavior during his life that suggested he most likely committed the assassination.[3] Oswald often sought attention and recognition throughout his life whenever he experienced major failures, and the fact that he failed to reconcile with his wife on the Thursday evening prior to the assassination suggests that he was in the mood to commit such an act. Finally, Oswald lied repeatedly to police investigators about a variety of subjects related to his life and his behavior on the days leading up to the assassination.

While a strong likelihood exists that Oswald committed the assassination by himself, an important piece of evidence that remains unresolved concerns Silvia Odio's story.[4] As discussed in previous chapters, Odio's story that she received a visit from Oswald and two Cubans in late September 1963, stands out as a disturbing piece of evidence that has not been explained to the satisfaction of many researchers. Odio suspected that Oswald and the two Cubans, who presented themselves as part of an anti-Castro group, were actually supporters of Castro attempting to obtain information from her. After their visit to Odio's home, one of the Cubans contacted her and described Oswald as an ex-Marine who was "kind of nuts" and then mentioned that Oswald wanted to assassinate Kennedy. Some researchers have attempted to discredit Odio because she had been receiving psychiatric treatment for emotional distress at the time of the alleged visit. However, the House Select Committee on Assassinations (HSCA) in 1979 concluded that Odio was telling the truth. The Warren Commission also implied in its report that she was being truthful and the visit from Oswald and the two Cubans probably happened. To this day, Odio maintains that she is positive Oswald visited her with the two Cubans in late September 1963.[5]

While Odio's story implies a conspiracy in the Kennedy assassination with Oswald as a participant or patsy, it is also possible that Odio's story might be true and yet Oswald still may have committed the assassination by himself. Such behavior would have been consistent with Oswald's need for attention and recognition and also fits with his pattern of speaking publicly at times during his life about killing other political leaders such as President

Eisenhower and Vice-President Nixon. In 1955, a fifteen–year–old Oswald and Palmer McBride were both messenger boys for Pfisterer Dental Laboratory. Oswald told McBride on one occasion that Eisenhower was exploiting the workers of the United States and that he would like to kill Eisenhower.[6] On April 21, 1963, Oswald had read in the newspaper that Nixon was about to visit Dallas, Texas. Marina Oswald told the Warren Commission that, when Oswald heard this news, he put on a suit and got his pistol and stated that he wanted to get "a look" at Nixon. Since this episode was only days after Oswald's April 10, 1963, assassination attempt on General Walker, Marina assumed that Oswald was going to try and kill former Vice-President Richard Nixon. Marina told the Warren Commission that she thwarted Oswald's attempt on the life of Nixon by locking him in the bathroom.[7] Therefore, while the Odio story is a favorite among conspiracy theorists from across the spectrum, it can also be used logically to conclude that Oswald was simply being himself in boasting about a possible assassination to gain attention. Hence, it is entirely plausible that Oswald might have made such a comment about killing Kennedy to the Cubans without the comment necessarily proving the existence of a conspiracy.

A second piece of information that remains unresolved by investigators concerns Joseph Milteer and his claim that he had foreknowledge of the assassination. As noted in chapter 2, Milteer was tape-recorded in Miami, Florida, by a police informant and detailed a plan to assassinate Kennedy using a high-powered rifle from a tall building with an innocent man being picked up off the streets by police immediately afterward.[8] Milteer noted that a high powered rifle could easily be disassembled and taken up in pieces into a tall building without anyone noticing.[9] On the day of the assassination, Milteer supposedly contacted the informant and boasted that the right-wing conservatives had outsmarted the communists by getting them to carry out the assassination without any direct involvement by the radical conservatives. The informant also reported that Milteer claimed to have been in Dealey Plaza to witness the assassination. A photograph of someone resembling Milteer near the TSBD on the day of the assassination has intrigued researchers seeking to prove a conspiracy. The Federal Bureau of Investigations (FBI) questioned Milteer and the HSCA also investigated his claim but the FBI and HSCA could not prove that Milteer was in Dealey Plaza at the time of the assassination.

While conspiracy theorists often refer to Milteer as "The Miami Prophet" who predicted the assassination with great accuracy and may have even witnessed the event, critics note that Milteer made his comments to the informant while he was discussing the many Kennedy "look-alikes" who traveled with the president in order to provide security against an assassination attempt.[10] Milteer also mentioned in the tape-recording that someone named Jack Brown would murder Kennedy, but no such person has ever been linked to the assassination. In regard to Milteer's discussion of a disassembled rifle being taken into a tall building to shoot the president, those comments were made within the context of an assassin shooting at Kennedy while the president stood on the balcony of the White House. Finally, Milteer's presence in Dealey Plaza on the day of the assassination was refuted by a Secret Service Report from its Atlanta Office which concluded that Milteer was in Quitman, Georgia, on November 22, 1963. It should also be recognized that the police informant, William Somersett, who provided the tape-recording of Milteer to federal authorities was, at times, unreliable and prone to exaggeration. In 1961, the federal government discontinued its use of Somersett as an informant after he threatened to expose another informant employed by the federal government and also because he was labeled as a "professional informant" who only provided information in exchange for cash. In sum, a closer examination of Milteer's comments and the credibility of the police informant raises serious doubts concerning whether Milteer knew about the assassination beforehand.

Richard Case Nagell's intriguing story is a favorite among conspiracy theorists. Nagell claimed to have been employed as a Central Intelligence Agency (CIA) counter-intelligence agent for over a decade in the 1950s and 1960s. In the fall of 1962, he was allegedly given an assignment by the CIA to infiltrate Alpha 66 to determine if the anti-Castro organization was planning an assassination of the president. Nagell told author Dick Russell that he acquired foreknowledge of three assassination plots by members of Alpha 66 against President Kennedy during the period from December 1962 until September 1963. Nagell maintained that his alleged CIA contact for the Alpha 66 project turned out to be a Soviet intelligence agent and he was ordered to eliminate Oswald in order to prevent the assassination of the president. The Soviets supposedly wanted to avoid the embarrassment of being linked to the assassination through Oswald's history of living in Russia, even though the Soviets had nothing to do with the assassination plots.[11]

As noted in chapter 2, Nagell fired two gunshots inside a bank in El Paso, Texas, on September 20, 1963, for the sole purpose of getting arrested so as to avoid any connection to the Kennedy assassination in Dallas, Texas. Nagell also was reported to have knowledge of the conspirators involved in the Kennedy assassination which included David Ferrie, Clay Shaw, Guy Banister, and "Angel" and "Leopoldo," the two Cubans who allegedly visited the home of Silvia Odio with Oswald in late September 1963.[12]

While Nagell was a decorated war hero in Korea with a Purple Heart and a Bronze Star, he lacked credibility because an Army psychiatrist concluded that Nagell was detached from reality and was mentally unbalanced to the point of being unable to understand the difference between right and wrong. Nagell's mental impairment was a product of serious injuries suffered in battle during the Korean conflict and a 1954 plane crash where he was the only survivor. The plane crash left Nagell with a permanent indentation on the left side of his head as well as organic brain damage.[13]

In 1958, Nagell married Mitsuko Takahashi, a citizen of Japan, and the couple had two children. Mitsuko left Nagell when the children were still infants and he entered a Veterans Administration (VA) hospital expressing his sorrow at the failure of his marriage, his inability to maintain employment, and his fantasies of murdering his wife. Nagell was later arrested on a charge of being intoxicated and disorderly after he broke down the door to Mitsuko's apartment. A short time later he showed up at a VA hospital with a bullet wound to his chest and claimed that he had been shot by his wife. However, the physician who treated Nagell suspected that the gunshot wound was self-inflicted.[14]

Nagell apparently was cognizant of his mental deterioration because he tried a number of times to receive psychiatric treatment, however, he would strangely refuse such treatment when it was offered by the VA. After Nagell fired the gunshots inside the El Paso bank, he surrendered peacefully and reportedly informed two FBI agents that he was frustrated with the court system in California which had denied him the opportunity to visit with his two young children who were in the custody of his ex-wife.[15]

In addition to the issues concerning his mental state, the CIA has denied having any professional relationship with Nagell and, in fact, the source of his CIA relationship is none other than Nagell himself. Critics also maintain that Nagell started to put his bizarre story together in 1967 when Jim Garrison, the District Attorney of New Orleans, began his investigation in the Kennedy assassination which resulted in the unsuccessful prosecution of Clay Shaw. Nagell's account of the persons involved in the assassination conspiracy, such as David Ferrie, Guy Banister, and George De Mohrenschildt, appears to have been created from the media accounts connected to the Garrison investigation as well as the research conducted by Edward Jay Epstein for his 1978 book, *Legend: The Secret World of Lee Harvey Oswald*.[16]

In addition to the inconsistencies and contradictions in statements made by Nagell over the years until his death in 1995, he failed to produce any of the so-called "evidence" that he professed to have secured as insurance to validate his story. Nagell repeatedly promised to investigators that he would deliver the receipt for the September 17, 1963, letter that he supposedly mailed to J. Edgar Hoover warning him of the assassination attempt on Kennedy, the tape recording from August 1963 of the four alleged conspirators discussing the assassination, and the Polaroid photograph of he and Oswald together in New Orleans in September 1963. However, these three pieces of evidence were never produced by Nagell or located by investigators.[17]

As noted in earlier chapters, the acoustical analyses of the gunshots fired in Dealey Plaza on November 22, 1963, have produced conflicting results. At the time of the assassination, the Dallas police communicated by way of two radio channels. Channel 1 was recorded on a Dictaphone belt recorder and related to basic communication between officers. Channel 2 was recorded on an Audograph disc machine and was connected directly to the presidential motorcade. A dispatcher announced the time at one–minute intervals on both channels. According to Channel 2, the assassination occurred between 12:30 pm and 12:31 pm while a radio microphone from the motorcycle of a Dallas police officer, H. B. McClain, in the motorcade was stuck in the "on" position and took over Channel 1 during the time of the assassination from 12:28 pm until 12:34 pm. Channel 1 recorded static-like noises at about 12:30 pm that have been interpreted by some scientists as gunfire.

While some studies of the acoustical evidence have argued for a second shooter from the grassy knoll in Dealey Plaza, the National Research Council in 1982 and Michael O'Dell challenged the assumptions of this research by concluding that a shot fired from the grassy knoll was highly unlikely.[18] Until the scientific community is able to reach an agreement, this area of research will remain unsettled. Factoring in the complexities of echoes from gunfire in an urban area such as Dealey Plaza and the fact that the reenactments of gunfire in Dealey Plaza were conducted without any knowledge of the position of the motorcycle microphone, the results from any scientific study of the acoustical data are suspect at best. In fact, Dallas police officer H. B. McClain expressed serious doubts that the sounds recorded on Channel 1 were actually from his motorcycle microphone.[19] In addition to the problems created by the poor quality of the tape recordings, the recordings must be questioned because each channel used a different type of machine, each with its own flaws, to record the event. For example, according to the NRC study, the Audograph machine used to record the noise on Channel 2 was thought to skip and repeat sections. Moreover, each machine was designed with a system to stop recording if no noise occurred for four seconds.[20] This obviously creates a serious problem in terms of aligning the two channels together to analyze the sounds accurately. Hence, it is probably safe to assume that the acoustical data recorded at Dealey Plaza can be manipulated by way of statistical analysis. Because of the inherent difficulties in arriving at an absolute conclusion in terms of the acoustical analysis, the data analysis cannot be trusted from either side of the debate. The use of a null hypothesis and the process of falsification in statistical analysis do not provide definitive conclusions.[21]

As described in chapters 2 and 3, David Lifton's research provides a meticulous account of the president's head wounds as described by hospital personnel at Parkland Hospital in Dallas and government officials at Bethesda Naval Hospital.[22] In addition, Lifton documents in detail the location of the president's casket on Air Force One as well as how it was transported by the Secret Service personnel on its way to the official autopsy at Bethesda. Lifton concludes that Secret Service members used an alternate casket to transfer the president's body from Andrew Air Force Base to Walter Reed Medical Center in order to have surgery performed on the president's head wounds. After the surgery was conducted to make the head wounds appear as if the president had been shot from above and behind the presidential motorcade, the body was then taken to Bethesda Naval Hospital for the official autopsy. Lifton's conspiracy theory maintains that the president was, in fact, shot by assassins from the front and to the right of the motorcade, probably from the grassy knoll area of Dealey Plaza.

Lifton claims that the unknown conspirators had the opportunity to remove the president's body from the casket when Air Force One was on the tarmac at Love Field in Dallas.[23] However, it would have been impossible for the conspirators to make off with the president's body because the casket was never left unattended long enough for anyone to steal the body.[24] Brigadier General Gordon McHugh, who was an aide to the president, never left the casket except for a few moments when he checked to inquire as to why the plane had not departed Love Field. Secret Service agent Richard Johnsen and the First Lady, Jacqueline Kennedy, also stayed close to the casket throughout the entire trip on Air Force One. In addition, there were several other individuals who were watching the coffin during the flight from Dallas to Andrews Air Force Base.[25] If by chance the unknown conspirators tried to snatch the president's body during the few moments that it may have been unattended, it would have been obvious because the body was drenched with blood and other fluids and would have left a trail of evidence that it had been removed from the casket.[26] In addition, the casket was being held down with steel cables in order to prevent it from shifting during the flight. It would have been impossible for the conspirators to remove the steel cables quickly enough and put them back in place without anyone noticing such actions.

While Lifton's theory is intriguing and well-documented, it is largely based upon a FBI report produced by two agents, James Sibert and Francis O'Neill, who were among many individuals who observed the official autopsy at Bethesda. Sibert and O'Neill reported that surgery had been performed on the president's head area prior to the autopsy. However, in his testimony before the HSCA, Sibert admitted that he assumed surgery had been performed on the president's head prior to the autopsy because a large piece of bone was missing from the president's skull.[27] However, the piece of bone was eventually found in the presidential limousine and delivered to Bethesda during the latter part of the autopsy. Hence, Sibert wrongly interpreted that, because the president had a large piece of bone missing from his skull, a pre-autopsy surgery must have been performed on the head area.

In sum, Lifton's argument for a conspiracy is weakened by two facts: 1. it would have been impossible for the president's body to be removed from the casket on Air Force One and 2. Sibert and O'Neill's report wrongly interpreted that surgery had been performed on the president's head. It is unimaginable that a large number of conspirators could successfully steal the president's body, perform surgery on the head at Walter Reed, return the body to Bethesda, and switch it back to the original casket, while concomitantly manufacturing additional evidence against Oswald and remaining collectively silent for fifty years.

The most important piece of information relevant to solving the mystery of the Kennedy assassination begins and ends with Jack Ruby's murder of Lee Harvey Oswald. Chapter 1 presents a compelling argument that Ruby acted independent of any conspiracy by portraying Ruby as overly emotional about the assassination. Ruby has been viewed by the lone gunman theorists as an individual possessing the classic tendencies of an egocentric personality seeking publicity. By murdering the alleged assassin of a beloved president, Ruby expected to redeem the city of Dallas and become a hero in the eyes of the world.

While the theories used to explain Ruby's actions in the previous chapters range from the plausible to implausible, an aspect of the Oswald murder that has received little attention is the possibility that one or more members of the Dallas Police Department may have played a role in assisting, influencing, or coercing a mentally unbalanced person such as Ruby to murder Oswald. Seth Kantor refers to the possibility that Ruby was manipulated into murdering Oswald as "the most significant" lead that was not investigated by the Warren Commission.[28] It is logical to assume that the members of the Dallas Police Department were affected more personally by the murder of a Dallas police officer, J. D. Tippit, than by the assassination of President Kennedy. Because close bonds exist among police officers and a vigilante mindset definitely existed among some members of the Dallas Police Department, it is conceivable that Oswald was targeted by more than a few officers who wanted revenge for the murder of Tippit. A few officers may have influenced Ruby by playing upon his volatile temper and mental instability. It would not have been difficult to convince an unstable person such as Ruby that he would be hailed as a national hero and the savior of Dallas if he murdered the assassin of a beloved president. According to Attorney Jim Martin who spoke to Ruby while he was in jail, Ruby believed that he would not serve any time in prison for the murder of Oswald.[29] It is conceivable that one or more police officers may have even assisted Ruby in gaining access to the press conferences where Oswald was on display as well as to the basement of the Dallas city jail where Oswald was eventually shot and killed.[30] It is well documented that Ruby had close ties with members of the Dallas Police Department because Ruby was employed as an informant for the department and he also had been known to cosign bank loans for police officers. In addition, many of the officers frequented Ruby's night clubs and he also was in close contact with police officers in the time period immediately following the murders of Kennedy and Tippit.

Interestingly, the .38 caliber Colt Cobra revolver used by Ruby to murder Oswald was registered to a member of the Dallas Police Department. The .38 Colt Cobra that Ruby used to murder Oswald was registered to Ruby's friend, Dallas Police Detective Joe Cody. The pistol was supposedly purchased by Cody for Ruby because police officers in Texas at the time did not have to pay a sales tax on the purchase of a gun. Cody and Ruby went to Ray Brantley's hardware store in West Dallas where Cody purchased the pistol for $62.50 and was later reimbursed by Ruby who used the weapon for protection when he carried around the cash receipts from his nightclubs.[31]

While there was only one eyewitness, Howard Brennan, to the shooting of the president, there were several eyewitnesses who confirmed that Oswald murdered Tippit.[32] Hence, unlike the shooting of Kennedy, there was a sense of certainty that Oswald murdered Tippit. Oswald's arrogant and disrespectful behavior during the interrogation at the Dallas Police Department inflamed the animosity for Oswald among the Dallas police. It is interesting to note that Oswald was murdered as he was leaving the Dallas city jail, where the Dallas police department had jurisdiction, and was in the process of being transferred to the custody of another jurisdiction, the Dallas county jail. At the county jail, the Dallas police would have had limited access to Oswald.

In testimony before officials of the Warren Commission, Ruby asked to be taken out of Dallas, Texas, and placed in protective custody in Washington, D.C.[33] After this request, Ruby informed the members of the Commission that he had had a one–hour conversation with Harry N. Olsen, a Dallas police officer, on the morning of Saturday, November 23, 1963.[34] Olsen, who was in the company of one of Ruby's strippers, told Ruby that Oswald should be "cut inch by inch into ribbons" and he also said that he admired Ruby as a great guy. According to Dallas Police Chief Jesse Curry, departmental records indicated that Olsen had a reputation for being violent and unstable. In fact, the Dallas Police Department as a whole had a reputation for being corrupt and violent in the early 1960s which Ruby himself often referred to as a "homicidal city."[35] Olsen admitted to the FBI that he had the conversation with Ruby on Saturday morning after the assassination but denied suggesting to Ruby that he murder Oswald. Olsen left the Dallas Police force in December 1963 for undetermined reasons and also left the city of Dallas. The connection between Ruby and the Dallas Police Department remains an unresolved area because the Warren Commission relied on the Dallas Police Department who, after investigating itself, found that Ruby had not colluded with any Dallas police officers in the murder of Oswald.[36]

In sum, it is possible that Ruby was manipulated into murdering Oswald because the presidential assassin was also a "cop-killer," and not because Ruby was instructed to silence Oswald by the shadowy forces involved in the assassination. Hence, Ruby's murder of Oswald may have been independent of a larger conspiracy to assassinate Kennedy. This scenario raises the possibility that Oswald may have been the lone assassin in Dealey Plaza on November 22, 1963, and a conspiracy within the Dallas Police Department, separate from the Kennedy assassination itself, may have provided the impetus for Ruby's behavior.

Some researchers claim that Ruby's murder of Oswald was a spontaneous act and occurred as the result of a series of coincidences that happened to place Ruby in the right place and the right time. However, it is obvious Ruby was stalking Oswald based upon the fact that he showed up a number of times at the Dallas police station where Oswald was being held.[37] At roughly 7:00 pm on the Friday evening of November 22, 1963, only seven hours after the assassination, Ruby tried to enter the Homicide Bureau Office on the third floor of the Dallas Police Department where Oswald was being questioned by the Dallas police captain, Will Fritz, and other investigators. However, Ruby was prevented from entering the room by a police officer. Ruby even attended one of the impromptu press conferences at midnight on Saturday, November 23, where Oswald was paraded in front of the media. Here, Ruby famously corrected District Attorney Henry Wade's statement to the press that Oswald belonged to the Free Cuba Committee, which, in fact, was known as the Fair Play for Cuba Committee (FPCC). During this press conference, Ruby was carrying a loaded revolver in his right hand pocket but he could not get close enough to Oswald because of the large crowd of reporters and photographers. It is obvious that the opportunity to murder Oswald presented itself only after several attempts by Ruby to get close enough to Oswald. Ruby told a Dallas police detective, Don Ray Archer, immediately after the shooting that he intended to shoot Oswald three times which would suggest a premeditated plan of murder.[38] Hence, the fact that Ruby secured an opportunity to shoot Oswald does not necessarily indicate a spontaneous act caused by a series of coincidences and leaves open the possibility of a conspiracy. A lawyer, Joe Tonahill, who represented Ruby during his murder trial, stated that "Ruby could have been used" by others to murder Oswald and "[i]t wouldn't have been any problem to . . . get Ruby to do something like this."[39] On March 14, 1964, a Dallas jury found Ruby guilty of murder with malice and he was sentenced to death.

Finally, it is also possible (although less probable than Ruby acting on behalf of the Dallas police) that Ruby committed the murder because Oswald possessed sensitive knowledge of criminal activity connected to organized crime and the intelligence community. Along the same lines as Ruby murdering Oswald on behalf of the Dallas Police Department, Oswald may have been silenced for some other reason than to conceal a conspiracy in the assassination of the president. A number of authors have established such conspiracy theories grounded upon Oswald's connections to the world of organized crime in New Orleans operated by Carlos Marcello and government agencies involved in intelligence operations. Oswald was clearly immersed in the milieu of New Orleans with its anti-Castro exiles, Mafia figures, and intelligence personnel who specialized in assassination plots, gunrunning, and drug trafficking. If Oswald had stood trial for the murder of President Kennedy, his alleged roles as an informant for the FBI, a contract agent for the CIA, or a low-level employee with the New Orleans Mafia through his uncle, Charles "Dutz" Murret may have surfaced as part of his defense and would have been damaging and embarrassing for many powerful individuals. Hence, the decision to silence Oswald would have appeared as an attractive option to many interests.

While the murder of Oswald by Ruby evokes conspiratorial overtones, it is also probable that Oswald was murdered for reasons independent of a larger conspiracy to murder President Kennedy. Quite simply, Ruby may have acted on his own for attention or for a host of other reasons such as his fascination with the Kennedys or Ruby's own psychological problems. From a more complex perspective, Oswald's murder of Dallas police officer, J. D. Tippit, may have caused some members of law enforcement to influence Ruby in seeking their revenge or Oswald's knowledge of sensitive information about the world of organized crime or the activities of U.S. intelligence agencies may have caused such forces to use Ruby to silence Oswald. These complex explanations for Ruby's actions are as logical as a wider conspiracy to murder the president.

A PLAUSIBLE SCENARIO: OSWALD AS CONSPIRATOR (20 PERCENT PROBABILITY)

There is no shortage of conspiracy theories when it comes to Lee Harvey Oswald and the Kennedy assassination. A number of conspiracy theories consist of Oswald working in conjunction with a rogue element of the CIA, Mafia, and/or anti-Castro Cubans. Oswald was clearly immersed in the milieu of the intelligence community and the organized crime syndicate as well as the pro-Castro and anti-Castro groups operating in New Orleans and Dallas. Oswald's connections to David Ferrie, Clay Shaw, Guy Banister, Carlos Bringuier, Carlos Marcello (through his uncle, Charles "Dutz" Murret), as well as the Soviet and Cuban embassies in Mexico City imply that he may have been involved with individuals, or groups, plotting the assassination of the president. If Oswald was recruited during his service in the Marine Corps to perform the tasks of a CIA contract agent or FBI informant, then he may have become involved with a rogue element of the intelligence community planning the assassination. Interestingly, conspiracy theorists have suggested that Oswald's stay in the Soviet Union was part of an intelligence operation designed to allow fake defectors the opportunity to gather information about life inside a communist country. The fact that Oswald worked for his uncle, Dutz Murret, in New Orleans during the summer of 1963 has generated conspiracy theories related to the Mafia because Murret worked as a mid-level bookie for Carlos Marcello, the leader of the organized crime syndicate in New Orleans. During this time, Oswald also interacted frequently with pro-Castro and anti-Castro Cubans in New Orleans. Oswald's communist affiliations and defection to the Soviet Union as well as his subsequent marriage to a Russian woman whose uncle was a lieutenant in the Soviet Secret Police (KGB) have raised suspicions that perhaps Oswald acted on behalf of an international communist conspiracy. Oswald's mysterious trip to Mexico City six weeks before the Kennedy assassination wherein he met with Soviet and Cuban officials at their respective embassies raised serious concerns, particularly since he met with Valeriy Kostikov, the head of Department 13 for the KGB in charge of assassinations and sabotage.

Oswald's trip to Mexico City in September–October 1963 also raised allegations that Cuban intelligence operatives knew in advance that Oswald was involved in a plot to assassinate the president. Oswald was alleged to have informed officials at the Cuban consulate in Mexico City that he might attempt to assassinate President Kennedy. It is unknown whether Castro or Cuban intelligence agents were involved directly in the assassination but some conspiracy researchers claim that Castro knew about Oswald's visit to the Cuban Embassy and his desire to murder the president to prove his loyalty to the communist revolution in Cuba. In the aftermath of the assassination, Thomas Mann, the U.S. ambassador to Mexico, attempted to raise the issue with the Warren Commission that Oswald may have been working for Castro and the Cubans. However, Mann was told by the State Department to keep quiet. President Lyndon Johnson and the CIA supposedly withheld information from the Warren Commission about Oswald's connections to Cuban intelligence to avoid a confrontation with Cuba and the Soviet Union which could have started a nuclear war. Today, it is well known that the Hotel del Comercio where Oswald stayed during his time in Mexico City was a haven for Cuban spies.[40]

Silvia Odio's story discussed repeatedly throughout this book obviously provides support for a conspiracy in the Kennedy assassination. Interestingly, the Warren Commission and the HSCA concluded that Silvia Odio most likely told the truth in her testimony about Oswald and two Cubans visiting her in Dallas in late September 1963.[41] As noted above, Odio was suspicious that Oswald and the Cubans were supporters of Castro presenting themselves as anti-Castro in order to gather information from her. Conspiracy theorists note that Odio's story is consistent with Oswald's behavior at this time. For example, during the summer of 1963 in New Orleans, Oswald met with Carlos Bringuier and attempted to infiltrate his anti-Castro organization, only to be confronted by Bringuier a few days later after Oswald was seen passing out pro-Castro leaflets. Oswald was arrested after a scuffle with Bringuier but, while he was in custody, he met privately with FBI agent, John Quigley. Some conspiracy theorists argue that such behavior was typical of Oswald who was known to oscillate between expressing pro-Castro and anti-Castro sentiments in order to perform his role as an intelligence operative and/or a FBI informant.[42] This pattern of behavior demonstrated by Oswald coupled with Odio's claim that the assassination of Kennedy was discussed with one of the Cubans who accompanied Oswald to her home provides circumstantial evidence that Oswald may have been part of a conspiracy to assassinate Kennedy. However, because of Oswald's mysterious behavior, it is difficult to ascertain whether he would have been working with pro-Castro or anti-Castro-Cubans in the assassination plot. If Oswald conspired with pro-Castro Cubans, then Fidel Castro and the Soviet Union may also have been part of the plot. If Oswald conspired with anti-Castro Cubans, the intelligence community and organized crime might be considered likely accomplices in the murder of the president.

While Joseph Milteer's story has its deficiencies based upon the analysis above, it coincidentally fits perfectly with Carlos Marcello's prediction that President Kennedy would be assassinated and a "nut" would be arrested for the assassination to insulate the Mafia from any culpability. While the Warren Commission in 1964 investigated and concluded that Marcello was not involved in the assassination, the HSCA in 1979 found that a conspiracy existed in the assassination and pointed the finger at the Mafia. Robert Blakey, chief counsel for the HSCA, argues that organized crime bosses, Marcello of New Orleans, Santos Traficante of Tampa, and Sam Giancana of Chicago, were behind the planning of the assassination carried out by Oswald and a second gunman firing from the grassy knoll area.[43]

The credibility of Richard Case Nagell obviously was weakened by his documented history of mental incompetence, his failure to produce any evidence to support his claims, and the appearance that he acquired much of his information related to the Kennedy conspiracy through public channels, such as Jim Garrison's investigation and Edward Jay Epstein's research. In regard to Nagell's mental competence, it is worth noting that a 1966 psychiatric report from the Springfield Medical Center in Springfield, Missouri, where he was being held as a federal prisoner after his arrest in El Paso, concluded that he possessed no evidence of any brain damage.[44] Interestingly, Nagell was apparently given intelligence training and Top Secret security clearance by the military, after the time period when he supposedly became mentally unstable because of his military combat experience and the plane crash in

1954. It has been suggested that Nagell's counter-intelligence role included voluntary admission to VA hospitals for psychiatric treatment and part of the legal defense strategy after his arrest in El Paso was simply designed to establish mental incompetence. In short, conspiracy theorists have argued that any idea of Nagell as a mentally unstable person was simply a myth.[45]

Evidence of Nagell's role as an intelligence operative was uncovered from his own belongings. When Nagell was arrested in El Paso, Texas, on September 20, 1963, the FBI found two spiral notebooks in his possession with the names of two Soviet officials and seven individuals listed as "CIA." When the FBI asked the CIA about the seven names, a CIA inquiry discovered that all of the seven individuals were actively involved in intelligence operations. The CIA, in turn, asked the FBI how Nagell had come into possession of the seven names but the mystery was never resolved. The notebooks also revealed that Nagell had had previous contact with the FBI prior to his arrest in El Paso suggesting rendezvous points for transferring information to the FBI, possibly for secret operations. In addition, the notebooks contained a reference to the FPCC and a telephone number referencing the Cuban consulate in Mexico City. While the FPCC could arguably only connect Nagell to Oswald in a loose fashion, the telephone number to the Cuban consulate provided a more direct link as the number, "11-28-47," was identical to the one found among Oswald's belongings after his arrest. Finally, and perhaps most intriguing, the FBI found a Minox spy camera in the trunk of Nagell's automobile. The Minox spy camera was the exact same type of camera found in Oswald's possession after he was arrested for the assassination of the president.[46]

While evidence of Nagell's mental competence and a review of personal items found among his effects does not establish with certainty that he was privy to various plots to assassinate the president, it provides circumstantial evidence that Nagell was an intelligence operative and suggests that he may well have infiltrated conspiratorial plots in 1962-1963 involving members of Alpha 66 and Lee Harvey Oswald. Interestingly, Nagell correctly identified and described a number of anti-Castro Cuban exiles presumed to be directly involved in the plot, including Sergio Arcacha, Angel (identified as Tony Cuesta), and Leopoldo. Some researchers suggest that Nagell may have been the person in charge of recruiting Vaughn Marlowe and, later, Oswald as a communist sympathizer assigned the task of shooting the president in order to initiate American military action against Cuba as revenge for the Kennedy assassination.[47]

The physical evidence in favor of Oswald being involved in a conspiracy to assassinate the president is limited to the acoustical evidence and David Lifton's claim that surgery was performed on the president's body to disguise the fact that shots were fired at the president from in front of the motorcade near the grassy knoll area of Dealey Plaza. In regard to the acoustical evidence, the HSCA in 1979 and D. B. Thomas's research in 2001 concluded that a strong probability existed a shot was fired from the grassy knoll area which would indicate a conspiracy in the assassination of President Kennedy.[48] Eyewitness and ear-witness testimony from individuals within Dealey Plaza at the time of the assassination also supports the idea that shots were fired from the grassy knoll area.[49] Witnesses observed smoke rising from the grassy knoll area at the time the president was shot as well as other suspicious activity in and around the area to the front and right of the presidential motorcade.

David Lifton's evidence in support of a conspiracy is based upon a preautopsy report submitted by two FBI agents, Sibert and O'Neill, who noted that surgery had been performed on the president's head prior to the official autopsy.[50] As noted above, Sibert testified before the HSCA that he incorrectly assumed that surgery had been performed on the president's head prior to the autopsy because a large piece of skull was missing from the head area. The piece of skull was eventually discovered in the presidential limousine and delivered to Bethesda during the autopsy.

While the Sibert and O'Neill report cannot necessarily be used to support a conspiracy theory, Lifton's research still is useful because of the fact that medical personnel at Parkland Hospital in Dallas observed wounds to the head area that suggested the president was shot from the front and to the right of the motorcade.[51] For example, Dr. Malcolm Perry of Parkland Hospital told reporters that the president's throat wound was an entrance wound and it appeared as if the bullet was coming at him when he was struck in the throat.[52] In addition, most medical personnel at Parkland who observed the wound to the back of the president's head concluded that it was an exit wound based upon its large size suggesting a shot from the front of the presidential motorcade.[53] The conflict between how the Parkland physicians described the president's head wounds compared to the observations of medical personnel during the official autopsy at Bethesda has not been resolved in a satisfactory manner, regardless of the repeated attempts by critics to discredit Lifton's research.

As noted above, Lifton's research concerning whether the president's body was removed from the casket has been the subject of much criticism because it appears as if the casket was closely guarded during the specific time frame when Lifton hypothesized that the body was stolen by the conspirators. However, in response to his critics, Lifton has revised his theory and concluded that the president's body was probably removed when the casket was loaded on to Air Force One.[54] At this time, Lifton notes that the president's entourage was still on the tarmac at Love Field in Dallas. He further argues that the president's body was then most likely taken off of Air Force One and placed onto Air Force Two.

Most conspiracy theories argue that Ruby was a central figure in the assassination of Kennedy. Ruby's connections to the world of organized crime and the intelligence community obviously create the possibility that Ruby was silencing Oswald to protect other persons or organizations involved in the assassination. Ruby was in close contact with organized crime figures in the months leading up to the assassination of Kennedy, although the substance of the numerous telephone calls between Ruby and persons connected to the Mafia remains unknown.[55] Based upon the Warren Commission's psychological profile of Ruby as a violent and unstable individual desperate to become an important person, it is plausible that Ruby was manipulated by the intelligence community or organized crime to silence Oswald based simply upon the belief that he would become a heroic figure. Hence, Ruby may not have even understood that he was being used to conceal a conspiracy.

A LESS LIKELY SCENARIO: OSWALD AS PATSY AND HERO (>5 PERCENT PROBABILITY)

As discussed in detail throughout chapter 3, some researchers view Oswald as a heroic figure performing his duty for the United States as a counter-intelligence operative working for the CIA and/or FBI. In the process of gathering information for the federal government regarding extremist organizations, Oswald may have stumbled upon a plot to assassinate the president and then was set up by the conspirators as a patsy to take the fall for the murder of the president.

Silvia Odio's story can easily be interpreted as an attempt to frame Oswald for the assassination. After Odio received the visit from Oswald and the two Cubans in late September of 1963, she received the telephone call from one of the Cubans a few days after the visit and he specifically asked about her impressions of Oswald. During the telephone conversation, the Cuban told Odio that Oswald was thinking about assassinating President Kennedy. It would appear that the groundwork was being laid to frame Oswald for the assassination roughly two months prior to the event. However, it is unknown whether the Cubans behind the attempt to frame Oswald were supporters of Castro perhaps protecting international communists who were intent on committing the assassination or anti-Castro Cubans connected to organized crime or the U.S. intelligence community.

As noted in the previous section, Joseph Milteer's story to the Miami police informant that President Kennedy would be assassinated with a high-powered rifle from an office building and someone would be picked up on the streets to throw off the public fits perfectly with the scenario that Oswald was a patsy. Milteer also told the informant after the assassination that Oswald didn't know anything suggesting that Oswald was innocent of any involvement in the assassination.

Richard Case Nagell's story clearly defines Oswald as the patsy in the conspiratorial plot to assassinate Kennedy but, unlike Milteer, Oswald is not viewed as an innocent or heroic figure but rather an active participant in the assassination. According to Nagell, Oswald was recruited into the plot as a shooter by members of Alpha 66 posing as G-2 intelligence agents of Castro. As stated above, the Alpha 66 members, most likely Angel and Leopoldo, had hoped to trigger an invasion of Cuba by the United States once Oswald, a communist sympathizer, was framed for the assassination.

The acoustical evidence examined by the HSCA raised the real possibility that two shooters fired at the president's motorcade in Dealey Plaza on November 22, 1963. The HSCA concluded that a strong probability existed that three shots were fired from the sixth floor of the TSBD and at least one shot was fired from the grassy knoll area to the right and in front of the motorcade. Oswald was seen in the second floor lunchroom immediately prior to the assassination by a fellow employee of the TSBD, Carolyn Arnold, and was also seen by a Dallas police officer, Marrion Baker, in the same area of the second floor lunchroom drinking a Coke less than two minutes after the assassination. Oswald was not out of breath or excited when he was confronted by Officer Baker and the fact that he was drinking a Coke means that, after firing three shots at the motorcade, Oswald would have had to race down to the second floor from the sixth floor, operate the vending machine, open a bottle of Coke, and begin drinking it all in less than two minutes. Interestingly, a witness for the Warren Commission, Victoria Adams, testified that she was on the stairway during the time period that Oswald would have had to travel from the sixth floor to the second floor and she saw no one during this time period.[56] Hence, circumstantial evidence suggests Oswald may not have been in position to be involved in the assassination.

In support of the narrative that Oswald was a patsy, David Lifton argues that Oswald's rifle and shell casings discovered on the sixth floor of the TSBD, the two bullet fragments discovered inside the presidential limousine, and the "magic bullet," also known as CE 399, found on a stretcher at Parkland Hospital were planted by members of the Secret Service who had fired the bullets from Oswald's rifle prior to the assassination.[57] Lifton also documents the number of times that Oswald emphatically denied shooting President Kennedy, including statements that he made at the time of his arrest and during his transport to the Dallas police station as well as his statements made during the interrogation conducted by the police.[58] Finally, Lifton points to Oswald's famous claim to reporters that he was "just a patsy."

The murder of Oswald by Jack Ruby would have been the final piece of the puzzle to frame Oswald and protect the real assassins who murdered the president. If Oswald had lived to stand trial for the assassination, he would have been given the opportunity to defend himself and perhaps prove that he was framed by sinister forces involved in the conspiracy.

Each piece of evidence discussed above might seem implausible as it relates to Oswald being framed for the assassination. However, a collective examination of the evidence interestingly provides reinforcement for such a theory. The acoustical evidence combined with Lifton's arguments as well the intriguing stories from Odio and Milteer cannot be dismissed casually as coincidence. Moreover, Ruby's role in eliminating Oswald continues to fascinate researchers and has solidified the belief among many investigators as well as a majority of the American public that Oswald was framed for the assassination of President Kennedy.

THE LEAST LIKELY SCENARIO: THE "RUSSIAN" OSWALD (>1 PERCENT PROBABILITY)

Because Oswald's life has been shrouded in mystery and the circumstances surrounding the Kennedy assassination provide little clarity, it is worth examining the possibility that, while Lee Harvey Oswald left the United States for the Soviet Union in 1959, he may not have returned. Instead, Oswald may have been replaced by a Russian "look-alike" who came to the United States in 1962 as part of an international communist conspiracy to assassinate President John F. Kennedy.

Lee Harvey Oswald had only been in the Soviet Union about eight months when the Director of the FBI, J. Edgar Hoover, expressed serious concern in a memorandum on June 3, 1960, to the State Department that a Russian impostor might be using Oswald's birth certificate. Hoover's memorandum coupled with a number of physical discrepancies provides a modicum of circumstantial evidence for the "Russian Oswald" theory. For example, Lee Harvey Oswald possessed a two–inch scar behind his left ear as a result of a surgery to remove his mastoid bone when he was six years old. Although Oswald's military records noted the scar in 1956 and 1959, the scar is not visible in photographs of Oswald after his arrest on November 22, 1963. Moreover, the autopsy performed on Oswald after he was murdered by Jack Ruby fails to document the scar behind his left ear. The autopsy also did not account for three scars on Oswald's left arm as well as a vaccination scar that had been noted in his Marine medical record from the late 1950s. Finally, Oswald's height has become a point of contention because Marine records show that Oswald was five feet and eleven inches. However, after his return to the United States in 1962, Oswald's height was consistently reported as five feet and nine inches on numerous occasions. Family members also commented on significant changes in his physical appearance upon his return to the United States, even though he had only lived in the Soviet Union for a few years.

Oswald's language skills have also become a source of debate among conspiracy theorists. When Marina Oswald was first introduced to Lee Harvey Oswald in Minsk, she stated that his Russian language skills were so good she assumed that he was a native Russian. However, prior to leaving the United States for the Soviet Union, Lee Harvey Oswald apparently did not possess such language skills based upon a Russian language examination given to him in 1959 by the military wherein he scored a rating of poor in every category. Oswald took a Russian equivalency examination on February 25, 1959, and scored poor in reading, writing, and understanding. He also completed an aptitude exam on the Russian language and scored a rating in the lowest category. Richard Snyder, the consul at the U.S. Embassy in Moscow, was quoted as saying Oswald probably could not have "gotten along on his own in Russian society" based upon his poor language skills.[59] Priscilla Johnson McMillan and Aline Mosby, both of whom interviewed Oswald in Moscow, concurred that his skills in the Russian language were very bad.

Oswald's sudden improvement of his language skills raises the remote possibility that he may have been replaced by a Russian impostor after he arrived in the Soviet Union. Interestingly, after his return to the United States, Oswald's family members said that he appeared to have acquired an accent during his stay in the Soviet Union and a language expert from Southern Methodist University concluded that English was not the native language of Oswald based upon audio recordings of his voice produced after his return to the United States.[60]

The Silvia Odio story fits neatly into the "Russian Oswald" scenario if the Cubans traveling with Oswald were pro-Castro Cubans supportive of the Soviet Union. As noted, Odio suspected that the Cubans were pro-Castro but were pretending to be anti-Castro in order to get information from her. If the Odio story is examined within the context of Oswald's trip to Mexico City a few days later, it would seem logical that the "Russian Oswald" would be traveling with pro-Castro Cubans on his way to visit the Cuban and Russian embassies in Mexico City where he might have received his instructions to assassinate President Kennedy. Is it simply a coincidence that Oswald met with Valery Kostikov, a KGB officer in command of Department 13 renowned for assassination plots, at the Soviet Embassy in Mexico City?

Joseph Milteer's premonition of the Kennedy assassination included his claim that the conservatives had outsmarted the communists by getting them to carry out the assassination without direct involvement from the ultra-right wing movement. Milteer's "innocent man scenario" coupled with Lifton's evidence of a government conspiracy and subsequent cover-up as well as the acoustical data suggests that perhaps the "Russian Oswald" was sacrificed as the patsy in order to conceal the conspiracy. Such a scenario would have involved sinister forces within the intelligence agencies of the U.S. government manipulating the communists to carry out the assassination on their behalf.

Richard Case Nagell's story that he was hired by Soviet intelligence to eliminate Oswald in order to stop the assassination obviously creates a fascinating scenario perhaps involving the "Russian Oswald." Nagell intimated that the Soviet Union was not part of the assassination plot against Kennedy but that the Russians simply wanted to prevent the assassination because of Oswald's history of having lived in the Soviet Union. Hence, the Soviet Union wanted Nagell to eliminate Oswald because of the fear that the assassination would have been blamed on the Russians who were not involved but had simply discovered the plot by using Nagell as an intelligence source.[61] Nagell's claim about the Russians, if true, appears suspect at best. A simpler and more logical explanation would seem to be that the "Russian Oswald" had been ordered by the Soviet government to commit the assassination and then the Soviets suddenly had a change of heart at the last moment but had lost track of or control over the "Russian Oswald." In order to protect themselves and their reputation across the globe, the Soviet Union may have found it in their best interests to mislead Nagell about the actual reason why the "Russian Oswald" needed to be murdered.

As detailed in chapter 5, in the aftermath of the assassination, the "Russian Oswald" was subsequently murdered by Jack Ruby, who was allegedly performing the role of a low-level operative working for Russian intelligence. Ruby's murder of the "Russian Oswald" would then have been imperative to hide the role of the international communists in the assassination of an American president. Of course, as noted above, it is also possible that Ruby murdered the "Russian Oswald" without any knowledge of any type of conspiracy.

CONCLUSION

Even though interesting questions and circumstantial evidence have surfaced in the Kennedy assassination suggesting a conspiracy, no researcher has delivered concrete evidence to resolve the most important questions surrounding the Kennedy assassination. G. Robert Blakey, chief counsel for the HSCA, has examined all of the JFK files yet to be released by federal agencies and maintains that no smoking gun exists to satisfy the conspiracy theorists who will continue to be disappointed.[62] However, conspiracy theorists can always rely upon the argument that the CIA, organized crime, or Soviet intelligence would have covered their tracks completely if a plot of such magnitude was carried out in 1963.[63] From this counter-intuitive perspective, the absence of evidence will always provide conspiracy theorists with a platform to support their beliefs.

Hence, the life of Lee Harvey Oswald remains shrouded in mystery and intrigue and has undergone a historical evolution of epic proportions. In reality, most of the American public remains uncertain and perplexed about the identity of Oswald, even after fifty years of debate and analysis from professional researchers and investigators. While Oswald was initially depicted as the lone assassin by the Warren Commission, researchers have subsequently argued forcefully and, at times, effectively, that Oswald's role in the assassination may have been that of a conspirator, patsy, hero, or Russian impostor. In the final analysis, this book has sought to provide a comprehensive review of the various dimensions of Lee Harvey Oswald and the relevant evidence connected to the Kennedy assassination in order to allow each reader to decide for themselves the role played by Oswald in one of the most significant events in American history.

NOTES

1. Norman Mailer, *Oswald's Tale: An American Mystery* (New York: Random House, 1995), 778.
2. *Investigation of the Assassination of President John F. Kennedy: Hearing before the President's Commission on the Assassination of President Kennedy*. 88th Congress. (1964) [Warren Commission Report here in WCR], vol. II (1964), 353–358 (statement of J. Humes) (describing Kennedy's fatal wounds in detail).
3. James Clarke, *Defining Danger: American Assassins and the New Domestic Terrorists* (Piscataway, N. J.: Transaction Publishers, 2007), 104–124.
4. Jim Marrs, *Crossfire: The Plot That Killed Kennedy* (New York: Carroll & Graf, 1989), 147–155.
5. Bugliosi, *Reclaiming History,* 1308.
6. Gerald Posner, *Case Closed: Lee Harvey Oswald and the Assassination of JFK* (New York: Random House, 1993) 17; FBI report of November 26, 1963 (affidavit of Palmer McBride) Commission Document 75, Commission Exhibit 1386, WCR, 251–252.
7. Marina Oswald's Testimony, WCR, vol. V, 388–389.
8. Anthony Summers, *Conspiracy* (New York: McGraw-Hill, 1980), 404.
9. Dan Christensen, "JFK, King: The Dade County Links," *Miami Magazine* (September 1976), 12-76.
10. John McAdams, "The Kennedy Assassination: Joseph Milteer: Miami Prophet or Quitman Crackpot?" *The Kennedy Assassination*, accessed January 25, 2013. http://mcadams.posc.mu.edu/milteer.htm.
11. Dick Russell, *The Man Who Knew Too Much* (New York: Carroll & Graf, 1992).
12. Ibid.
13. Dave Reitzes, "Truth or Dare: The Lives and Lies of Richard Case Nagell," accessed June 21, 2013, http://mcadams.posc.mu.edu/nagell1.htm
14. Ibid.
15. Ibid.
16. Ibid.
17. Ibid.
18. O'Dell, "The Acoustics Evidence in the Kennedy Assassination."
19. Posner, *Case Closed,* 240–241.
20. National Research Council, "Reexamination of Acoustic Evidence," 61–64.

21. Mark H Maier. *The Data Game* (Armonk, N.Y.: M. E. Sharpe, 1999); Chava-Frankfort Nachmias and David Nachmias, *Research Methods in the Social Sciences* (New York: Macmillan, 2000), 437–453.
22. David Lifton, *Best Evidence: Disguise and Deception in the Assassination of John F. Kennedy* (New York: Macmillan, 1980), 308–338.
23. David. R. Wrone, *The Zapruder Film: Reframing JFK's Assassination* (Lawrence: University Press of Kansas, 2003), 133–137.
24. Robert Groden and Harrison Livingstone, *High Treason: The Assassination of President John F. Kennedy and the New Evidence of Conspiracy* (New York: Conservatory Press, 1989), 35.
25. Wrone, *The Zapruder Film,* 133; Godfrey McHugh, "Letter to the Editor," *Time,* (February 17, 1981); William Manchester, *The Death of a President: November 1963* (New York: Harper & Row, 1967), 309–310.
26. Wrone, *The Zapruder Film,* 133.
27. *Investigation of the Assassination of President John F. Kennedy: Hearing before the House, Select Committee on Assassinations* (HSCA), 95th Congress. (1979) [House Select Committee on Assassinations, herein HSCA)], doc. 002191, staff interview of James W. Sibert (August 29, 1977).
28. Seth Kantor, *The Ruby Cover-Up* (New York: Kensington Publishing, 1978), 412.
29. Gary Willis and Ovid Demaris, *Jack Ruby: The Man Who Killed the Man Who Killed Kennedy* (New York: DeCapo Press, 1994), 72–73.
30. Kantor, *The Ruby Cover-Up,* 142.
31. Bugliosi, *Reclaiming History,* 1077.
32. Posner, *Case Closed,* 274.
33. WCR, vol. V, 210 [Testimony of Jack Ruby].
34. Kantor, *The Ruby Cover-Up,* 28.
35. Ed Reid and Ovid Demaris, *The Green Felt Jungle* (New York: Buccaneer Books, 1963).
36. Kantor, *The Ruby Cover-Up,* 28–30.
37. Ibid., 95–102.
38. Ibid., 221–223.
39. Ibid., 103. Seth Kantor interviewed Joe Tonahill on July 15, 1976, in Jasper, Texas.
40. Brian Latell, *Castro's Secrets: Cuban Intelligence, the CIA, and the Assassination of John F. Kennedy* (New York: Palgrave Macmillan, 2012).
41. Bugliosi, *Reclaiming History,* 1308.
42. Ray and Mary La Fontaine, *Oswald Talked: The New Evidence in the JFK Assassination* (Gretna, La.: Pelican Publishing Company, Inc., 1996), 181–183, 302–303.
43. G. Robert Blakey and Richard Billings, *Fatal Hour: The Assassination of President Kennedy by Organized Crime* (New York: Berkeley Books, 1992).
44. Dick Russell, *The Man Who Knew Too Much,* 406–407.
45. Larry Hancock, "The Man in the Middle: Richard Case Nagell's View of an Evolving Conspiracy," *Kennedy Assassination Chronicles.* (Winter 1999), 16.
46. Dick Russell, *The Man Who Knew Too Much,* 6.
47. Larry Hancock, "The Man in the Middle," 16.
48. Thomas, *Echo Correlation Analysis,* 21–32.
49. Josiah Thompson, *Six Seconds in Dallas: A Micro-Study of the Kennedy Assassination* (New York: Random House, 1967).
50. Lifton, *Best Evidence,* 681–690.
51. Lifton, *Best Evidence,* 308–337.
52. John McAdams, The Kennedy Assassination "Parkland Hospital Press Conference: Dallas Doctors First Statements," accessed March 31, 2013, http://mcadams.posc.mu.edu/press.htm.
53. Lifton, *Best Evidence,* 317.
54. Joel Grant, "Body Snatchers at Love Field?" accessed March 31, 2013, http://mcadams.posc.mu.edu/b_snatch.htm.

55. Lamar Waldron and Thom Hartmann, *Ultimate Sacrifice: John and Robert Kennedy, The Plan for a Coup in Cuba, and the Murder of JFK* (New York: Carroll & Graf, 2005), 586–587.
56. Lifton, *Best Evidence,* 350–351.
57. Ibid., 359–373.
58. Ibid., 352.
59. Posner, *Case Closed,* 64.
60. Gary Mack, "Who Was Really in Oswald's Grave? Parts 1–3." *Cover-ups!* (Feb.–April 1983), 1–3.
61. Dave Reitzes, "Truth or Dare."
62. Posner, *Case Closed,* 471.
63. Scott Shane, " C.I.A. Is Still Cagey about Oswald Mystery," *New York Times*, October 16, 2009, accessed June 25, 2013, http://www.nytimes.com/2009/10/17/us/17inquire.html?pagewanted=all&_r=1&.

Bibliography

Adamson, Bruce C. *Oswald's Closest Friend: The George de Mohrenschildt Story.* Santa Cruz, Calif.: Self-published, 2001.
Albanese, Jay. *Organized Crime in Our Times.* Newark, N.J.: Matthew Bender & Co., Inc., 2010.
Armstrong, John. *Harvey and Lee: How the CIA Framed Oswald.* Arlington, Tex.: Quasar, 2003.
Bamford, James. *The Shadow Factory: The NSA from 9/11 to the Eavesdropping on America,* New York: Random House, 2009.
Banta, Thomas. "The Kennedy Assassination: Early Thoughts and Emotions," *Public Opinion Quarterly* 28 (1964): 216–220.
Barger, J. E., S. P. Robinson, E. C. Schmidt, and J.J. Wolf. *Analysis of Recorded Sounds Relating to the Assassination of John F. Kennedy.* Cambridge, Mass.: Bolt, Baranek & Newman Inc., 1979.
Berman, Harold J. *The Trial of the U-2.* Chicago: Translation World Publishers, 1960.
Bishop, Jim. *The Day Kennedy Was Shot.* New York: Funk and Wagnalls, 1968.
Blakey, G. Robert and Richard Billings. *Fatal Hour: The Assassination of President Kennedy by Organized Crime.* New York: Berkeley Books, 1992.
Bohni, Don. *The Castro Obsession: U.S. Covert Operations Against Cuba, 1959–1965.* Dulles, Va.: Potomac Books, Inc., 2006.
Bowart, W. H. *Operation Mind Control: Our Government's War Against Its People.* New York: Dell Publishing, 1978.
Brennan, Howard and J. Edward Cherryholmes. *Eyewitness to History: The Kennedy Assassination as Seen by Howard L. Brennan.* Waco, Tex., Texian Press, 1987.
Breo, Dennis L. "JFK's Death: The Plain Truth from the MDs Who Did the Autopsy," *Journal of the American Medical Association* 267 (May 27, 1992): 2794-2803.
Brown, Peter Harry and Pat H. Broeske. *Howard Hughes: The Untold Story.* Cambridge, Mass.: Da Capo Press, 2004.
Brown, Walt. "You Know about Albert Guy Bogard: What about Ed Brand," *JFK/Deep Politics Quarterly* 4 (April 1999): 14–16.
Bugliosi, Vincent. *Reclaiming History: The Assassination of President John F. Kennedy.* New York: W. W. Norton & Co., 2007.
Butbul-Aviel, Y. & D. Miron, R. Halevy, A. Koren, and W. Sakran. "Acute Mastoiditis in children: *Pseudomonas aeruginosa* as a Leading Pathogen," *International Journal of Pediatric Otorhinolaryngology* 67 (March 2003): 277-81.
Christensen, Dan. "JFK, King: The Dade County Links," *Miami Magazine* 7 (September 22, 1976): 1–16.

"CIA Link to L.A. Police Reported," *Los Angeles Herald Examiner*, January 12, 1976.
"CIA Murder Plots Weighing the Damage to U.S." *U.S. News and World Report* 1 (December 1975): 13–15.
Clarke, James. *Defining Danger: American Assassins and the New Domestic Terrorists*. Piscataway, N.J.: Transaction Publishers, 2007.
Committee on Ballistic Acoustics, National Research Council. "Reexamination of Acoustic Evidence in the Kennedy Assassination," *Science* 218 (Oct. 8, 1982): 127–133.
Condon, Richard. *The Manchurian Candidate*. New York: McGraw-Hill, 1959.
Corn, David. "The Same Old Dirty Tricks," *The Nation* 246 (August 27, 1988): 157–160.
Crenshaw, Charles A. with Jens Hansen and J. Gary Shaw. *JFK: Conspiracy of Silence*. New York: Signet, 1992.
Davis, John. *Mafia Kingfish: Carlos Marcello and the Assassination of John F. Kennedy*. New York: McGraw-Hill, 1989.
Deitch, Scott M. *The Silent Don: The Criminal Underworld of Santos Traficante*. Fort Lee, N.J.: Barricade Books, Inc., 2009.
DeYoung, Karen and Walter Pincus. "CIA Releases Files on Past Misdeeds," *Washington Post*, June 27, 2007, A01.
Dobbs, Michael. "Myths Over Attacks on U. S. Swirl Through Islamic World: Many Rumors Lay Blame on an Israeli Conspiracy," *Washington Post*, October 13, 2001, A22.
Durham, T. Mack. *The Innocent Man Script: Cui Bono–To Whose Advantage?* Lincoln, Neb.: Writer's Showcase, 2000.
Eddowes, Michael. *The Oswald File*. New York: Clarkson N. Potter, 1977.
Ellsberg, Daniel. *Secrets: A Memoir of Vietnam and the Pentagon Papers*. New York: Penguin Books, 2003.
Epstein, Edward Jay. *Legend: The Secret World of Lee Harvey Oswald*. New York: Reader's Digest Press, 1978.
———. *Inquest: The Warren Commission and the Establishment of Truth*. New York: Viking, 1966.
Fetzer, James H., ed. *Assassination Science: Experts Speak Out on the Death of JFK*. Chicago: Catfree Press, 2001.
Exner, Judith. *My Story*. New York: Grove Press, 1977.
Final Report of the Assassination Records Review Board. Washington, D.C.: Government Printing Office, 1998.
Fonzi, Gaeton. *The Last Investigation*. New York: Thunder's Mouth Press, 1993.
Garrison, Jim. *On the Trail of the Assassins*. New York: Sheridan Square Press, 1988.
Grant, Joel. "Body Snatchers at Love Field?" Accessed March 31, 2013, http://mcadams.posc.mu.edu/b_snatch.htm
Hancock, Larry. "The Man in the Middle: Richard Case Nagell's View of an Evolving Conspiracy," *Kennedy Assassination Chronicles,* Winter 1999, 16.
Hill, Gladwin. "One Bullet Fired: Night-Club Man Who Admired Kennedy Is Oswald's Slayer," *New York Times*, Nov. 25, 1963, 1a.
Groden, Robert and Harrison Livingstone. *High Treason: The Assassination of President John F. Kennedy and the New Evidence of Conspiracy*. New York: Conservatory Press, 1989.
Hartogs, Renatus and Lucy Freeman. *The Two Assassins*. New York: Thomas Y. Crowell, 1976.
Holloway, Diane. *The Mind of Oswald*. Victoria, B.C.: Trafford Publishing, 2000.
"How the CIA Tried to Break Defector in Oswald Case," *Washington Star,* September 16, 1978.
Hurt, Henry. *Reasonable Doubt: An Investigation into the Assassination of John F. Kennedy*. New York: Henry Holt & Co., 1985.
Investigation of the Assassination of President John F. Kennedy: Hearing before the House, Select Committee on Assassinations (HSCA). 95th Congress (1979).
Investigation of the Assassination of President John F. Kennedy: Hearing before the President's Commission on the Assassination of President Kennedy. 88th Congress (1964).
Janis, Irving. *Groupthink: Psychological Studies of Policy Decisions and Fiascoes*. Boston: Wadsworth, 1982.

Johnson, Scott P. "The Prosecution of Lee Harvey Oswald," *South Texas Law Review* 48 (2007): 101–127.
Kantor, Seth. *The Ruby Cover-Up.* New York: Kensington Publishing, 1978.
Kornbluh, Peter. *Bay of Pigs Declassified: The Secret CIA Report on the Invasion of Cuba.* New York: New Press, 1998.
La Fontaine, Ray and Mary La Fontaine. *Oswald Talked: The New Evidence in the JFK Assassination.* Gretna, La.: Pelican Publishing Company, Inc., 1996.
Lane, Mark. *Plausible Denial: Was the CIA Involved in the Assassination of JFK?* New York: Thunder's Mouth Press, 1991.
———. *Rush to Judgment.* New York: Dell, 1966.
Lardner, George, Jr. "Study Backs Theory of Grassy Knoll: New Report Says Second Gunman Fired at Kennedy," *Washington Post*, March 26, 2001, A03.
Lasswell, Harold. *Power and Personality.* New York: W. W. Norton, Inc., 1948.
Latell, Brian. *Castro's Secrets: Cuban Intelligence, the CIA, and the Assassination of John F. Kennedy.* New York: Palgrave MacMillan, 2012.
Lawrence, Jill. "Americans Served as Guinea Pigs for Radiation Testing," *Fort Collins Coloradoan* 25 (October 1986): A-10.
Lifton, David. *Best Evidence: Disguise and Deception in the Assassination of John F. Kennedy.* New York: Macmillan, 1980.
Lopez, Edwin. "Report on Lee Harvey Oswald's Trip to Mexico City," *House Select Committee on Assassinations (HSCA)*, 1979.
Mack, Gary. "Who Was Really in Oswald's Grave? Parts 1–3," *Cover-ups!* (Feb.–April 1983): 1–3.
Mahoney, Richard D. *Sons & Brothers: The Days of Jack and Robert Kennedy.* New York: Arcade, 1999.
Mailer, Norman. *Oswald's Tale: An American Mystery.* New York: Random House, 1995.
Maier, Mark H. *The Data Game.* Armonk, N.Y.: M. E. Sharpe, 1999.
Mallon, Thomas. *Mrs. Paine's Garage and the Murder of John F. Kennedy.* New York: Pantheon, 2002.
Malone, William Scott. "The Secret Life of Jack Ruby." *New Times*, January 23, 1978, 46–51.
Marchetti, Victor and John D. Marks, *The CIA and the Cult of Intelligence.* New York: Alfred Knopf, 1974.
Marrs, Jim. *Crossfire: The Plot That Killed Kennedy.* New York: Carroll & Graf, 1989.
Martinez, Michael and Brad Johnson. RFK assassination witness tells CNN: "There was a Second Shooter," CNN: Justice, Accessed June 4, 2013, http://www.cnn.com/2012/04/28/justice/california-rfk-second-gun/.
McAdams, John. "The Kennedy Assassination: Joseph Milteer: Miami Prophet or Quitman Crackpot?" *The Kennedy Assassination*, Accessed January 25, 2013, mcadams.posc.mu.edu/milteer.htm.
McAdams, John. "The Kennedy Assassination—Parkland Hospital Press Conference: Dallas Doctors First Statements." Accessed March 31, 2013, http://mcadams.posc.mu.edu/press.htm.
McMillan, Priscilla Johnson. *Marina and Lee.* New York: Harper & Row, 1977.
Meagher, Sylvia. *Accessories After the Fact: The Warren Commission, the Authorities, and the Report.* New York: Vintage, 1992.
Mills, C. Wright. *The Power Elite.* New York: Oxford University Press, 1956.
Morley, Jeffery. "The JFK Murder: Can New Technology Finally Crack the Case?," *Reader's Digest* (March 2005): 84–91.
Morrow, Robert D. *Betrayal: A Reconstruction of Certain Clandestine Events from the Bay of Pigs to the Assassination of John F. Kennedy.* Chicago: Chicago Henry Regnery Co., 1976.
Mosby, Aline. *The View from No. 13 People's Street.* New York: Random House, 1962.
Moseley, Jack. "Body of JFK Assassin Is under Guard in FW," *Fort Worth Press*, November 25, 1963.
Mosk, Richard M. "Conspiracy Theories and the JFK Assassination: Cashing in on Political Paranoia," *Los Angeles Lawyer*, Nov. 1992.

Nachmias, Chava-Frankfort and David Nachmias. *Research Methods in the Social Sciences*. New York: Macmillan, 2000.

Nathan, James A. and James K. Oliver. *Foreign Policy Making and the American Political System*. Baltimore: Johns Hopkins University Press, 1994.

Nechiporenko, Oleg Maximovich. *Passport to Assassination: The Never-before-Told-Story of Lee Harvey Oswald by the KGB Colonel Who Knew Him*. New York: Carol Publishing, 1993.

Newman, John. *Oswald and the CIA*. New York: Carroll & Graf, 1995.

———. "Oswald, the CIA and Mexico City: Fingerprints of Conspiracy," *Probe* (September–October, 1999): 1-29.

Norton, Linda, James A. Cottone, Irvin M. Sopher, and Vincent J. M. DiMaio. "The Exhumation and Identification of Lee Harvey Oswald," *Journal of Forensic Sciences*, 29 (1984): 19-38.

O'Dell, Michael. "The acoustics evidence in the Kennedy assassination," Accessed February 9, 2013, http://mcadams.posc.mu.edu/odell/.

Oswald, Robert. *Lee: A Portrait of Lee Harvey Oswald by His Brother*. New York: Coward McCann, 1967.

"Oswald Grave Now Battle Site," *Fort Worth Star-Telegram*, October 1, 1979.

Philbrick, Herbert. *I Led Three Lives: Citizen, "Communist," Counterspy*. New York: McGraw-Hill Book Co., 1952.

Phillips, David Atlee. *The Night Watch: 25 Years of Peculiar Service*. New York: Antheneum, 1977.

Popkin, Richard H. *The Second Oswald*. New York: Avon, 1966.

Posner, Gerald. *Case Closed: Lee Harvey Oswald and the Assassination of JFK*. New York: Random House, 1993.

Powers, Francis Gary with Curt Gentry. *Operation Overflight: The U-2 Spy Plane Pilot Tells His Story for the First Time*. New York: Holt, Rinehart & Winston, 1970.

"Project Minaret," *Newsweek*, 10 (Nov. 1975): 31–32.

Random House Webster's College Dictionary. New York: Random House, 1997.

Reid, Ed and Ovid Demaris. *The Green Felt Jungle*. New York: Buccaneer Books, 1963.

Reitzes, Dave. "Truth or Dare: The Lives and Lies of Richard Case Nagell," Accessed June 21, 2013, http://mcadams.posc.mu.edu/nagell3.htm.

Ridgeway, J. and K. Jacobs. "Onward Christian Soldiers," *Village Voice*, 17 (March 1987): 32ff.

Roebuck, J. and S. C. Weeber. *Political Crime in the United States: Analyzing Crime by and against Government*. New York: Praeger, 1978.

Russell, Dick. *The Man Who Knew Too Much*. New York: Carroll & Graf, 1992.

Sauvage, Leo. "The Oswald Affair," *Commentary* (March 1964): 55–65.

Schlesinger, Arthur M. *The Imperial Presidency*. New York: Houghton Mifflin Co., 2004.

Scott, Peter Dale. "From Dallas to Watergate," in *Government by Gunplay: Assassination Conspiracies from Dallas to Today*, eds. Sid Blumenthal and Harvey Yazijian, 113–129. New York: Signet, 1976.

———. *Deep Politics and the Death of JFK*. Berkeley: University of California Press, 1993.

Shane, Scott. "CIA Is Still Cagey About Oswald Mystery," *New York Times*, October 16, 2009, accessed February 12, 2013, http://www.nytimes.com/2009/10/17/us/17inquire.html?pagewanted=all&_r=1&.

Shipler, David. "Living under Suspicion," *New York Times*, February 7, 1997, A33.

Simon, David R. *Elite Deviance*. Needham Heights, Mass.: Allyn & Bacon, 1999.

Smist, Frank J., Jr. *Congress Oversees the United States Intelligence Community, 1947–1989*. Knoxville: University of Tennessee Press, 1990 .

Stafford, Jean. *A Mother in History*. New York: Farrar, Straus & Giroux 1966.

Stone, Oliver and Zachary Sklar. *JFK: The Book of Film*. New York: Applause Books, 1992.

Summers, Anthony. *Conspiracy*. New York: McGraw-Hill, 1980.

Szalavitz, Maia. "The Legacy of the CIA's Secret LSD Experiments on America," *Time: Health & Family*, March 23, 2012. Accessed January 2, 2013. http://healthland.time.com/2012/03/23/the-legacy-of-the-cias-secret-lsd-experiments-on-america/.

"The CIA's Hit-List," *Newsweek*, 1 (December 1975): 28–32.
"The Crusade to Topple King," *Time* 1 (December 1975): 11–12.
"The FBI's 'Black-Bag' Boys," *Newsweek*, 28 (July 1975): 18–21.
The Fourth Decade: A Journal of Research on the John F. Kennedy Assassination 3 (March 1996): 35–37.
"The Phantom Battle That Led to War," *U.S. News and World Report*, July 23, 1984, 56–67.
Thomas, D. B. "Echo Correlation Analysis and the Acoustic Evidence in the Kennedy Assassination Revisited," 41 *Science & Justice* (2001): 21–32.
Thompson, Josiah. *Six Seconds in Dallas: A Micro-Study of the Kennedy Assassination.* New York: Random House, 1967.
Waldron, Lamar and Thom Hartmann. *Ultimate Sacrifice: John and Robert Kennedy, the Plan for a Coup in Cuba, and the Murder of JFK*. New York: Carroll & Graf, 2005.
Weiss, M. R. and A. Ashkenasy. *An Analysis of Recorded Sounds Relating to the Assassination of John F. Kennedy*. Department of Computer Sciences, Queens College, City University of New York, 1979.
"Who's Chipping Away at Your Privacy," *U.S. News and World Report*, 31 (March 1975): 18.
Willis, Gary and Ovid Demaris. *Jack Ruby: The Man Who Killed the Man Who Killed Kennedy*. New York: DeCapo Press, 1994.
Wise, David. *The Politics of Lying: Government Deception, Secrecy and Power*. New York: Random House, 1973.
Woodward, Bob. *State of Denial: Bush at War Part III*. New York: Simon and Schuster, 2006.
Wrone, David R. *The Zapruder Film: Reframing JFK's Assassination*. Lawrence: University Press of Kansas, 2003.
Zegart, Amy. *Spying Blind: The CIA, FBI, and the Origins of 9/11*. Princeton, N.J.: Princeton University Press, 2007.

Index

Abbott, John, 77
Acre, Danny, 63
Adams, Victoria, 63, 117
Air Force One, 27, 68, 107, 108, 115
Air Force Two, 116
Alba, Adrian, 52
Aleman, Jose, 39
Allende, Salvador, 60
Almeida, Juan, 69
Almon, John, 82
Alpha 66: and Richard Case Nagell, 34, 35, 62–63, 104, 114, 117; and the framing of Oswald, 62, 117; infiltration of by Oswald, 30; and Antonio Veciana, 30, 59
American Communist Party, 3, 36, 44, 48, 95
AMSPELL, 53–54
Andrews Air Force Base, 27, 107
Angel (or Angelo), 36, 83, 104, 114, 117
Applin, George J., 66
Archer, Don Ray, 110
Armstrong, John, 75
Arnold, Carolyn, 63
Arcacha-Smith, Sergio, 36, 114
Ayers, Bradley, 30
Azcue, Eusebio, 58, 84–85, 95

Baker, Marrion, 63, 117
Banister, Guy, 30, 36, 52–53, 57, 62, 77, 86, 104, 105, 111

Barnes, W. E., 65
Bates, Pauline, 48
Batista, Fulgencio, 38
Baumgartner, Alan, 98
Bay of Pigs, ix, xix, 6, 21–22, 35, 38–39, 51, 77
Becker, Edward, 37
Benavides, Domingo, 9
Berlin wall, ix
Bertrand, Clay, 53
Bethesda Naval Hospital, 26–27, 68, 106–108, 115
Betrayal (novel), 36, 62
Blakey, Robert, 39, 113, 120
Bledsoe, Mary, 60
Bogard, Albert Guy, 79–80, 80
Bolden, Abraham, 33
Bond, James, 44
Boone, Eugene, 63
Brennan, Howard, 8, 63, 102, 109
Brewer, Johnny Calvin, 65
Bringuier, Carlos, 54, 86, 111, 113
Brown, Jack, 103
Brown, Oran, 80
Bugliosi, Vincent, x, 32
Bundren, Jim, 35
Bush, George H. W., 21

Callaway, Ted, 9
CAP. *See* Civil Air Patrol
Carr, Richard Randolph, 63

131

Carr, Waggoner, 61
Castro, Fidel: U. S. attempts to overthrow, xix, 21, 28, 36, 38, 51, 54, 69–70; CIA plots to assassinate, 21–22, 24, 44, 50; Oswald's fascination with, xviii, 5, 112; and Kennedy assassination, xviii, xx, 112, 113; Cuban 1959 revolution, 38
Central Intelligence Agency: assassination plots against foreign leaders, 21–22, 50; and the Bay of Pigs, 22, 38; and conspiracy theories related to the JFK assassination, 19–24, 59, 111–112; cover-up after the assassination, 23; and George de Mohrenschildt, 31; domestic surveillance of citizens, 23; and exhumation of Oswald's body, 97–98; and Martin Luther King Jr., 50; and military industrial complex, x, xvi; and Robert Morrow, 36; and Richard Case Nagell, 34, 114; and Harvey Oswald, 75; and Lee Harvey Oswald, xvi, 30, 43, 53–54, 56–60, 85, 111–112; and LSD experiments, 23–24; and murder of Lee Harvey Oswald, 110–111; and plots to assassinate Fidel Castro, 21–22, 44, 57; and Jean Rene Souetre, 31–32
Civil Air Patrol, 27, 44, 52
CIA. *See* Central Intelligence Agency
Clarke, James, x
Clemons, Acquilla, 65
Cody, Joe, 109
The Collective manuscript, 48
Cohen, Mickey, 25
Colby, William, 23
Cole, Alma, 75
Coleman, William T., 45
Connally, John, 11, 47–48, 78
Conspiracy: definition of, 19; Mossad, 1; Oswald as conspirator, 25–40, 111–116; scientific method and, 19; September 11, 2001 terrorist attacks, 1; theories and the JFK assassination, xvi–xix, xx, 1, 16, 19, 43, 89, 111–121; theory in assassination of Martin Luther King, 23; theory in assassination of Robert F. Kennedy, 25
Cornwell, Gary, 86
Craig, Roger, 63
Cuban Missile Crisis, ix, 34, 69

Cuban Revolutionary Council (Junta), 39, 83
Curry, Jesse, 109

Dannelly, Lee, 78–79
Davis, Barbara, 9
Davis, Virginia, 9
de Gaulle, Charles, 31
De Laparra, Eugene, 37
DeLaunne, Gary, 67
de Mohrenschildt, George, 31, 50–51, 105
Dealey Plaza, xix, 11, 12, 26, 34, 63, 66, 103, 106–107, 110, 114, 117
Deslatte, Oscar, 76–77
Devlin, Larry, 22
Diem, Ngo Dinh, xvi, 22, 50
Donneroummus, Frank, 25
Dougherty, Jack, 63
DRE. *See* Student Revolutionary Directorate
Duran, Silvia, 58, 84, 95

Echevarria, Homer S., 33
Eddowes, Michael, x, 98
Eisenhower, Dwight D., 22, 103
Ekdahl, Edwin, 2
Epstein, Edward Jay, 105, 113
Eunis, Amos, 63
Exner, Judith Campbell, xix

Fadlallah, Sheik Mohammad Hussein, 50
Fain, John, 93–94
Fair Play for Cuba Committee, 5, 9, 30, 36, 51, 55, 61, 66, 94, 95, 110, 114
FBI. *See* Federal Bureau of Investigation
Federal Bureau of Investigation: airtel message on November 17, 1963, 39–40, 54; contact with Lee Harvey Oswald, xvi, 48, 52, 54, 93–94; and Chicago assassination plot against Kennedy, 33; conspiracy theories related to, xvi; cover-up after the assassination, 23; domestic surveillance of citizens, 23; and Martin Luther King Jr., 50; questioning of Joseph Milteer, 103; Lee Harvey Oswald as informant for, 30, 40, 43, 53–54, 61, 111, 112, 116; and Marina Oswald, 7, 30, 40; note left by Oswald at FBI office in Dallas, 7, 61;

Index 133

and alleged palm print on rifle, 67
Ferrie, David, 27, 36, 52, 69, 104, 105, 111
Ferrell, Mary, 31
Fetzer, James, x
Fleming, Ian, 44
Fonzi, Gaeton, x, 30, 84
FPCC. *See* Fair Play for Cuba Committee
Frazier, Buell, 7, 9, 60–62, 81
Friends of Democratic Cuba, 76–77, 86
Fritz, Will, 110

Garrison, Jim, x, 27–28, 36, 48, 64, 70, 77, 84, 105, 113
Gaudet, William, 57
Giancana, Sam, xix, 38, 70, 113
Graham, Robert, 34–35
Grand Prairie Sportsdrome, 73
Gregory, Peter, 48, 50
Groden, Robert, 6, 56
Groody, Paul, 67, 97, 98, 98–99
Guinyard, Sam, 9
Guzman, Jacobo, 21

Hall, Loran Eugene, 84
Harris, Jones, 82
Helms, Richard, 53
Hemming, Gerry Patrick, 29
Hemstock, Philip, 77–78
Hickey, Edward, 89
Hill, Gerald, 66
Hoffa, Jimmy, 39
Hoover, J. Edgar, 24, 35, 44, 65, 85, 89, 97, 105, 118
Hosty, James, 7, 40, 61
Hotel del Comercio, 84, 112
House Select Committee on Assassinations: acoustical analysis of gunshots fired in Dealey Plaza, 12–14, 26, 117; chief counsel Robert Blakey, 38, 113, 120; conspiracy in assassination of John F. Kennedy, xix, 20, 22, 113; conspiracy in assassination of Martin Luther King, 23; investigation of Joseph Milteer, 33–34, 103; organized crime as source of conspiracy, 25, 113; scientific study of backyard photographs of Oswald, 2; and Silvia Odio, 102, 112; testimony of Jose Aleman, 38; testimony of James Sibert, 107; testimony of William Walter, 54; investigation of threats to President Kennedy in 1963, 32–34
HSCA. *See* House Select Committee on Assassinations
Hughes, Howard, 65
Humes, James, 12
Hunt, E. Howard, 22
Hunter, Gertrude, 74
Hutchison, Leonard E., 80, 81

I Led Three Lives (television show), 44, 54
Irving Sports Shop, 74

Jackson, Kenneth, 82
Jaffe, Sam, 97
Jaggers-Stiles-Stovall, 5, 48, 51
January, Wayne, 82–83
Jarman, Junior, 63
JFK (film), x, xvii, 64
John Birch Society, 49
Johnsen, Richard, 107
Johnson, Lyndon, ix, xvi, 21, 70, 75, 112
JURE. *See* Cuban Revolutionary Council (Junta)

Kantor, Seth, x, 66, 108
Kennedy assassination: Acoustical data of gunshots fired, 12–14, 26, 106, 117, 120; autopsy photographs and X-rays, 12, 27; and CIA/Mafia/anti-Castro coalition, xvii, 51, 54, 69–70, 111, 116; conspiracy theories, xvi–xix, 19–40, 43, 51, 57, 89, 95–96, 111–116; grassy knoll area, 12–14, 113, 114, 117; Lone gunman theory, xv; Mafia involvement in, xviii–xix, 25, 37–39, 68–70; 7.65 Mauser rifle, 63; and Joseph Milteer, 33–34; and Richard Case Nagell, 34–36; and the Secret Service, 27, 32, 68; Single bullet, or magic bullet, theory (CE 399), 11, 68, 117; and Soviet intelligence (KGB), xviii, 34–35, 89; testimonies that foretold of the event, 32–40; Thorburn position, 11
Kennedy, Jacqueline, 14, 107
Kennedy, John F.: autopsy of, 12, 27, 67–68, 102; failure at the Bay of Pigs, ix, xix, 6, 22, 35, 38–39, 51;

construction of Berlin wall, ix; support for civil rights, ix, xvi; and Cuban Missile Crisis, ix, 69; Orange Bowl speech, 35; Oswald's view of, 15–16; personality of, ix; *PT-109* (film), 35; and policy on Vietnam, x, xvi, 23; and steel industry crisis, ix

Kennedy, Robert: assassination of and possible conspiracy, 25; deportation of Carlos Marcello, xvi, 27; prosecution of Mafia leaders as Attorney General, 43, 51, 70

KGB. *See* Soviet State Security Service

King, Martin Luther Jr., 23, 50

Kostin, Valeri Dmitrevich, 95–96

Kositkov, Valery, 59, 95, 112, 119

LaFontaines, Ray and Mary, 53–54

Lane, Mark, x, 64, 70

Latona, Sebastian, 67

Lee, V. T., 61

legend, 29, 54

Leopoldo, 6, 36, 39, 55, 83, 104, 114, 117

Liebeler, Wesley, 86

Lifton, David: conspiracy in the Kennedy assassination, 26–27, 67–68, 101, 106–108, 114–116, 120; planting of evidence against Oswald, 117, 118; removal of Kennedy's body from casket, 27, 107, 115–116; Secret Service involvement in conspiracy, 27, 107; Sibert and O'Neill report, 26, 107–108, 115

Livingstone, Harrison, 6, 56

Long, Joe, 67

Lonsdale, Gordon, 90

Lovelady, Billy, 63

Lumumba, Patrice, 22, 50

Lyon, K. E., 66

The Mafia.: conspiracy theories involving JFK assassination, xviii–xix, 19–20, 37–39, 51, 57, 68–70, 113; assassination attempts against Fidel Castro, xvii, 24, 44, 57; enemy of President John F. Kennedy, xvi; assassination of Robert F. Kennedy, 25; silencing of Oswald, 68–70; and Richard Nixon, 24; and Watergate scandal, 24. *See also* Organized Crime Syndicate

Maheu, Robert, 38

Mailer, Norman, x

The Manchurian Candidate (film), xviii

Mann, Thomas, 112

Mannlicher-Carcano rifle, 5, 8, 10–11, 11, 49, 62, 67, 68, 74, 79, 102

Marcello, Anthony, 37

Marcello, Carlos: deportation of, xviii, 27; and FBI informants, 37, 69; and House Select Committee on Assassinations, 25; alleged role in the Kennedy assassination, xviii, 27, 37, 43, 51, 57, 68–70, 111–112; and the framing of Oswald, 51, 68–70, 113

Marchetti, Victor, 30, 43

Markham, Helen, 9

Marlowe, Vaughn, 35–36, 114

Marrs, Jim, x, 84

Martello, Frank, 76

Martin, Jim, 108

McBride, Palmer, 103

McClain, H. B., 106

McDonald, M. N., 65

McGarvey, Patrick, 30

McHugh, Gordon, 107

McMillan, Priscilla Johnson, 2, 119

Meagher, Silvia, 6

Mercer, Julie Ann, 66

microdots, 31, 48

Mills, C. Wright, 20, 25

Milteer, Joseph, 33–34, 101, 103–104, 113, 116–117, 118, 119–120

Minox spy camera, 31, 114

Monterey School of the Army (Defense Language Institute), 29

Moore, Joseph, 76

Morales, David, 57

Morrow, Robert, 36, 62

Mosby, Aline, 75–76, 119

Moseley, Jack, 67

Murret, Charles "Dutz", xviii, 37, 51, 69, 111–112

Nagell, Richard Case, 34–36, 62–63, 101, 104–105, 113–114, 117, 120

National Aeronautics and Space Administration, 52

Index

NASA. *See* National Aeronautics and Space Administration
National Research Council, 12–13, 14, 26, 106
National Security Act of 1947, 20
National Security Agency, 23
Newman, John, x, 58–59, 85
Nixon, Richard M, xvi, 21, 103
Norman, Florence, 78
Norman, Harold, 63
Nosenko, Yuri, 29, 91

O'Dell, Michael, 13–14, 106
Odio, Silvia, 5–6, 36, 39, 55–56, 83–84, 86, 101, 102–103, 104, 112–113, 116, 118, 119
Office of Naval Intelligence, 29, 43, 44, 46, 52, 90
Olsen, Harry N., 109
O'Neill, Francis, 26, 107–108
ONI. *See* Office of Naval Intelligence
Operation Mongoose, xix, 38, 44
Organized Crime Syndicate: and Air America, 24; assassination attempts against Fidel Castro, xvii, 22, 24, 44, 57; conspiracy theories related to JFK assassination, xviii–xix, xx, 25, 27, 37–39, 40, 43–44, 51, 68–70, 113, 116; history of, 24–25; murder of Lee Harvey Oswald, 110–111, 116. *See also* The Mafia
Oswald, Audrey Marina Rachel, 7
Oswald, June, 4
Oswald, Lee Harvey: and 544 Camp Street, 30, 77, 86; use of alias Alex Hidell, 5, 9–10, 17n39, 49; use of alias O. H. Lee, 7, 60–61; and anti-Castro Cubans, 5–6, 30, 39, 55, 56, 70, 77, 86, 111–112, 113, 116; arrested in New Orleans, 5, 54; arrested at Texas Theater in Dallas, 9, 11, 65; assassination attempt on General Edwin Walker, 5, 49–50, 51; in Atsugi, Japan, 3, 28, 90; autopsy of, 92; behavioral pattern of, xx, 2–10, 16, 19, 102–103; birth certificate, 89; and CIA 201 file, 30, 43, 58; connections to Central Intelligence Agency, xvi, 28, 43, 53, 112, 116; contact with Cuban embassy in Mexico City, 6, 57–59, 84–85, 95, 111–112; connection to Cuban intelligence, 112; as counterintelligence operative, 44–46, 116; and Dallas car salesman, 79–80; Defense Department Identification card, 43, 62; exhumation of body, 97–99; financial transactions of, 29; as hero, xx, 43, 70, 101, 116; impersonations and sightings, 73–86; doubled as KGB agent, 90, 95; as lone assassin, 1–16, 101–111; habitual lying of, 9–10, 50; at Irving Supermarket, 80–81; *Life* magazine photographs of, 67; service in the Marines, 3–4, 16, 44–45, 90, 112; interest in Marxism, 3, 4, 54–55; language skills in Russian, 92, 119; mastoidectomy scar, 91, 98, 118; trip to Mexico City, 6, 9, 56–60, 61, 84–85, 86, 95–96, 111–112, 119; employment at Minsk radio factory, 4, 47; North Dakota impersonator, 75–76; and paraffin tests on, 66; as patsy, xviii, xx, 10, 37, 43–70, 85, 101, 116–118; alleged palm print on rifle, 11, 67; and Mrs. Lovell Penn's Cow Pasture, 79; and Harvey Oswald, 75; physical evidence against, 10–13, 19, 101–102; physical discrepancies before and after defection, 91–94, 118–119; political personality of, 15; and pro-Castro Cubans, 39, 53, 55, 56, 70, 77, 111–112, 113, 119; prosecution of, xi, 1, 16; contact with Russian embassy in Mexico City, 6, 57–60, 61, 84–85, 95, 111; at Selective Service Headquarters, 78–79; and Soviet intelligence connections, 29–30, 95–96; defection to Soviet Union, xvii, xx, 4, 28, 46–47, 51, 89; return to the United States from the Soviet Union, 4, 29, 47–48, 93; Smith and Wesson .38 revolver, 5, 11, 102; State Department loan, 29, 47; suicide attempt, 4, 46–47, 97; obtains job at Texas School Book Depository, 7; murder of Officer J. D. Tippit, 2, 8–9, 11, 65, 94, 102; Two Oswalds, xx, 73–86; at voter registration drive in Clinton, Louisiana, 52; whereabouts at time of assassination, 63, 117; and

Wisconsin barber, 77–78
Oswald, Marguerite, 2–3, 37, 66, 89, 92–93, 97
Oswald, Marina: and knowledge of assassination attempt on General Edwin Walker, 49–50; exhumation of Oswald's body, 98, 99; and James Hosty, 7, 40, 61; relationship with Lee Harvey Oswald, 4, 7–8, 16, 47, 74, 92, 94, 119; relationship with Ruth Paine, 60, 74, 80; and Russian community in Dallas, 50; Warren Commission testimony, xvi, xviii, 5, 50, 103
Oswald, Robert Sr. (father of Lee Harvey Oswald), 2
Oswald, Robert Jr. (brother of Lee Harvey Oswald), 2, 4, 9, 48, 67, 93

Paine, Lynn, 10
Paine, Michael, 7, 31, 60
Paine, Ruth, 6–7, 10, 31, 60, 74
Parkland Hospital, 26–27, 67–68, 106, 115
Penn, Lovell T., 79
Perry, Malcolm, 115
Philbrick, Herbert, 44
Phillips, David Atlee, 30, 36, 57, 59–60
Pic, John (half-brother of Lee Harvey Oswald), 2–3, 93
Pic, Marge, 3
Poe, J. M., 65
Poretto, Joseph, 37
Posner, Gerald, x, 19, 32, 80
Postal, Julia, 65
Powers, Francis Gary, 21, 43, 46, 91
Prusakova, Ilya (uncle of Marina Oswald), 92

Queen Bee nightclub in Tokyo, 28–29, 34, 45
Quigley, John, 54, 94, 113

Redbird Airport, 81–83, 97
Reily Coffee Company, 52
Reily, William, 52
Reynolds, Warren, 9
Roselli, Johnny, 38, 43, 57, 70
Rowland, Arnold, 63
Rubinstein, Jack. *See* Jack Ruby

Ruby, Jack: purchase of .38 Colt Cobra pistol, 109; manipulated by Dallas Police, 108–110; death of, 15; discrimination of Jewish people, 14–15; as low-level KGB agent, 96–97, 120; framing of Oswald, 62, 69; murder of Oswald, xvi, 10, 14–15, 68–69, 75, 78, 84, 96, 97, 108–111, 116, 117–118, 120; stalking of Oswald, 66, 110; murder trial of, 15, 110; connections to organized crime, 27
Rusk, Dean, 90
Russell, Dick, 35
Russian Oswald, xx, 29, 89–99, 101, 118–120
Ryder, Dial Duwayne, 74

Sauvage, Leo, 73–74
Schneider, Rene, 22, 50
Scoggins, William, 9
Sehrt, Clem, 38
Shaw, Clay, 27, 52–53, 62, 104, 105, 111
Sheep-dipping, 60
Sibert, James, 26, 107–108
Sirhan, Sirhan, 25
Skrivanek, Jesse, 78
Slawson, W. David, 45
Smith, William Arthur, 9
Snyder, Richard, 119
Socialist Workers Party, 36, 48
Somersett, William, 33–34, 103
Souetre, Jean Rene, 31
Soviet State Security Service (KGB), xviii, 28, 30, 47, 48, 59, 89, 94, 96, 96–97, 112
Stevenson, Adlai, 21
Stone, Oliver, x, xvii
Strykes, Sandra, 63
Stuckey, Bill, 54
Student Revolutionary Directorate, 30
Sturgis, Frank, 22, 38, 84
Summers, Anthony, 48, 57, 58, 70, 83, 99
Sweatt, Allan, 61

Tague, James, 11
Takahashi, Mitsuko, 105
TSBD. *See* Texas School Book Depository
Termine, Sam, 37

Texas School Book Depository, 7, 34, 60, 62, 63, 75, 102, 103, 117
Thomas, D. B., 13, 26, 114
Timmer, William, 75
Tippit, J. D., 2, 8–9, 65, 82, 94, 108–109, 111
Tonahill, Joe, 110
Traficante, Santos, 25, 37, 38–39, 43, 57, 68, 84, 113
Tregle, Ben, 37
Trujillo, Rafael, 22
Truly, Roy, 7, 60, 63
Tujague, Gerard F., 3, 77

U-2 spy plane, 3, 21, 28, 45, 46, 90

Vallee, Thomas Arthur, 32
Veciana, Antonio, 30, 59

Wade, Henry, 61, 63, 66, 110
Walker, Edwin, 5, 49–50
Walter, William, 54
Walthers, Carolyn, 63
Walter Reed Medical Center, 27, 107, 108

Warren Commission Report: behavioral pattern of Oswald, xv–xvi; financial transactions of Lee Harvey Oswald, 29; as myth, x, xvii; portrayal of Lee Harvey Oswald as disconnected Marxist, 3, 96; psychological profile of Jack Ruby, 116; testimony of Silvia Odio, 39, 102, 112; testimony of Marina Oswald, xvi, xviii, 5, 12, 75, 81, 103; testimony of Marguerite Oswald, 92; testimony of Jack Ruby, 15; testimony of Edith Whitworth and Gertrude Hunter, 75
Warren, Earl, 15
Webster, Robert, 29, 90
Weissman, Bernard, 15
Weitzman, Seymour, 63
White, Jack, 34
Whitworth, Edith, 74
Williams, Bonnie Ray, 63
Wilson, Eugene, 80
The Worker newspaper, 48
Wright, Mr. and Mrs. Frank, 65

Zapruder film, ix, 11

About the Author

Scott P. Johnson is a professor of political science, coordinator of the Law & Society Program, and pre-law advisor at Frostburg State University in Frostburg, Maryland. He holds a Bachelor of Arts degree in political science and history from Youngstown State University, a Master of Arts degree in political science from the University of Akron, and a Doctor of Philosophy in public law from Kent State University. He teaches courses on American politics, constitutional law, race and law, criminal justice, research methods, political psychology, comparative legal systems, and equal protection. In 2010, he published an encyclopedia with ABC-CLIO entitled, *Trials of the Century: An Encyclopedia of Popular Culture and the Law*. He also has authored numerous articles in such law journals and law reviews as *Judicature, West Virginia Law Review, South Texas Law Review, Pierce Law Review, New England Law Review, Ohio Northern University Law Review, South Dakota Law Review, Wayne Law Review, University of Toledo Law Review, Akron Law Review,* and *Wyoming Law Review*. His research interests include unanimous decision-making on the U.S. Supreme Court, the presidential pardon power, the John F. Kennedy assassination and the psychology of Lee Harvey Oswald, case complexity and opinion writing on the Rehnquist Court, and the career of Justice David Souter. Dr. Johnson resides in Frostburg, Maryland, with his lovely wife, Phaiboon Ladkubon Johnson, and his six beautiful cats, Tippy, Ploy, JJ, Poco, Bello, and Nellie.